Flight of an Eagle

MARGARET FORTE was born in England, but lived in New Zealand from the age of seven. Her education included three years at a Quaker school, the Friends School in Wanganui. She began her career as a journalist at *The Dominion* in Wellington, and over the next fourteen years she worked for the *Sydney Daily Telegraph*, the *Vancouver News Herald* and the Adelaide *News*. She married a professional engineer, and in the 1950s resigned from the *News* to be a full-time parent to their three sons.

The Vietnam war developed, and Margaret's commitment to non-violent resolution of conflict led her to join the Women's International League for Peace and Freedom, where she worked as secretary of the South Australian branch for thirty years. She has also worked for the National Trust of South Australia and for the South Australian Division of the United Nations Association. In 1986 she was awarded an OAM for services 'to International Relations and Peace'.

FLIGHT OF AN EAGLE

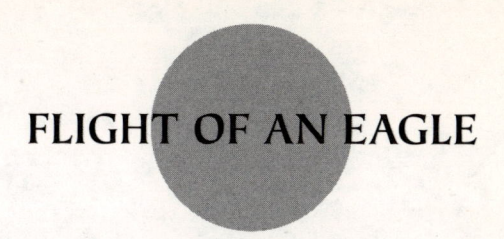

The Dreaming of Ruby Hammond

MARGARET FORTE

Wakefield Press

Wakefield Press
Box 2266
Kent Town
South Australia 5071

First published 1995

Copyright © Margaret Forte 1995

All rights reserved. This book is copyright. Apart from
any fair dealing for the purposes of private study, research,
criticism or review, as permitted under the Copyright Act,
no part may be reproduced without written permission.
Enquiries should be addressed to the publisher.

Edited by Simon MacDonald
Cover and book designed by Ann Wojczuk
Typeset by Clinton Ellicott, Adelaide
Printed and bound by Hyde Park Press, Adelaide

National Library of Australia
Cataloguing-in-Publication entry

Forte, Margaret.
Flight of an eagle: the dreaming of Ruby Hammond.

ISBN 1 86254 353 4.

1. Hammond, Ruby, d. 1993. 2. Aborigines, Australian –
Women – Biography. 3. Aborigines, Australian – Civil rights.
I. Title.

305.899915

Promotion of this book was assisted by the
South Australian government through the
Department for the Arts and Cultural Development.

Publication of this book was assisted by
the Commonwealth Government through the
Australia Council, its arts funding and advisory body.

*This book is a tribute to the memory
of Ruby Hammond's parents*

Ethel and Arthur Ahang

*. . . and beyond them to the great number of other
Aboriginal men and women who have striven,
and are striving, to make a good life
for their children.*

Author's Note

Aborigine is a word meaning 'original inhabitant'. The indigenous people of Australia accepted it in the early 1880s, but since then it has often been used in a derogatory way. Aborigines prefer to be called 'Aboriginal people'. We have used this term, but we have also used 'Aborigine', believing it to be a word they should carry with pride, and that the wider community should use it as a tribute. It is used in this way in *Flight of an Eagle*.

Contents

	Preface	ix
1	EXECUTIVE SECRETARY	1
2	LAUGHTER FROM THE PAST	22
3	DISCOVERING HERSELF	56
4	THE COUNCIL OF ABORIGINAL WOMEN	83
5	THE WISDOM PEOPLE	108
6	DISCOVERING CANBERRA	133
7	THE ABORIGINAL LEGAL SERVICE	154
8	REACHING BEYOND THE CITY	176
9	JUSTICE AND EQUALITY	197
10	NINGLA A-NA	209
11	OTHER LANDS – OTHER LIFESTYLES	243
12	'SISTER, IF YOU ONLY KNEW . . .'	277
13	NEW TASKS, NEW STRENGTHS	304
14	MAKING RECONCILIATION A REALITY	332
	Committees and Professional Bodies	351
	Notes	353
	Acknowledgements	364
	Bibliography	366
	Index	369

Preface

Ruby Hammond was born in 1936 and grew up in a relatively independent Aboriginal community in the south-east of South Australia. It was a time of 'assimilation' when the government was encouraging Aborigines to develop European standards and forget their indigenous past.

Ruby's parents, Ethel and Arthur Ahang, wanted the best for their eight children, and strove to give them education and middle-class Australian values. But Ruby was to discover, as all Aborigines did, that behaving like white people was not enough. If you looked like an Aborigine you were treated with racial discrimination, against which you had to fight if you wanted to retain your self-respect.

In the 1970s she went in search of her Aboriginality, seeking out the people who linked her to the land and its timeless history. She discovered their wisdom and understanding, the deep spiritual beliefs that are their Dreaming, and the hope and faith they have built into what they see as their 'land rights'.

She discovered their needs, and the dispossession that had brought them into the depressed poverty in which so many of them are still living. She determined to seek justice and equality for all Aboriginal people. This led her into work with the Council of Aboriginal Women, the Aboriginal Legal Rights Movement and the South Australian Public Service.

I first met Ruby in the 1960s, and we became close friends. I learnt more of the story of the Aboriginal people from her, and felt this story should be told more widely.

I wanted to tell it, and I persuaded Ruby to let me use her life as a background. Together we produced a book called *Brightening Landscape*, which was submitted for the 1978 Festival of Arts Literary Prize. It didn't win, and it didn't get published.

In 1993 when Reconciliation was a national issue we talked about updating the book, and relating it to this new concept. Ruby wanted the book to be re-written and published. Because she had shared so much of her thinking with me, she wanted me to do it. She was dying of cancer. I would have to do it without her.

It seemed an impossible task but she said to me, as she had said to so many women in the convincing way she had, 'Of course you can do it.'

As it has turned out, she was right.

Margaret Forte
Adelaide, South Australia
September 1995

ONE

EXECUTIVE SECRETARY

now, at last, she would fly high

*FLY HIGH WITH THE EAGLE, RUBY, FOR SHE IS YOUR DREAMING . . .
Fly like an Eagle on your new journey . . . Your song will be heard in the
winds from the sea, your footsteps in the colours of the earth, your
touch in the beat of that golden wing . . . our thoughts of you now,
Ruby, are of you singing and dancing in the wild flowers . . . a very
special black woman who touched many hearts, her achievements will
never be forgotten.*

These were among tributes that appeared day after day in long columns of the *Advertiser* for nearly a week after Ruby Hammond died on 16 April 1993.

Longer obituaries in the news columns carried recognition of her achievements, and in little notices on the back pages were scores of tributes of love and admiration from people who had known and worked with her. Non-Aboriginal people paid tribute, for Ruby was always willing to work hand-in-hand with all people who sought equality and justice. Government departments, public service officers and other groups with which she had worked acknowledged her with affection and high regard. The Commissioner for Public Employment and the staff of the Department of Labour typically paid tribute 'to Ruby, our colleague and friend who, by her vision and constant example, helped us to better understand her people's culture and needs'.

At her funeral the church was crowded. The governor of South Australia, Dame Roma Mitchell, was among those who came, together with members of parliament, heads of government departments, leaders of community groups, and hundreds of people who had known and loved her.

Ruby would have liked this, especially the governor being there. She loved recognition, not just for herself but because she knew that every tribute to an Aboriginal person was a step towards recognition that all Aboriginal people are of value in the human family.

She was only fifty-seven when she died, and her death drew together the South Australian Aboriginal community in a realisation of what can be achieved by one person devoted to their cause.

Through her father's mother Ruby belonged to the Tanganekald group of the Ngarrindjeri people of the Coorong area in the south-east of South Australia. Their beliefs included the concept of the 'ngatji',[1] or personal totem. Ruby had adopted the eagle as her personal totem when she was in her thirties and discovering her Aboriginality. She was fascinated by eagles, and when she began travelling for the Aboriginal legal service, it seemed to her that an eagle would always be there when she had a difficult decision to make. Her family and close friends have identified her with eagles for many years.

Her self-confidence, her pride and her belief in achievement reflected Ruby's faith in her eagle ngatji. She saw it as a link with her land, her people, and her ancestors, and as a part of her spiritual strength which stemmed from the dawn of time upwards and onwards to the vision she carried of the future. For her the ngatji was a reflection of Aboriginal Dreaming.

Through the Dreaming, Aborigines see themselves as part of the natural world, and as having responsibility for its survival. It is the well-spring of the deep and complex Aboriginal beliefs which are the source of the great strength that has enabled them to protect their culture through more than 200 years of European colonisation, and has brought them to the verge of the twenty-first century where the Australian government is seeking reconciliation with them.

The influence of the Dreaming is in every aspect of their daily lives. Dreaming stories teach Aboriginal children about right and wrong behaviour, about the laws of society and, above all, the land on which they live, and the care they owe to the land and the living things, animals and plants, with which they share it.

Dreaming stories vary across Australia, but all of them link the people to the land in a way that underlies the whole meaning of existence for them. Some of them may now be learning the European code that values land in dollars, but it is still alien to Aboriginal philosophy, and money is not the basis of the struggle for land rights.

Ruby first heard Aboriginal stories as a child. She was part of a community at Blackford near Kingston on the south-east coast of South Australia. In Aboriginal fashion a sense of kinship ran through the whole group and the men and women were 'uncle' or 'aunty' to the children. It was 'uncle' Milton Wilson, a frequent visitor to Ruby's home, who told the Ahang children the Dreaming stories of his own childhood.

All the Ahang children were sent to school. Ruby was a good reader. As she grew older she would read anything about Aborigines that came her way, or listen to what little came over the radio.

It was in 1968, when she was thirty-two, that Ruby listened to the Boyer Lectures. Entitled 'After the Dreaming', they had been well advertised on the ABC as being about black and white Australians. The speaker was W.E.H. Stanner, then Professor of Anthropology at the Australian National University, and Ruby was to remember for the rest of her life what he said about land:

> No English words are good enough to give a sense of the links between an Aboriginal group and their homeland ... A different tradition leaves us tongueless and earless towards this other world of significance and meaning.
>
> When we took what we call 'land' we took what to them meant hearth, home, the source and focus of life, and the everlastingness of the spirit.[2]

These words made little impression on the majority of Stanner's non-Aboriginal listeners, but Ruby recognised in them her own beliefs. For her the land was the source of Aboriginal spirituality, the foundation of philosophy and religion, the basis of dignity and self-respect. The phrase 'land rights' was indivisible from the equality and justice for which she was to struggle all her life.

Ruby took these perceptions with her in 1974 when she was appointed executive secretary of the Aboriginal Legal Rights Movement (ALRM). It was a prestigious position that offered opportunities she longed to have. She had been working as a field officer for the Council of Aboriginal Women, and for the Aboriginal Legal Rights Movement in its early years. She had tried her wings, and now at last she would fly high.

Thanks largely to the ALRM, the legal situation for Aborigines was slowly improving. In South Australia the movement had developed from work done voluntarily since the 1950s by a small group of lawyers led by Elliott Johnston.[3] It consisted mainly of Aboriginal people, and was responsible to a council elected by the Aboriginal community. By 1972 it had achieved a government subsidy, but it was not run by the government. It was run by Aborigines assisted by white people whom they themselves chose. The movement was so successful that Aborigines are at a loss to understand why the government will not accept it as a regular pattern for Aboriginal aid.

There was a real need for the work the ALRM was able to do. Aborigines, who were only one per cent of the Australian population, made up one-third of prison inmates – mainly for trivial offences.

It was a frequent matter for Aborigines to be arrested for drunkenness in places such as Victoria Square, and to have 'resisting arrest' and 'offensive language' added to the original charge. They would be taken to the watch house where, because they were unable to get bail, they would be put into a cell for the night. There was no one to bring them a clean shirt or their shaving materials and, dirty and unkempt, they would appear in court next day for a virtually automatic prison sentence. If they were fined they were unable to pay, so they went to prison anyway.

The legal service brought changes – legal representation in court, and a bail fund. Aborigines learnt that they could ask for bail, that they did not have to answer questions beyond those asking for name and address, and that they had the right to telephone the Aboriginal Legal Rights Movement as soon as they were arrested. They learnt that 'resisting arrest', no matter how unjust the arrest might seem, would only make matters worse; that certain words used freely in the city's hotel bars were mysteriously illegal in situations of police confrontation.

The ALRM was directly responsible for an improvement

in relations between Aborigines and police, and indirectly for setting up Aboriginal sobriety groups. It contributed to the raising of the status of Aborigines in their own eyes, and in the eyes of the community.

In Adelaide the ALRM's work was done from the overcrowded ground floor of 128 Wakefield Street. When Ruby became executive secretary there were twenty-three on the staff. Eighteen of them were Aboriginal, twelve were women.

Ruby was then thirty-eight. She'd had more schooling than many Aborigines and had learnt a lot from life. She knew about being poor, about being Aboriginal, and she had developed a sympathy which contributed a special quality to the work she did. Ruby had also learnt something of office procedure while working with the Council of Aboriginal Women, and with the legal service in its earlier years. She ran the legal service with great efficiency, but a dislike of 'red tape' kept her from rigid decisions. Her office was subtly different from the Australian Legal Aid Office, which operated out of a prestigious suite in a multi-storey city building to help the poor whites of the community.

Those with legal problems who shared the Aboriginal handicaps of poverty and lack of education envied the Aborigines their informal office with its sympathetic atmosphere. They sometimes came round looking for help, but to qualify they had to be Aboriginal in what has become the legal sense – they had to see themselves as Aborigines and be accepted as such by the communities in which they lived.

In Australian cities almost all Aborigines are of mixed heritage, but society dismisses as Aboriginal anyone in whom a part-Aboriginal inheritance is visible. These people share the discrimination that unites them and makes Aborigines of them all. Degree of caste is unimportant.

The ALRM office would make enquiries to see if all the

hopefuls who came in had some degree of Aboriginality, but all too often people had to be sent away.

The office was a democratic one, with frequent staff meetings and discussions. It was the days before equal opportunity and Ruby thought the men chafed a little at having a woman in the most senior position. Perhaps they also felt a little excluded from a sort of sisterhood that united the women on the staff. The women had similar domestic problems, and seemed to share a concern about their weight.

Ruby kept bathroom-type scales under the desk and the women weighed themselves once a week, writing the result on a chart. They were fond of saying to newcomers, 'You don't clock in here, you weigh in.'

These were small things, and there were no significant differences between the men and the women. On the whole the staff were closely united and, because Aborigines never take themselves too seriously, they were a cheerful group. They were also very dedicated. Some degree of commitment to a cause was felt by them all. Ruby took things under her wing. She felt concern for all the clients, and found it hard to confine herself only to the legal problems.

Guidelines proposed by the Department of Aboriginal Affairs for Aboriginal Legal Services stated in paragraph 9.6.3:

> Aboriginal Legal Services are not to engage in ancillary activities arising out of their operations as set out in 9.5., such as general welfare, adoption agencies etc., but may refer clients requiring help in these areas to appropriate agencies, and undertake such liaison as is necessary to ensure that the access of Aboriginals to such agencies is comparable to that available to other Australians.

Ruby conceded some wisdom in this, but she disliked the departmental style in which it was written, and she disliked it as a hard-and-fast ruling. She was not one to heed the niceties of departmental guidelines when someone was homeless or hungry. In those situations it was not an 'ancillary activity' for Ruby to do something about it, it was her way of life.

She believed the ALRM was involved inescapably with welfare work, and wanted to see this acknowledged by having welfare workers on her staff, working at her direction. She was fortunate in having field officers who were able to undertake welfare work. These officers were all Aboriginal, and had pioneered this work in Australian courts. They had been especially valuable in the Juvenile Court.

The term 'field officer' was used by the legal service to mean someone who did work in direct contact with the people who needed it, but who was not a graduate social worker. They were a liaison with people involved with the courts. Some of them were graduates of the Task Force course that the South Australian Institute of Technology had been running for Aboriginal students since 1973.

The work the field officers did was of tremendous value. By 1977 there were four of them in Adelaide, and four in country centres. Special field officer training had been established, with solicitors and court officials lecturing them on court procedures and the law.

Ruby liked this type of training. She had a deep respect for experience and knowledge, but she was suspicious of academic training, which seemed to her to teach people to 'think in boxes'. She had great faith in her field officers, and the practical ways in which they had acquired their skills.

In 1977 the four city staff field officers were Joanne Willmot, Shirley Peisley, Harry Taylor and Charlie Agius. They all shared Ruby's impulse to help whenever there was need for help, and this often kept them working long hours beyond the call of duty, or overtime payments. Ruby was dismayed by civil servants who went home at five o'clock, leaving not just unfinished reports on the desk, but people in need wondering what to do next.

She remembered as a typical case a sixteen-year-old boy from Point Pearce who was in Adelaide on a Juvenile Court charge, and in the care of the Department of Community Welfare. The department had expected the boy to be remanded to the McNally Training Centre, but Judge Newman released him. He did not have as much as five cents in his pocket. It was late in the afternoon, and no one from the department was in court. Fortunately Shirley Peisley was there, and it was she who saw that the boy had a meal and caught the bus back to Port Victoria.

Natascha MacNamara was a member of the ALRM executive at that time. She was the daughter of Olga Fudge, a respected Aboriginal woman from Point McLeay, who lived in Adelaide with her husband. Olga spent much of her time holding court in her kitchen, which was at the end of a long passage from her front door. Donald Dunstan, South Australian premier in the 1970s, was among those who would walk up this passage to the generous teapot and wise advice about Aboriginal matters.

Olga was immensely proud of Natascha's Teaching Diploma in Business Administration gained in 1971 from the South Australian College of Advanced Education. Both mother and daughter believed in education as the way to parity between black and white people, but Ruby mistrusted formal education, fearing it would erode her Aboriginality and undermine her sense of identity with the people who crowded into her office.

At the same time Ruby was grateful to Natascha for keeping her aware of the formalities without which an office can become disorganised. Many Aborigines in South Australia in the 1970s owed something to Natascha for their understanding of the strange committee rites that are part of the white man's tribal customs. The ALRM staff conducted their meetings with agendas and minutes, moving and seconding motions, suspending standing orders when they needed to, and deferring to the 'chair'. Many of them would rather have sat around and talked their problems into a consensus solution, but Natascha, and Aborigines like her, taught them that this would not win what they saw as their constant battle with the Department of Aboriginal Affairs.

The tendency of Aborigines to see the federal government and its departments as hostile elements would have dismayed many good public servants who saw themselves as 'helping' the Aborigines. Ruby acknowledged the help and concern of many individual public servants. The 'enemy' was bureaucracy itself. It was this, she believed, that constantly left Aborigines feeling that they were in a paternalistic situation – a situation that frustrated their aim to achieve in the fullest sense the right to manage their own affairs.

Ruby saw it as important that Aborigines retain their special understanding when they became members of government departments. The Department of Aboriginal Affairs was recruiting Aborigines, but Ruby feared that in the bureaucratic atmosphere some of them would develop 'public service attitudes', working to rules and by the clock.

When young Aborigines began new jobs with the department she urged them never to lose sight of their basic beliefs. She would say to them, 'Ask yourself about what you are doing all the time. Is it what your father would want, what your mother would want? Don't worry about what the government or the department would want. It is what the Aboriginal people want that matters.'

Ruby's working day began early. She was married with

three children, and was a typical working wife, worrying about what to cook for dinner, dashing to the shops on the way home, and catching up with the housework over the weekend. Her husband, Frank, supported her in every way, and so did the children, John, Sandra and Bruce. They all helped with the housework, and Ruby did not employ anyone at home.

The radio was switched on by the first one up. The family usually listened to station 5AD, a commercial station that combined a lively breakfast session with serious news announcements. Sometimes this radio news was the first intimation Ruby had of work that would be coming to her through the day. Since 1975, when discrimination became a legal offence in Australia,[4] the nationality of people in trouble with the law has generally been left out of news reports, but Ruby had an intuitive awareness when Aborigines were involved. Poverty was the underlying theme of almost all Aboriginal crime, and she knew the crimes that poverty led to and the places where the poorest Aborigines lived.

On Tuesday, 1 February 1977, the first news was that there had been an attempted armed robbery at the Wauraltee Hotel in Port Victoria on Yorke Peninsula, and that two boys had been shot dead by the licensee. Port Victoria was not far from the Point Pearce Aboriginal Mission.

This was not a typically Aboriginal crime, but Aborigines were learning 'white ways'. Ruby feared that the boys in this case were from Point Pearce. When she arrived at the office it was known that this was so. The names of the boys who had died were known, and all the staff knew the boys or people who were related to them. The feeling among them was as united as if they were all of one family as, indeed, in many ways they were. It was a tragic happening, and they shared their grief. It was a shameful thing, and they shared their shame.

The following morning it was anger that united the staff. There had been only a Stop Press reference to the tragedy in the *Advertiser* of 1 February. The next day a front-page story began, 'Police said yesterday it was unlikely that any charges would be laid against a Port Victoria publican who shot dead two armed bandits after they broke into his hotel.'

This statement angered Aborigines throughout South Australia. The boys had committed a serious crime, and deserved severe punishment, but they had not deserved to die. It seemed to them that the police had dismissed the whole matter without the enquiry which violent death demands. Is this the first news the public would have had of the event if two white boys had been killed? The staff of the legal service did not think so.

They believed the crime was related to the poor conditions on the reserve. Point Pearce Mission had been established in the days when it had been government policy to segregate Aborigines. Now integration was the policy. The government wanted Aborigines to leave reserves and become part of the general community. Ruby Hammond, and other educated Aborigines, could have supported this if it had been based on a program to prepare people for employment outside the reserve. There was no such program, and the reserve was allowed to run down so that people would want to move. The housing was substandard, and unemployment was at the shocking level of ninety per cent. People stayed there because they did not have the skills or the confidence with which to seek employment in the general community, and they knew that discrimination would handicap what skills they had.

The Wauraltee Hotel case could have been used as a basis for an enquiry into all the problems of Point Pearce. The legal service staff did not want the seriousness of the crime to be underestimated, nor did they want to see the deaths of two young Aborigines dismissed without proper investigation.

In April a Coroner's Inquest was held, and it was found that the publican had been justified in using his gun. No charge was laid against him. One of the boys had been shot in the back while running away, and many Aborigines were not happy with the finding. They accepted it passively because they felt powerless to do anything else, but they were bitter about what had happened, and the way the Adelaide papers had implied hostility between black and white people in early reports.

The legal service staff shared these feelings. Like any other group of twenty-three people they had their differences, and there was sometimes tension between them, but these were quickly lost to sight when situations that discriminated against Aborigines arose. Indignation over the way news was handled by press or television often drew them together.

They were united in anger again on the morning of 10 June 1977 when a House of Representatives Committee was taking evidence in Adelaide on drink-related problems among Aborigines. The *Advertiser* reported the first day's hearings under a large-type heading across the top of the front page – 'Enquiry told of Social Breakup. Drinking Hindering Aboriginal Progress.' It was the sort of statement that left the whole Aboriginal community depressed and angry.

'Don't they realise,' Ruby was saying at the Friday hearings, 'what it must be like for an Aboriginal child to go to school when the *Advertiser* has had that across its headlines? Don't they care? Drinking is hindering the progress of white people. Why don't they make that the news of the day?'

Her anger was still smouldering when, that afternoon, she and Elliott MacAdam, the legal service projects officer, gave evidence before the committee.

Giving evidence before statutory enquiries and commissions was often part of Ruby's work. She and Elliott MacAdam were the regular representatives of the Aboriginal Legal Rights Movement on these occasions. Until late in 1977, when he became administrator of the Aboriginal Cultural Centre, MacAdam was the research officer of the movement. A gifted Aborigine, his high intelligence and sensitive awareness of the needs of those with whom he was dealing made him an excellent man for giving evidence. He had been one of the first Task Force students, and had acquired a sound knowledge of legal procedure. He could advance the points he wished to make and support them in a way that quickly won the respect of the court. Both he and Ruby gave evidence in 1977 before the Royal Commission into the Juvenile Court Acts,[5] and to the House of Representatives Standing Committee on Aboriginal Affairs Inquiry into Alcohol-related Problems.[6] This evidence had to be prepared as well as presented, and could entail long hours of work.

Ruby also went to meetings of the Aboriginal–Police Steering Committee, and lectured to cadets at the Police Academy at Fort Largs. She tried to give these young men some idea of the often heart-breaking background to Aboriginal crime, to help them to see that it was related to poverty, discrimination, and the frustrations of substandard education, housing, employment opportunities, and even health.

Often it was the cadets' first experience of meeting an Aborigine, and Ruby recognised the responsibilities inherent in this. She found them, on the whole, less prepared and less responsive than the classes of school children to whom she sometimes talked.

The cadets asked such questions as, 'Why don't Aborigines stay at school and get some education?'

Ruby explained how discouraging it was for Aborigines to see other Aborigines who had a leaving certificate or matriculation and found they were refused jobs given to white school-leavers with less education. She had experienced this herself, but she could talk about it quite impersonally.

She had slides with which to illustrate her lectures. One sequence showed houses made of bits of old wood and galvanised iron. She remembered a cadet saying he thought they looked 'all right'.

'Do you really think so?' asked Ruby. 'Would you like to live there? There is no water, no sewerage, no light, no gas, no power. Cooking is done on the ground. It is draughty and the roof leaks. Would you like to live there?'

'Well, no, but they are not all that bad.'

'In other words you think they are good enough for Aborigines?'

'I suppose so, yes.'

'I hope,' said Ruby, 'that you will think about what you are really saying.'

She hoped desperately that she could make these young men aware that Aborigines were people seeking a social and economic justice to which they were unquestionably entitled. The task of dispelling their colour prejudices, if they had them, was more daunting, but she tried to break down the stereotyped ideas which many of them had.

Her work introduced her to policemen whom she liked and trusted, but there were still some with narrow prejudices at whose hands black people got only a second-rate chance. It was hard to prove, and harder to correct. She hoped there would be fewer of them graduating in the late '70s and the '80s.

She was a member of the Aboriginal–Police Steering Committee, which was seeking to develop 'guidelines' for police in situations involving Aborigines. She was grateful for the achievements of this committee, and for the concern that brought it into existence. Aboriginal–police relationships were improving, and she tried to build on this.

Problems with tribal and country children coming to Adelaide had to be dealt with. There was not enough accommodation for them, and Ruby and the field officers spent time finding places where these young people would not be too bewildered. Shirley Peisley has never forgotten the little Pitjantjatjara boy she once found at the McNally Training Centre, huddled in a corner unable to understand one word of English. He was awaiting trial, although the staff did not know what the charge was. Shirley later found Pitjantjatjara-speaking people with whom such children could stay.

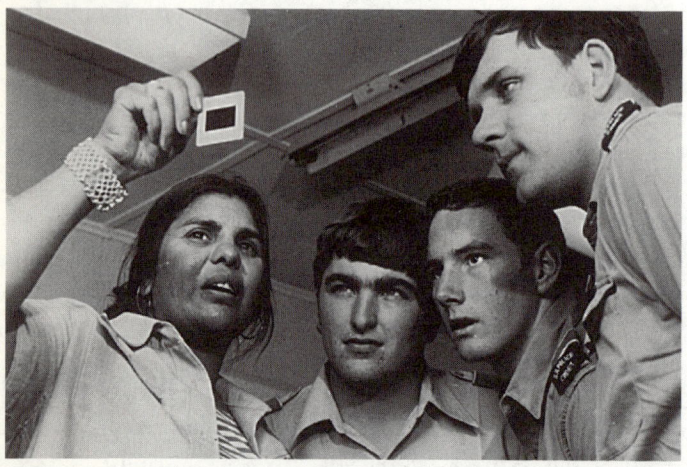

Lecturing to police cadets.

The ALRM was possibly the busiest legal office in Adelaide because cases of every type were dealt with – criminal, civil, traffic, accident, neglected children, worker's compensation, city cases, country cases, and cases from reserves and missions.

When the movement first started, all its work was in support of Aboriginal people in conflict with the police, but a positive move was made to include civil cases, so that all the legal and social rights of Aboriginal people would be covered. The ALRM staff handled such things as claims for damages in road accidents, claims for workers' compensation, claims in relation to tenancies. They advised communities in various matters, and considered general questions.

Many of the criminal cases the movement handled were alcohol related. Ruby was not a qualified social worker, but years of doing welfare work among Aboriginal people had developed in her a well of sympathy and concern for Aborigines caught up in the meshes of alcohol. She was impatient with theories that Aborigines react differently to alcohol from other people, or that some 'racial factor' made them especially liable to become alcoholics.

'They get drunk from drinking too much, just like white people do,' she used to say, 'and they drink from poverty, loneliness, frustration and despair, just like white people do. And the poverty, the loneliness, the frustration and the despair of the Aborigines arises from situations created by white society.'

When Aborigines were criticised for drinking she reacted as protectively as a mother with her children. Confronted with drunken Aborigines she could sit down on the ground beside them and talk quietly with them in a way that perceptibly raised their self-esteem.

Ruby had a rare understanding of the circumstances that gave rise to crime, and the ability to condemn a wrong without losing understanding for the person who had done it. She could be equally understanding with people who were charged with sexual offences.

One case that involved her concerned a sixteen-year-old boy charged with buggery. His whole family had been engulfed in shame to the point where the father was telling people that the boy was to be charged with breaking and entering. The boy believed that this was what would happen, and was in a state of desperate confusion.

Two 'aunties' offered to bring him up to Adelaide for the hearing. They stayed with Ruby, as so many Aborigines did, and she spent a long time talking with the boy.

'It is important you tell the truth,' she said to him. 'If you don't tell the truth how can we or the judge help you?'

He had been going to plead not guilty. His father had told him that if he pleaded guilty he would be put in a mad house.

Next day he said to Ruby, 'I want to tell you something, but I don't know how.'

'Try me,' she said.

'I did it, and I want to plead guilty.'

Ruby promised to stay with him all through the hearing, which she did. He was let off with a bond after his 'aunts' promised to care for him. They had already arranged for him to work on a station property.

'I'll never do it again,' he said to Ruby. 'Next time I'll have a girl.'

So Ruby sat down with him, and had a long talk about girls and their needs, and how important it was not to have sex unless you both wanted it, and understood what it could mean.

Ruby saw him as an innocent, lonely boy, hungry for education – not schooling, but an understanding of the conditions that surrounded him, and the work he was seeking to do. She tried to be tolerant and understanding of his father although she was troubled by his lack of sympathy for the boy.

'It was an incident that should have drawn the family together,' she said, 'but they succumbed to social pressures. I wish more people would realise that you have not achieved your own integrity if you are living up to someone else's standards.'

There was often a sense of great achievement for the ALRM staff, and this was especially so with cases involving the Juvenile Court. The two judges and two magistrates who sat on the bench in this court had shown outstanding concern in Aboriginal cases. On many occasions the court was adjourned to enable judges to discuss cases with the legal service field officers, who were included on the assessment panels for all Aboriginal children.

This was a heartening situation, but for the ALRM to make the fullest use of it they needed more staff, especially for welfare work.

Country children brought to the city had often committed quite trivial offences, and ought not to have been remanded to institutions. There was urgent need for less intimidating places for them to stay.

All this would have needed more money, but in 1977 there were cuts to the funds for Aboriginal Affairs as there were for many government departments. This angered Ruby. Aboriginal Affairs were at the very beginning of a long haul to overcome wrongs that had been building up for 200 years. Whatever economies had to be made in other departments, she believed that Aboriginal Affairs should be given whatever was needed. Of course the money should be spent effectively, and she saw this as meaning that less of it should go into white pockets and administration, and more of it directly to the people in need.

The telephone in the office rang all day long. It brought work, it brought problems and solutions to problems, it brought news, invitations, and requests for help; and it brought, sometimes maliciously, and sometimes casually and unintentionally, the undermining slur of racial prejudice.

Many people assumed that the staff were not Aboriginal because they were well-spoken, which in itself was a slight, and prejudiced people would reveal their prejudices.

Using the telephone to seek housing, employment, or other help for Aborigines, the staff had to suffer speculation, often from people who had never spoken to an Aborigine in their lives, that they would be lazy, or dirty, or have this 'walkabout syndrome', or some other supposed disadvantage.

The staff of the legal service had to put up with this sort of thing quite frequently from people who did not realise they were speaking to Aborigines. There was only a small satisfaction in saying 'I don't think this is necessarily so, I am Aboriginal and I am not lazy' (or whatever the supposed handicap was). This produced an embarrassed silence at the other end of the line, and it might have made a small point, but the total answer was too complex to give in a moment.

They could reply, 'Laziness and dirtiness are shortcomings of the poor. There are lazy, dirty people wherever there is poverty. If it worries you, poverty is what you should be attacking.'

It was hardly the moment to make points such as this, and there was certainly not time to tell the whole story of the Aborigines who, having been pushed into the outback of a land that was once wholly theirs, were trying desperately to find their way back.

The cool way the staff of the legal service, and Aborigines in responsible positions in other offices, handled these gratuitous insults was compelling evidence of their maturity. They would tell the caller courteously that they were Aboriginal, and that they did not agree, and they left it at that.

For Aborigines who have made a success of their lives, the telephone is the main channel through which discrimination reaches them, but it is not the only one. Every person whose skin is black and who lives in a predominantly white society has to suffer discrimination, and some of it is malicious and deliberate.

Occasionally Aborigines say of someone, 'You can't trust him.' They are not talking about his honesty, or his reliability, or his integrity. They mean you cannot trust him to treat Aborigines like fellow human beings.

Every Aboriginal person has to carry this burden of discrimination. At its most shocking level it denies them equality of education, housing, employment, and even health. Discrimination is a basic reason for Aborigines failing to make a successful transition into white society. Those who have succeeded have climbed to their success up a steeper hill than most people face, and even at the top they are not spared. People like Sir Douglas Nicholls, who was governor of South Australia, Neville Bonner, who was a Queensland senator, and Charles Perkins BA, who was a senior civil servant, have all had to endure discrimination in its covert forms.

Some successful Aborigines have learnt to ignore it. Others have built up defences, and some have integrated it so well it has deepened their understanding both of themselves and of other people. It has become part of an inner strength that is winning them the admiration of those who are fortunate enough to know them well.

All the legal service staff in Ruby's time learnt to come to terms with discrimination in some way or another. It was a factor that united them, not only with each other, but also with their clients who, every day, climbed the steep steps that led into the little hallway of the ALRM office.

TWO

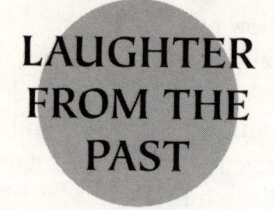

LAUGHTER FROM THE PAST

building defences
against hurt
and slight

MEMORIES OF A HAPPY CHILDHOOD WERE RUBY HAMMOND'S first source of strength when she was confronted by discrimination.

For most of her childhood her family lived independently in their own home within a small Aboriginal community in a scattered settlement at Blackford, about twenty-five kilometres from Kingston on the south-east coast of South Australia. They lived in real poverty but, because of the loving care of their parents, Ruby and her seven brothers and sisters were not aware of being poor. There was always enough to eat, and they did not know about other people with different material standards.

The community was self-supporting. They killed emus and kangaroos for meat. They had a few cows, kept chickens, and grew vegetables and fruit. There were rations for the unemployed – tea, flour, sugar, tobacco, and occasionally blankets, and those who had things shared with those who were in need.

Aborigines were not forbidden to live in the town, but

they were not encouraged to live there. In any case, few of them could afford the rent of a town house. The settlement became known as 'Blackford Reserve', although it was not a prescribed reserve subject to statutory government control. The people were independent and, although they were poor, it was not the stifling poverty that condemned uncounted numbers of Aboriginal children to the tragedy of malnutrition. The Ahangs were among the more fortunate Aboriginal children, neither separated from their parents nor forced into the regimented life of the reserves or the missions.

Ruby's mother had been a domestic help on a country property before she was married, and had learnt a style of middle-class housekeeping that she did her best to recreate for her own family. She sought to instil in them the middle-class virtues and values of the 1930s. In this she had her husband's support. Arthur Ahang had grown up at a time when Aboriginal people were being encouraged to forget their past, and adopt 'white ways'. His parents had wanted their children to have the best of this European life, and did not tell him a great deal of his Aboriginal or Chinese heritage. In 1971 Ruby went in search of it all.

Her father was Australian-born, his mother Aboriginal, and his father Chinese-Aboriginal. Kingston is not far from Robe, a port through which hundreds of Chinese entered Australia to go to the goldfields in Victoria in the 1860s.

Arthur Ahang's grandfather fell in love in the 1860s with an Aboriginal girl, married her and forgot the call of the goldfields. He stayed near Kingston, and is buried in the hills behind Sandys Hut, another little settlement not far from Blackford.

What Arthur knew of his Aboriginal ancestry he owed to 'Queen Ethel',[1] an Aborigine with long links with the Buandik people. Arthur's mother had a kinship with her, and she was 'Granny Ethel' to him and to his children. She lived with her husband, Harry Watson, along the Blackford Road. Kingston Aborigines felt themselves to be related to her, whether they were or not, and she instilled in them a self-discipline that gave Aborigines in that part of South Australia an unusually high reputation. She was the last full-blood Aborigine to live in the Kingston district.

Ethel Ahang with 'Granny Ethel' outside her house at Blackford, 1945.

Ethel and Arthur Ahang with Maureen, 1935.

A memorial to her, erected by the National Trust, stands in a little reserve on the banks of the Maria Creek, where she spent much of her childhood. The reserve is now on the edge of the town, but tales are still told of uncleared bushland, and about 200 Buandik Aborigines camping there in their wurlies. Some recall seeing the platforms in the tea trees on which their dead were placed, the corroborees at night, and the natives decorated with ceremonial clay.

Queen Ethel's monument was designed and created by Verne McLaren.[2] He was a grazier with a national and international involvement in conservation and cultural heritage, and was for many years the chairman of the Kingston branch of the National Trust.

'I don't know who first called her "Queen Ethel",' McLaren said, 'because obviously women didn't hold that sort of status in their old lives, but it was a merited title. She had a regal quality about her, and she was indeed the ruler of the Kingston Aboriginal community.'

Ruby remembered her as a warm-hearted, merry lady, who sang and danced easily. Queen Ethel certainly developed a streak of independence that is not traditional for Aboriginal women. A tale told by her granddaughter, Lola Bonney, relates that once on a drive into Kingston in a buggy drawn by a pair of horses, Ethel had a difference with her husband that resulted in her unhitching one of the horses from the buggy pole and riding home. Poor Harry Watson had to struggle home as best he could with the other horse, which, because of the pole, had to be harnessed to one side of the buggy.

When Arthur Ahang left school the depression still had a few years to run. Employment was hard to get, but there were plenty of rabbits to trap in the Blackford Hills and occasional jobs of stone-breaking on the roads.

Working in road gangs taught Arthur Ahang that the human race was one that all people belonged to, and that the colour of your skin was of no more importance than the colour of your boots, if you were lucky enough to have a pair.

These were hard times, but Arthur believed in making the best of every situation. He learnt a song in those days, an old Hollywood classic about 'painting the clouds with sunshine', and he would sing it if things were getting him down.

Arthur did not have much time for 'whingers', or for drunks or layabouts. In his young days there was no drinking for Aborigines, and he accepted this well enough. He thought, in fact, that it would have been better if this had not been changed.

When he got into the army Arthur discovered that he was the only one in his company not allowed to drink. This was discrimination, and he objected. He went absent without leave. The military police either did not look for him or did not catch up with him. He had a very short army career.

During the depression years Saturday was the highlight of the week. Friday night was bath night, and the young Blackford males made sure that their shirts were clean, their suits pressed and their shoes polished. These were standards to which the Watsons, the Steeds, the Ahangs and the other Aboriginal families in Blackford expected their children to conform.

The boys would be up early to catch the horses, racing on them along the road before they harnessed them up. Then off the families would go for a morning in town and an afternoon at the football.

Arthur Ahang played football well and he could have had the pick of the girls who came to cheer the local teams. With what proved to be great discernment, his choice fell upon Ethel Ellis.

Ethel was not a Kingston girl, but she had worked at a station homestead in the Kingston district, and had friends in Kingston whom she visited. She had spent her earliest years in the mid-north of South Australia, but she had grown up in Adelaide where her parents had gone to escape the 'protection'[3] of the government.

Her mother, Ruby Ellis, who had been Ruby Smith, had been brought up at the Hermannsburg Mission near Alice Springs. She had been taken from her mother in the ruthless fashion of the 1800s. This policy was based on a belief that part-European children were better off in an institution than with their mothers. It was implemented in a way that makes it one of the scandals of the colonising of Australia.

Ruby Hammond's aunt, Miriam Dadleh, had dreadful

memories of the forcible abduction of children. Her father was an Afghan camel-driver, and as she grew up she travelled all over the area between Alice Springs, Marree and Oodnadatta. She remembered seeing Aboriginal women in an agony of pain and grief after having their babies torn literally from their breasts.

Hermannsburg Mission was a place that took these children and, in the Christian traditions of the day, did its best by them. Little brown-skinned boys and girls were taught to speak English, and to sing Lutheran hymns. The girls were taught to cook and sew, and were generally prepared for a life of domestic service to white women. To make it easier (and one wonders for whom) they were given English names, and Ruby's grandmother became Ruby Smith.

She went to work at Anna Springs, which lies between Alice Springs and Marree, and here she met and married a white man, Charlie Ellis. There was no question of a white man and an Aboriginal woman not marrying if they wished to live together in those days. The man would be up on a charge of consorting unless he was married.

They lived for a time in Marree, but they began to fear the government would take their children from them. They went to Adelaide and their four children, Ida, Ethel, Myrtle and Ernie, all went to the Sturt Street primary school.

Ernie Ellis was to return to Marree and re-identify so closely with his mother's Adnyamathanha people that he became an initiated elder. The three girls stayed closer to the city, and the 'white ways' of their upbringing. Ruby and Charlie Ellis believed, like Arthur Ahang's parents, that adopting European standards and customs offered their children the best hope for the future.

Ethel Ellis eventually went into domestic service, as her mother had done before her. She learnt eagerly from the women for whom she worked and her ideas of cooking, housekeeping and child care were those of her employers.

When she married Arthur Ahang they found a little timber and galvanised iron shack at Sandys Hut. She took her domestic service values and customs with her and preserved them faithfully for her children.

Ethel Ahang is well remembered by the people of Kingston. 'She was a lovely woman,' says Mary Cameron. 'She was a marvellous person,' says Verne McLaren. Both of these people were neighbours of the Ahangs, and their high regard for Ethel is echoed by all who knew her. She was fun-loving, courageous, resourceful, kind, and utterly devoted to her children.

She and Arthur were married in 1934. Jobs were hard to get then, but they kept a couple of cows at Sandys Hut, and sold the milk. They trapped rabbits, and sometimes Arthur would get a job on the roads. He had to be away for a week at a time on these occasions, but he would always get back for the weekend. He would pack a couple of loaves of bread, some butter and meat, and a tin of jam into a home-made haversack and, if no one came by to give him a lift, he would walk the five kilometres to the little timber and iron house where he and Ethel lived.

While they were living there they had two daughters, Maureen, born in 1935, and Ruby, born in 1936, and two sons, Fred in 1938, and Jack in 1940. When the babies were about to be born Arthur would take Ethel into Kingston to stay with his sister, Dossie Hartman, and her husband, Bill. The children were born in a house on the corner of Holland and Agnes Streets, where the midwife lived.

The war years brought greater prosperity. Jobs were easier to get, and Arthur decided to move closer to Kingston. Sandys Hut was too far from the little school at Blackford for the children to walk there, and in those days there was no school bus. Arthur and Ethel Ahang wanted education for their children.

Ruby's first lessons were around the kitchen table at Sandys Hut. Because they were Aborigines, an officer from the Department of Aboriginal Affairs would come to visit them once a year. The Ahangs were lucky. Marjorie Angas was assigned to them. She was a young woman then, just starting out on her career, but even then she saw Aboriginal families as people with whom to make friends. She also recognised that people in need of help also needed understanding. These attitudes were not by any means the general rule in the 1940s.

Marjorie Angas impressed on Ethel Ahang the need for the children to study by correspondence, and Ethel, with a few years of primary education to guide her, gathered together some primers and other early reading books, and helped the children pick out the words and copy them down.

When Ruby was six her parents moved to Bullocky Town so that the children could go to school. It was a long walk, more than six kilometres, but she and Maureen trudged the distance every morning, and later Fred came too.

The highlight of their journey was crossing the bridge over the Maria Creek. Sometimes they would stop to play. They had been well taught about the dangers of water, and never went near the edge.

Not far from the bridge is an island where black swans nest. It is a tiny island, but when Ruby was a child it looked big. She longed to go on it and explore. Years later she remembered this island poignantly when she was on another island, thousands of kilometres away, in the Yenisey River in the heart of the Soviet Union.

After a year or two in Bullocky Town, a chance came for the Ahangs to move to what had been a boundary rider's stone cottage in Blackford, on a property belonging to Verne McLaren. He and his wife, Jean, were the kindest of neighbours and became the Ahangs' life-long friends. The cottage was not too far for the children to walk to the little school where Arthur had once studied, and memories of the past filled it with promise.

By this time the family consisted of Maureen, Ruby, Fred, Jack, Irene and Kingsley; Kevin and Marie were yet to be born. For all of them the little house at Blackford was to become a place of great happiness.

In 1976 Ruby made a nostalgic visit back to Blackford with her son Bruce. The little house was still standing although a cyclone had torn off the iron roof. The stone walls were intact, and inside the little rooms were the remains of furniture. The frames of stuffed chairs lay around the old fireplace in the tiny living room; in the kitchen the oven where Ethel had baked their bread was rusting in a corner; and in the little back room was all that remained of the old wooden and iron bed in which Ethel and Arthur had slept.

'It was so tiny,' Ruby said after this visit. 'At the time I thought we had quite a big house.'

The family was poor, but Arthur Ahang was a resourceful man. He could cut timber, make fences, train and break-in horses, and eventually he developed an established round as a shearer, but this was all seasonal work, often hard to get, and in the 1940s it was not well paid. They had eight children, and although the government introduced child endowment in 1941, it was only a few shillings a week.

The Ahangs managed as well as they could in the little house. There was no glass in the windows, and when it was cold and wet Ethel and Arthur moved sheets of galvanised iron across to keep out the weather. The roof leaked. Ruby later remembered that when it rained heavily they would put buckets to catch the drips.

The children would hear the 'ting, ting, ting' of water dripping into the buckets. When it went 'plop, plop, plop' it was time to empty them.

Sometimes Arthur would find a sheet of galvanised iron and go up and mend the roof, but it was always old iron, and a heavy shower usually meant a run for the buckets.

There was no electricity, no running water, no bathroom. On bath night the bath was put in front of the fire in the living room, and was filled with water heated in buckets on the kitchen stove. If there was a good fire going the children had to be careful not to burn themselves on that side of the bath, and if it was left there overnight they had to beware of stumbling into it in the dark, or slipping on the soap.

The little house was still standing.

These were things they accepted without complaint. It was the way it was. They were never hungry, and if they were cold they got used to it.

Their parents set store by the children looking nice when they went out, and they always had school clothes that were cleaned and pressed. The clothes were usually second-hand, but their mother altered them to fit. Ruby remembered Ethel making and mending on a hand-turned sewing machine. Ethel used to make pants for the boys from the legs of their father's worn trousers, lining them with material from flour bags.

Ruby loved to recall her mother at the clothes line at the back of the house where Ethel so often had a big wash blowing in the wind.

Above: Fred, Kingsley and Irene with Banker and pups, 1945.
Below: Ethel Ahang with Maureen (L) and Ruby (R), 1938.

Fred and Jack ready for school, 1945.

Ruby would smile, remembering laughter from the past, and blue days with steam rising from the 'washing machine' with the manual plunger, which was a great feature of their household routine. It stood outside the back door, and Ruby could recall it against the green hillside under the vast sky. The hill sloped gently to the plain that extended to the sea, so the sky at Blackford was a greater dome than it ever was in the city, or in mountainous country, and Ruby's memories were backed with blue skies or great tumbling cloud patterns.

The Ahang children all recall helping their mother with

the housework and washing and ironing as part of the routine of their early days. Every weekend clothes would be on the long line, which was pushed up by the prop Arthur had made from the spindly trunk of a tea tree.

'Keep plunging,' Ethel would call, and the children would take it in turns to push the plunger up and down; or they would go down the hillside to the waterhole from which they had to bring up all the household water. Two of them would carry water up in a bucket suspended on a broom handle. Years later Ruby would still dissolve into laughter remembering times when she did this with Kingsley, younger and in those days much smaller, so that it was a problem to keep the broom handle level and the bucket from spilling.

The children ran barefoot at home, and could race over stones and the roughest of ground, but they each had a pair of shoes to wear to school, or 'for best'. Ruby remembered a family whose children went to school in torn clothes, or with hems dropping down. Ethel would never let her children go out in anything that needed mending. The Ahang children were always clean and neat. They were expected to behave well, and they did.

Verne McLaren remembers the little boys going off to school in their grey suits, and the girls in jumpers and skirts. 'They were always well dressed and well behaved,' he says, 'and they were all pretty smart at their school work.'

The children remember that their mother 'did everything'. She used to bake their bread, sending to Melbourne for the yeast, which came, in blocks, COD to the post office. Baking days had a special mystique. Ethel would mix the dough and put it to rise in a big preserving pan with a cloth over it. Then woe betide any child who created a draught, or bumped into it, or otherwise caused it to subside.

'We used to creep about and not make any noise when the dough was rising,' Ruby said, recalling these days.

She remembered a tale of bread-making as a favourite story of her mother's days in service. Ethel thought one batch of dough had gone wrong and was not going to rise, so she buried it in the garden. It was summer time, and next day when the sun came up it rose after all, pushing up through the ground like a giant mushroom and causing considerable amazement to her employers.

Near Blackford was a tiny school that hardly seemed big enough for ten children, but twenty or more of them used to fit into it, divided into seven grades with a single teacher.

The school was furnished with Education Department double desks, with sloping tops and ink wells, and seats on hinges to allow the pupils to rise and say, 'Good morning, sir,' when the teacher came in.

Arthur Ahang received all his formal schooling at these desks, but he claimed he got his education after he left.

'They just used to drum things into you at school,' he used to say. 'They didn't give you time to think about anything. It wasn't until I got away from school, and mixed with people, and thought about what I saw and heard, that I really began to learn anything worthwhile.'

All the Ahang children went to this school. Mostly they walked the three kilometres, but sometimes a farmer going by with a horse-and-trap would give them a lift, and sometimes one of the neighbours who had a car would pick them up. Ruby remembered it as 'a tiny little car with about seven kids jammed in the dickey seat at the back'.

The little one-roomed school, still standing in the 1990s, is a tiny building in the middle of a great paddock. It is smaller than any cottage in the district, and there is no notice or other sign to mark it as a school. Passersby wonder what on earth it is, but those enterprising enough to climb the locked gate and look through the broken window can see the 'blackboards' painted on the two side walls. At one end is a fireplace, and at the other a row of old-fashioned hooks where the children hung their coats. An old, sagging cupboard spills out a deteriorating supply of hymn books and Bibles, revealing that the building's last function was as a church and Sunday school.

'Where was the playground?' asked Ruby's city-bred son Bruce, gazing round at a more splendid play area than any suburban school staff could dream of.

'It's all here,' Ruby told him, pointing to the great gums, and the pepper trees that were planted on Arbor days when her father was a boy, and in whose branches they used to swing and climb. They used to play makeshift cricket on the hillside with piles of stones for wickets and sticks for bats. Across the road was the bush where they had gone birdnesting. The posts where some of the pupils had hitched their horses still supported the fence. Ruby could point to the bushes where she used to hide her father's boots, which she would sometimes wear over her own shoes in wet weather.

Further on towards Kingston was the group of cottages where Queen Ethel had lived. These cottages still had their roofs, and although their contents were crumbling away it was possible to find among them enough evidence to piece together in great detail the way in which their owners must have lived.

There was a big fireplace in each house, and near it the remains of the big, stuffed chairs that were in vogue in the era between the two world wars. *Women's Weekly* pictures had been pasted on the kalsomined walls, and kalsomined bags that once formed the ceilings hung down like strands of giant cobwebs.

All these little houses had plastered walls and bag ceilings that were constantly painted over with kalsomine. Ruby could remember bringing back bags of powdered kalsomine in their jinker, from Kingston. It would be mixed with water in the preserving pan, and the family would take turns with a big brush to paint it on and give all the rooms a new lease of life. She remembered the excitement when coloured kalsomine first came in and the walls could be painted pink or blue.

When Ruby was showing these places to Bruce, the kalsomine had powdered off, and only traces of the once bright linoleum remained on the floors. An old treadle sewing machine lay in one room with the remains of an old 'Mrs Potts' iron, parts of a cream separator, and piles of the loops of fencing wire that were used for drying rabbit skins.

Outside, the remains of a windmill were rusting away. The gardens were overgrown and encroaching into the house, but fruit trees remained, a patch of mint gone wild, and lilacs and gladioli and geraniums.

Uncle Milton's old blue utility was still under the trees where he had last parked it more than twenty years earlier, and Uncle Colin Watson's tractor and farm implements looked almost as though they could be revived for use.

The house where the Ahangs had lived was on a rise which sloped to the road where the children had waited for the school bus. Ruby recalled the younger children waiting by the gate, and signalling up to her and Maureen and Fred when the bus was coming, and racing down to catch it.

Fig trees that had been growing near the house were gone, but the pine trees that Ruby remembered were still there. Black cockatoos were screeching in them as they did when she was a child. They came for the pine nuts, which the children used to eat too.

Under the pines lay the rusting wheels and the rotting shafts of the old jinker, which had meant excitement when Ruby was young. It was in this old jinker that the Ahangs had gone off on visits to the families down the road, and on their rare trips to Kingston.

The Watsons had been the hub of the social life for the Aboriginal people in the area. Queen Ethel had married Harry Watson. Bill Watson was their son, and his children, Linda, Vi, and Colin, were friends of the Ahang children. They had an old wind-up gramophone, and the children acquired a taste for cowboy music from the Slim Dusty and Tex Moreton records that Linda and Vi Watson used to collect. Later they had a 'wireless', which was the wonder of the times, and soon the children became expert at switching to all the cowboy sessions. Yodelling became one of their skills.

Arthur Ahang was often away shearing or fencing. When he was at home he would do the Kingston shopping, riding off on a bicycle for the twenty-five kilometre journey with a game bag slung over his shoulder. He would set off early in the morning, and return in the afternoon with flour and sugar and things they could not grow or harvest from the surrounding countryside.

When Arthur returned from his shearing trips he would sometimes bring other things – toys for the children, saucepans and household gadgets for Ethel. On one memorable occasion he turned up with a 'wireless'. In those days there were no transistors or 'portables' and this wireless was a sizeable domed wooden box, worked off a car battery, stained dark brown, with a loudspeaker and the first knobs the Ahang children learned to turn.

Arthur had managed to get a lift out in a utility that was going out to Blackford, and he arrived home with his prize after the children were in bed. Ruby remembered hearing him arrive, and the music being turned on, and their mother walking up and down the room in excitement, waiting for the children to wake up and come and see what Dad had brought home.

Sometimes it was necessary to go to Kingston when Arthur was away. If it was school holidays they could take a weekday for the excursion, but in the term time it had to be on Saturday morning. This meant rising at four am because they had to be on the road at first light in time to get their shopping done before the shops closed at midday.

On the previous day the children would have carried bath water up from the waterhole, and it would have stood all night on top of the wood-burning stove. The bath would have been set ready in front of the fire in the living room, where Ruby and Irene slept in one bed, and Kevin in another. Clean clothes for everyone would have been laid out.

Before daylight Ruby would hear her mother building up the kitchen fire, and soon she would be in the front room, rekindling the fire too. Everyone would be up and involved in the bathing and breakfast preparations, catching and harnessing the horse, packing up the jinker, tidying up the house. Soon after dawn all would be ready, and they would crowd into the jinker, with Ethel in the driving seat, and set off on the long ride to town.

Ethel never seemed at a loss when Arthur was away. Although she did not like shooting, she would go out and kill an emu or a kangaroo if they were short of meat. Emus used to come to feed on the seeds of the karli bushes, and Ethel would creep out silently to catch them down-wind, and shoot the one that promised the most tender meat.

She had not had much education, but she could read what she needed, and this included a battered old 'home remedy' book, from which she would treat the children when they were sick.

Ruby grew up in a household where the mother was often in charge, confidently making decisions and directing the life of the family. Long after 1975 Ruby still had on the bumper of her car an International Women's Year sticker that said 'A Woman's Place is Everywhere'. Her earliest life patterns had prepared her for ready acceptance of this slogan of the '70s.

The Ahang children wonder now whether Ethel was ever nervous when their father was away and she had only the children with her in the isolated little house at night, and whether she worried when food was short and she had not heard from her husband.

'She must have worried,' they say, 'but she never let us know about it.'

Mary Cameron (Mrs Johnny Cameron), who was a neighbour, remembers a day when she went out on her verandah and saw a big snake climbing up a cross-bar supporting the roof. She got a short-handled spade and held it against the post, sending one of the children for something to kill it with. The child ran for Mrs Ahang, and in minutes she was there with an iron bar with which she attacked the snake without wasting a moment.

On another occasion a particularly ferocious goat had become loose. It came charging into the yard of the Ahang house, and with head down ran for one of the children who rushed, terrified, into the house. The goat tried to get in through the front door. Ethel slammed the door and gathered the children into the house through the back door.

'Quickly, get on the table,' she cried. Five children crowded onto the kitchen table while she got a stock whip and chased the goat off the premises.

Eventually the little Blackford school was closed, and the Education Department ran a bus that picked up children over a radius of about fifty kilometres and took them into the Kingston school.

The Ahang children would race down to catch it, clutching their school bags with their homework books and a cut lunch, which all too often they would eat on the ride in.

When they got home again it would be late in the afternoon. The first thing they did was take off their good school clothes and hang them up. Then, in older clothes, they

Ethel would shoot the emu that promised the most tender meat.

would set about helping with what was still to be done, bringing in the firewood, carrying up the water, fetching and milking the cow, collecting the eggs, and, without fail, cleaning their shoes for the following day.

After their evening meal Ethel would wash up with the younger children, keeping them quiet while the all-important homework was done at the kitchen table.

The house had no power, indeed, it had no services at all. The fire kept them warm, and kerosene lamps and candles supplied the light. If these ran short their mother made 'dripping lights' – enamel mugs of dripping with wicks of string or old cloth.

The weekends were busy too. There was the washing to be done, and the ironing. This was a hated chore, and one that was always done by the mother or the daughters. They used irons that had to be filled with live coals, and often had to be taken outside to be swung about in the wind to cool them off. The ironing used to pile up, and they would run to cover the mound with a sheet or a tablecloth if visitors came up the path. Ruby often thought of these mounds of ironing. All her life she found the ironing to be a chore that eluded her, and piled up.

Weekends also brought exciting excursions – hunting with their father, rabbit trapping, gathering the wattle and tea-tree bark which they sold to the tanners, or cutting flax and heavy grasses that the women wove into baskets. Hunting meant killing kangaroos and emus for food, or foxes for the skins they could sell.

These often meant long trips, setting off at dawn and returning after dark. Sometimes their father would camp out overnight. The children seldom went on these excursions, but when they were older, the boys would go.

From the front of the house there was a wide view of the Kingston plains, now largely cleared, but which in Ruby's childhood was mostly virgin bush. Immediately over the road was a swamp, which the Ahang children learnt to know and fear. It was a dangerous maze of quicksand and once, to their horror, they lost a cow in this dreadful quagmire. The children knew the safe paths, and if their father was late home from a hunting trip they would light a fire on the hill to guide him back. He would light bushes along the track and a communication would be set up.

The Blackford drain has reduced the menace of this swamp, but it is still a frightening place to the uninitiated.

The Ahangs did not go away for holidays, although when Ruby was in her teens they acquired a second-hand Dodge which they all learned to drive. In the summer they would pile into it and go to Long Beach for picnics, and sometimes to sleep overnight.

She remembered going to Adelaide with her mother to stay with Granny Ruby Ellis when her brother Kingsley was born. She had warm memories of her grandmother, who was loving and kind and indulgent to the little ones. She loved the name 'Ruby', given to her for her dark, proud grandmother, Ruby Ellis, whose blood linked her to the Adnyamathanha people of the far north.

Her granny had a magpie that used to say, 'Who's that Ruby? Who's that?', which delighted the little girl whose name was Ruby too.

Ruby was about seven when Kingsley was born, and inevitably she wanted to know where the baby came from.

'The doctor brought him.'

'How did the doctor bring him?'

'In a chaff bag.'

Ruby was used to things coming in a chaff bag, and this satisfied her. Her mother belonged to a generation that had been taught that it was 'not nice' to be frank about sex, and Ruby got her sex education, like most of her contemporaries, from observation and hearsay, supplemented by playground chatter.

Ruby's other early contacts with Adelaide were through her father's sister Maureen, who lived in Port Adelaide with her daughter, Noelene. They would sometimes come to Blackford for holidays, Aunty Rene bringing boxes of apples and oranges from the Central Market, which were a great treat for the Ahang children.

Noelene, who was a year older than Ruby, always seemed a very sophisticated person. Ruby used to envy the dresses and shoes she would bring up with her. She had a special memory of a pair of black patent leather shoes with silver buckles. Ruby longed for a pair like them.

Noelene was a city kid, and the Ahang children used to scare her about the 'dangers' of the bush. Noelene had her revenge when once or twice Ruby came to stay with her. After Noelene had warned her about the dreadful boys who might sit next to her at the Port Adelaide Ozone Theatre, Ruby was sure the city was much more frightening than the bush could ever be. In town she was just a country bumpkin, scared of getting lost.

She went to stay with Noelene during school holidays when she was fourteen. Noelene wanted a job for the holidays, and Ruby said she would like one too. They got work with some hardware merchants, Colton Palmer and Preston, making lamps. Noelene had to press out a screw-on fitting. Ruby's job was to stand by the spray painter, moving up the unsprayed lamps, and then hanging up the painted ones on a rack to dry. At the end of the first day she thought she had rheumatics; at the end of the week she knew this was not the sort of job she wanted. This was a factor in encouraging her to do three years at secondary school.

On Sundays the little school served as a church. Ruby thought it was Methodist. Sometimes the family would go.

There was a little pedal organ that had been there when Arthur was a boy, and Ruby later remembered the music and singing hymns.

A neighbouring Lutheran family persuaded Arthur to have the children baptised, and later an Anglican priest persuaded them to come to his church. What Ruby remembered most of church were Christmas parties, with Father Christmas, presents and balloons.

When she was at school she would tag along to religious instruction with whichever girl she was most friendly with that week, but she remembered nothing of those lessons.

Her own philosophy was to accept gratefully all that was good in her life, all that was offered in kindness, and to return to those in need. This was not too far from what she might have learnt in church, but it was not in church that she learnt it. It was absorbed from her parents through all that was best in her happy childhood.

Ruby never went to church after her school days. What she knew of Christian philosophy was gleaned from newspapers, radio, and television. It seemed to her that Christianity was preoccupied with sin, whereas her own philosophy was concerned with goodness. The Church, she felt, had more to say about massage parlours than about substandard housing for Aborigines, more to say about abortion than about infant mortality in Aboriginal communities. It did not attract her.

Her parents, having accepted that assimilation offered the best future for their children, taught them nothing of Aboriginal law or morality. They taught them to behave and conform in the terms of the best they knew of white society. What the children heard of the Aboriginal past were just a few stories, a few memories.

Ethel Ahang had memories of Marree, which became for Ruby the place that symbolised the Aboriginal past. She remembered especially her mother's stories of the 'mutha puttaye', the strange 'old grey man' of Coward Springs who could be summoned up like a bunyip from the spring by anyone who knew the secret of stirring the waters. Her mother had raced, terrified, down the hill when she had first seen it, and the story used to stir fears in the Ahang children.

Even more frightening were the stories Uncle Milton Wilson told. He lived with the Watsons down the road, and it was he who first awakened Ruby's feeling for her Aboriginal inheritance. He was a regular visitor to the Blackford house, and Ruby had vivid memories of him.

Outside it would be cold and dark. Inside the fire would be burning. The only other light was the kerosene lamp in the kitchen where their mother would be cutting lunches for the next day. The children were crowded into the front room because Uncle Milton had come to tea, and now he was telling stories, eerie tales of the spirits of the bush, the little green men outside, the big dog with red eyes, and the red kangaroo at the Jip Jip rock. This rock is in a national park to the east of Kingston. Aborigines never stay there after dark, even though they are not afraid of the bush at night.

Uncle Milton told them stories of the minka bird that cried like a baby, and which no one wanted to hear because it brought a message of death. After someone had died he would point to the sagging roof of the house they had lived in and say to the children, 'Look, that's where the minka bird perched,' and the children would go some roundabout way to avoid this benighted place.

The stories were not morality tales. It was not a question of what would happen to you if you were not 'good', but for Ruby they were her earliest source of thinking about those things which lie beyond what we know. They were linked with indefinable fears.

Years later when Andrew Collett was working as a solicitor with the Aboriginal Legal Rights Movement he was talking seriously with Ruby about ways of introducing Aboriginality into court procedures.

'What puts the fear of God into you?' he asked.

'I don't know,' said Ruby, 'the minka bird, I suppose,' and she told Andrew Collett of Uncle Milton's stories.

'Well,' said Andrew, only half jokingly, 'perhaps we could have 'minka bonds' and 'minka paroles' for Aboriginal offenders.'

Aborigines have deep responses to death, but surely this is something we all have in common. There are cemeteries in many cities that councils would convert into parks, or put to a more mundane use if it were not for public feeling about places associated with the dead. Yet in Kingston a refuse depot was established at the site of an ancient Aboriginal burial ground at the mouth of the Maria Creek. Following protest from the Aboriginal Legal Rights Movement the actual burial site was fenced off with a few old posts and some fencing wire. There was no marker for the site, and no notice to tell passersby that this was a sacred site for Aborigines. It was given only token recognition, and you could dump your rubbish around it while the cheapest of fences discouraged you from actually dumping on it. The National Trust became aware of this situation, and promised something would be done when money was available.

Money didn't become available and local Aborigines decided to restore it themselves. A large number of native shrubs were planted and a walkway developed. In December 1989 the site was dedicated to the memory of the early Aborigines, with a plaque marking the occasion. The Aboriginal flag now flies over it, and it is cared for by an Aboriginal committee led by Ian Steed.

Death came into the lives of the Ahang family when Ruby was fifteen, the only serious tragedy that was to touch them while they were young. Maureen died. She developed a throat infection which Ethel could not cure. They took her to the Kingston hospital. An ambulance was sent for to take her to Naracoorte, but Maureen died before they could get there.

Her death was a tremendous grief to them all. She had been the eldest, and had been the leader in many things. She was the one who helped them all with their school work. She could dance better than any of them, and she was the first of them to show a talent for drawing.

The whole family loved music and dancing, and Ruby had special memories of exhibition nights at the home of Kingston's dancing teacher, Shirley Curkpatrick, where Maureen was the star performer. They would be held in the summer, when the audience could sit on the lawn while the pupils danced on the verandah. European traditions were the ones that were followed here too. The dance at which Maureen especially excelled was the highland fling.

Her death left Ruby as the eldest, and the one to whom all the younger ones would turn.

Their mother bore her deep grief stoically, and Ruby and Irene drew closer together. Although Ruby was the older by five years the bond between them was always close and strong. Sometimes they felt there was almost a telepathic communication between them.

Each of the girls thought the other was like their mother.

'Ruby is like her,' Irene would say. 'I never feel unsure about things when I am with Ruby. She seems to know what is right all the time, just like Mum did. She says, "Don't worry, it will all work out." I don't remember Mum using these words, but it was Mum's philosophy.'

It was their father's philosophy too. There was a lot of her father in Ruby.

Ruby claimed that Irene was the one who was really like their mother. 'She is always concerned for others, but content to stay in the background, fulfilling herself through her family; and she is gentle, just like Mum was.' She was Ruby's beloved sister, a source of strength to her all her life.

All Irene's early memories centre around the house at Blackford. She remembers a life of great contentment there, in which little things were the ones that mattered, highlighted with 'excitements' that were often quite simple things.

Irene remembers occasions when her parents would go off to visit friends, leaving her in the care of the older children. They would contrive 'surprises' for them, especially their mother – little things like tidying out a cupboard, or putting clean paper in the cutlery drawer.

The most memorable of these 'surprises' for Irene was an occasion when she was ten and she and Jack, who was then twelve, killed a kangaroo for their parents. They had gone out with the dogs, and the dogs bailed up a big red kangaroo. They had no gun, because the children were never allowed guns when they were alone, but here was a kangaroo and Irene and Jack knew the house was out of fresh meat. With sticks, and the help of the dogs, they killed it as quickly as they could, and dragged it home.

'I don't know how far we dragged it,' Irene says. 'It took us hours and hours. We had to get it home. Having killed it, we couldn't leave it, and we knew there was no meat at home.'

When they got in sight of the house Irene ran on ahead and got Kevin's old pram to bring it the last few hundred yards. When they finally got it home the surprise and praise of their parents was splendid reward, and they had fresh meat for dinner that night. They were late back, but their mother did not seem worried, only delighted to see them.

Their parents were always very strict about guns. The children were all taught how to carry a gun properly, how to care for it, how to shoot with it, and how to keep it so that it was safe all the time.

Ethel Ahang was always busy – washing, ironing, cooking,

sewing, knitting, looking after the animals, and tending the beautiful flower garden she had at the front of the house. The children remember tomatoes growing, but not many other vegetables. What they remember are the lilies and the daisies, the larkspurs and the snapdragons, and the little ground flowers in the rockery under the flowering plum trees.

Ethel loved to knit, and she made jumpers for all the children. She used to get the *New Idea* (a women's magazine renowned for its knitting patterns), and she would produce colourful jumpers with Fair Isle patterns or nursery rhyme figures on them. These are the memories Irene loves to recall, and she is indeed like her mother.

Irene can remember magical Christmas mornings. A few days before Christmas their mother would kalsomine the walls. They used to get smoky, but she would kalsomine them, and make them fresh again.

Then, on Christmas morning, the children would wake up to find the house bedecked with streamers and a Christmas tree cut from the pines outside standing in a corner.

There were always animals at home, and the children always kept pets. At Blackford they had cows for their milk, a horse to pull the jinker, chickens that roosted in the pines and laid eggs under the bushes, dogs for hunting, and innumerable pets. They always had dogs and at least one cat. There were often birds that were tame enough to be considered part of the household, and, most memorably, there was Irene's kangaroo, Betty.

Sometimes there would be a young kangaroo in the pouch of a kangaroo killed for meat, and the children would try to raise it, but not often with success. It was Irene who managed to keep alive the little grey doe that became 'Betty', the dearest of all the family pets.

It was devoted to Irene and would try to follow her to school. She would have to stand up in the bus, leaning out and calling, 'Go home, Betty, go home, Betty,' and Betty would be waiting for her when she came back in the afternoon.

Betty had to sleep outside, but as soon as Ethel was up in the morning the kangaroo would come scratching at the door. Ethel would make herself tea and toast, and give Betty a saucer of toast and milk. Then the little kangaroo would hop over to Irene's room, and curl up on the bed with her until she got up.

One winter Betty got too close to the coals of a dying fire, and burnt her fur. When it regrew it was white, so Betty was a very distinctive little kangaroo. The dogs learnt quickly that she was part of the family, and not only never threatened her, but would never attack grey kangaroos the same size as Betty.

Sometimes Irene would dress Betty up, put mascara on her beautiful long eyelashes, and put nail-polish on the nails of her little paws. Betty loved this.

When Irene went away after she was married, Betty pined for her, and used to hop along the road, presumably looking for her, until one day she met the inevitable fate of kangaroos who spend too long on the road. She was killed by a speeding car.

It was from this home that Ruby used to race down the hill to catch the bus that took her to school in Kingston. She loved school. She did well at her work, and she was always in the basketball team. On four occasions she won the school trophy for the 'best and fairest player'.

Her prizes were things like crystal glasses, and a brush and comb set. She longed for a 'cup'. The only year at school in which she failed to win this award was the only one in which a 'cup' was given.

Perhaps it was just coincidence, but Ruby believed that, from the kindest of motives, the school thought an Aborigine would not know what to do with a 'cup'; that they were unable to realise the extent to which their Aboriginal pupils had identical hopes and aspirations, tastes, standards and ideals with those of the other students.

Irene and Betty at Blackford, 1956.

This was the type of racism, often well enough intentioned, that Ruby encountered at school. No one ever told her that there were people in whose eyes it was somehow more praiseworthy to be white than black, but it was one of those things that are learnt without being taught.

She saluted the flag every morning, repeating with the others: 'I love my country, the British commonwealth. I honour her King, King George VI. I salute her flag, the Union Jack, and promise faithfully to obey her laws.' Then she would march into school with the others, and like them accept unquestioningly all that she was taught.

A few years ago her son Bruce, who comes from a home where Aboriginality is proudly acknowledged, stood up in school and objected to the teacher saying that Captain Cook had discovered Australia. This was well received, and Ruby was invited to tell the class of the history of the Aboriginal Australians.

This sort of questioning of what is taught would not have been sympathetically received in Kingston in the 1950s. Ruby and other Aboriginal pupils were occasionally sent outside to practice basketball and football while their fellow students were learning 'facts' of some sort about the Aboriginal people, which the teachers thought it better not to tell their Aboriginal pupils. One wonders how they reconciled the school teachings of those days with the 'best and fairest player' outside who so often came top of her class.

Whatever it was they were hearing, Ruby was not often troubled by discrimination from her classmates. When she went to the pictures the Aborigines had to sit in the front, but she did not mind this. The people in the front were her friends. Occasionally she would go to the pictures with a white boy, and sit at the back with him, but she felt vaguely disloyal. Her special friends were the Aborigines who lived on Blackford Road, and she usually went with them.

Ruby's first feeling of resentment came when she was soon to leave school, and her mother showed her her 'exemption certificate'.[4] These certificates were bitterly resented by the Aboriginal people, who referred to them as their 'dog licences'. They were headed 'Limited Exemption from the Aborigines Act, 1934–1939'.

Signed by the chairman and secretary of the Aborigines Protection Board,[5] Ruby's certificate said:

> In pursuance of the powers conferred by Section IIa of the Aborigines Act, 1934–1939, the Aborigines Protection Board being of the opinion that Ruby Florence Ahang of Sandys Hut, by reason of her character and standard of intelligence and development, should, subject as hereinafter provided, be exempt from the provisions of the Aborigines Act 1934–1939, does hereby declare that, during the time this declaration remains in force, the said Ruby Florence

> Ahang shall cease to be an aborigine for the purposes of the said Act.
>
> This declaration is made subject to the condition that, if at any time the Aborigines Protection Board is of the opinion that the said Ruby Florence Ahang is not of such character and standard of intelligence and development as to justify the continuance of this declaration, the Aborigines Protection Board may revoke this declaration.

'... shall cease to be an aborigine' (spelt without a capital 'A'!). What on earth did that mean? How can you cease to be an Aborigine when you are one?

'... the Aborigines Protection Board may revoke this declaration'! What sort of threat was that?

Ruby always resented this certificate. It was issued in 1943 when she was seven years old and, though she did not know it then, conferred on her some safeguard from being taken from her parents and put in an institution. At least when she left school she knew that she had it.

Shirley Peisley, who was brought up in the same sort of Europeanised household as Ruby, first heard of her exemption certificate when she was seventeen years old. She was sitting in a car with a white boy a year or two older than she was when a police car drew up. Two policemen came over and stood one on each side of the boy's car.

'Where's your exemption certificate?' asked the policeman on Shirley's side.

'Don't you know you can be had up for consorting if she hasn't got one?' said the policeman on the other side. Shirley had no more idea than the average non-Aboriginal girl would have had of what an exemption certificate was. Like Ruby she was well educated, well spoken and well mannered, and she succeeded in reassuring the police, but she has never forgotten the incident.

> **SOUTH AUSTRALIA.** No. 22
>
> **LIMITED EXEMPTION FROM THE PROVISIONS OF THE ABORIGINES ACT, 1934-1939.**
>
> In pursuance of the powers conferred by Section IIa of the Aborigines Act, 1934-1939, the Aborigines Protection Board, being of opinion that RUBY FLORENCE ABANG of SANDYS HUT, by reason of her character and standard of intelligence and development, should, subject as hereinafter provided, be exempted from the provisions of the Aborigines Act, 1934-1939, does hereby declare that, during the time this remains in force, the said RUBY FLORENCE shall cease to be an aborigine for the purposes of the said Act.
>
> This declaration is made subject to the condition that, if at any time the Aborigines Protection Board is of opinion that the said RUBY FLORENCE ABANG is not of such character and standard of intelligence and development as to justify the continuance of this declaration, the Aborigines Protection Board may revoke this declaration.
>
> The seal of the Aborigines Protection Board was hereunto affixed on the 20th day of OCTOBER, 1941, in the presence of
>
> W R Penhall, Secretary
>
> Deputy Chairman.
>
> Member.

Exemption certificate, 20 October 1941.

Exemption certificates lapsed in 1967. In that year ninety-one per cent of Australian electors voted 'Yes' to a referendum question that gave citizenship to the Aboriginal people. It was no longer necessary for them 'to cease to be an aborigine', to be citizens in the country their ancestors had lived in for more than 60,000 years.[6]

It was when she left school that discrimination became a fact of life for Ruby. She left school at fifteen after she had completed her Intermediate year. She was the first Aborigine in South Australia to gain an Intermediate certificate. During the year she had continually vied for top place in class with two other girls, one of whom was the headmaster's daughter. She knew without being told that they could get jobs that would be closed to her.

This knowledge, at first only dimly perceived, was Ruby's first crippling experience of the discrimination that follows Aboriginal people like a curse. They believe that only those who experience it can understand the problems of damaged identity and undermined self-confidence that this discrimination forces on them.

Some Aboriginal people are bewildered by it, but many of them have learnt that racism has no truth in it, that there are no measurable differences in intellect or capacity between the peoples that make up the human race. There are individual differences. Not everyone can get a university degree or an olympic medal, but these are individual differences, and are the same among all racial groups. There is a true and basic equality of human beings in the face of which racial characteristics, such as features and skin colouring, have no meaning at all. Scientists and other scholars are supporting this truth, and men and women of all races are beginning to perceive it.

THREE

DISCOVERING HERSELF

the beginning
of a new
maturity

RUBY'S FIRST JOB WAS AS A WAITRESS AND HOUSEMAID IN the Crown Hotel in Kingston's main street. It was not the job she really wanted, but nevertheless she enjoyed it. She knew she did it well, and she liked waiting on the guests. It opened up a new adult world to her.

It also gave her spending money, and she began to be interested in clothes and shoes, especially shoes. With her very first pay she bought a pair of shoes.

She thought it went back to Noelene's patent leather shoes with silver buckles. Ruby had longed for a pair like them, but by the 1950s patent leather and chromium were not so fashionable. Spike heels were just coming in, and the shoes Ruby bought with her first pay had higher heels than she had ever worn before.

Ruby could no longer travel in the school bus, and it was too far to travel home each evening by any other way. She had to board in Kingston, going home each weekend. Her brother Fred used to call for her on Saturday afternoons in the old Dodge. He became aware that Ruby was trying to impress the neighbourhood, and to tease her he would wear his oldest clothes, start up the engine with the maximum noise, and loudly hail his friends in the street. Ruby used to shrink down in her seat, hoping that none of the hotel guests would see that this was the way their smart little waitress travelled home.

But home, when they got there, was wonderful. It was a joyous reunion every weekend. Ruby wondered how she would have fared without these few sustaining hours each week, because the other days were often very lonely. She boarded with people who were kind enough to her, and she had many friends in the town, but she was lonely nevertheless, and the curse of racism often cut down her self-esteem.

Her memories of those days were part of the 'there but for the grace of God go I' feeling which helped her to understand the despair, the loneliness and even the sense of worthlessness that leave some Aborigines feeling that the struggle is not worth the effort.

She longed to work in a shop, and at last an opportunity came. Mr Basheer, who ran a big mixed store, offered her a job. She was the first Aborigine in Kingston to work in a shop, but it was not behind the counter. He put her down at the back, weighing up flour and sugar. She did it to the best of her ability, hoping for promotion.

'I'm sorry, Ruby,' Mr Basheer said. 'You know how it is. I'd like to see you serving here, but the customers wouldn't like it.'

It was so often like this. It was not the person you were speaking to who was the racist standing in your way. Oh no, he was the most enlightened of people. It was someone else, someone out of sight, behind the scenes, who was the stumbling block.

Vi Watson remembers this too. She once tried to assert her right to sit in the back stalls at the pictures. The girl selling the tickets told her she hated having to make Aborigines sit in the front, but she had to because the manager insisted. Vi went to see the manager who explained that it was not his fault either. It was the owner.

'And,' says Vi, 'the owner didn't even live in Kingston.'

Vi remembers that her brother Colin, who had been good at mathematics at school, had wanted to work in a bank. His teacher approached the bank managers on his behalf. They were most sympathetic. They would have loved to

Left: Their smart little waitress.
Above: The Crown Hotel, Kingston, 1940s.
Below: L–R Kevin, John, Marie, Fred and Ruby.

employ this bright boy, they said, only their clients would not have liked it.

Shirley Peisley believes this may well have been true of the clients. Her mother, Betty Watson, got a job with a laundry. After a week or two the manager called her in, and apologetically dismissed her. Some of his customers had threatened to go to the rival establishment.

At the same time many women were employing Aboriginal girls in their homes to do cleaning and laundry work, and to mind their children. Irene had a particularly happy job on a nearby station helping to care for two children. She had her mother's gentle firmness, and the family kept in touch with her long after she left to get married.

A subtle racism pervaded the town. It would come through even when Aborigines did well, because people would accept it with surprise or special praise. Aborigines were not expected to do well.

In this atmosphere Ruby was not really happy, and sometimes she felt the coldness of depression. This is the fearful coldness that drives men and women to seek warmth wherever they can find it. Ruby sought it in what, in those days, was unwise love.

When she was sixteen she became pregnant. It was a dreadful thing to have to confess to her father and mother who were so proud of her. They were dismayed, but they were not rejecting. Ruby went to Adelaide to have her baby in the Kate Cocks Home, a Methodist refuge that for many years gave kindly help to girls in what was then a shameful plight.

The Ahangs have always had their values right, and Ruby was able to go home proudly with her beautiful baby boy. Ethel Ahang's motherly heart opened warmly to him, and he spent his first years in the happiest of homes. Ethel, still caring for her youngest children, had no trouble adding this new baby, John, to her family. It seemed best to do it that way, and let Ruby go back to work. The Crown Hotel gave her back her job as a waitress.

Kingston seemed to have little to offer her, and she longed to go to Adelaide. Many of her friends had already gone there. Vi and Linda Watson were working in the telephone exchange, where Vi had risen to the position of monitor.

Ruby did not want to go without her parents' consent, and at last they gave it. With very little money in her purse she set off for the city. She was eighteen, and the next ten years were to bring her times of failure and success, happiness and stark unhappiness, laughter and the most despairing tears she hoped she would ever shed. Looking back, she saw them as the years in which she learnt to know and understand herself.

Because she had so little money she spent the first night in a cheap hotel, and set off in the morning with the *Advertiser* situations vacant column tucked into her handbag.

She got a job very quickly as a waitress in the Parkside Hotel. It was a good job. It was work she knew and could do well, and it was a more exciting hotel than the Crown. It was a 'live-in' job, and Mr and Mrs Falland, who were in charge, were very kind to her.

But she wanted something better than waitressing. That was why she had come to Adelaide. She went to the Royal Adelaide Hospital and put her name down for training as a nurse, and Vi Watson persuaded her to sit for the public service examination and apply for a job in the telephone exchange. She would have liked to have been a nurse, but the telephone exchange position came up first, and she took it.

There were 300 girls who worked in three shifts. Vi and Linda Watson were both still working there. Before Ruby left, Vi became a supervisor, the highest position then open to women in the telephone exchange.

Ruby quickly made friends. Basketball was one of her skills, and before long she was captain of the Postal Institute

A Grade team. She was captain in 1954 when they won the Ridgeway Cup, a trophy for the team that scored the most goals for the season.

She could sing well and was chosen to represent the post office in Employees Playtime, a radio talent quest of the '50s. In 1955 she won a place for them.

At this time the only Aborigines she knew in Adelaide were her Aunty Maureen, cousin Noelene, and a few other people who had come up from Kingston, especially Vi and Linda Watson, Betty Watson, who was a friend of her mother, and Betty's daughter Shirley, who was to marry Cliff Peisley and later became a legal service field officer.

Aborigines in Adelaide tended to form groups, depending on where they had come from. People from the Point Pearce and Point McLeay reserves were the largest and most strongly-knit groups, and many of them had such a wide and satisfying circle of Aboriginal friends that they had no need for any others. Some of them criticised Ruby for having too many white friends. Her happy childhood had given her the capacity to make friends easily, and eventually she had friends of many nationalities. Everyone she met was potentially her friend.

When she left the Parkside Hotel she went to live at Willard Hall, a 'guest house' in Wakefield Street run by the Women's Christian Temperance Union. Vi and Linda Watson lived there. Ruby did not mind its 'no drinking, no smoking' restrictions, even though she had discovered the sophistication of cigarettes, and liked to drink at parties. What she disliked was what she felt to be an institutional atmosphere. She wanted to be with a family.

Ruby looked for a place to board, and here she was lucky. She found just the sort of warm family situation she was looking for with Hans and Emmy Haman in Carrington Street in the city. They had three little girls, Sylvie Ann,

Ingelore and Ellen, all with a charming German accent in which they learnt to call Ruby 'Miss Robbie'.

Emmy was a light-hearted, optimistic person whose outlook on life sorted well with Ruby's. They became good friends. Hans was the head waiter at the Paprika nightclub and sometimes, when they could get a babysitter, Ruby and Emmy would go in there for supper. The Hamans knew all the nightclub people, all the restaurateurs, and were often involved in parties at which Ruby was always welcome.

Emmy and Hans had come from Germany, and Ruby began to learn German while she was with them, especially German songs. It would delight the Hamans' German friends to hear this Aboriginal girl with her beautiful voice singing in the language of their homeland.

Ruby was living very much among Europeans, but she was regularly seeing her cousin Noelene and the Watsons, and all things Aboriginal appealed to her. She and Vi Watson barracked for the West Adelaide football team because they had an Aboriginal player, Bertie Johnson, and they followed the boxing career of Ron Karpany.

The Hamans moved from Carrington Street to suburban St Peters, and Ruby went with them. Life was happy enough, but from time to time incidents reminded her that there were disadvantages to being an Aborigine, and also that there were disadvantages to being a woman.

She discovered the hazards of the late shift. There was only one door by which to leave the trunk exchange, and every night boys would be lined up outside it. Some of them would be friends of the girls, but others were looking for 'pick-ups'. Ruby knew there were men among them who expected her to be more accessible, and more promiscuous, because she was an Aborigine.

She hated going-home time when she was on the late shift. One night when she was going home a volkswagen pulled up, and a young man got out and tried to pull her into the car. There were people about but, although she screamed for help, nobody came to her aid. She managed to free herself and run away.

On another occasion when a man was bothering her she jumped into a taxi. He got into another taxi and followed her. When her driver realised she seriously wanted to escape from the pursuing car he drove into the grounds of the Adelaide Hospital and lost it in the maze of roadways there.

What would have happened, Ruby asked, if she had not had the money for a taxi. She could have found herself in a situation in which she would have been the victim and, she knew, 'the victim as often as not gets the blame'.

Her most unpleasant experience was with a man with whom she'd had coffee occasionally. He asked her to go to a party with him, and on the Saturday night took her to a house in Mocatta Place. They went upstairs and he took her into an empty room in which the main furnishings were a bed and a camera.

She tried to leave, and he tried to stop her. She screamed, and the landlord came in. He had no word of complaint for the young man who had so obviously set the situation up, all he had was abuse for Ruby.

'Get out of here, you black slut,' he said.

She ran off, the landlord shouting abuse after her.

Ruby was often frightened in those years, but she did not go to the police about any of these things. Aborigines in Adelaide did not regard the police as friends in the 1950s, and she knew that a great many women, white as well as Aboriginal, did not regard them as friends either.

International Women's Year (1975) was a time of hope for women. If a time was coming when they would be able to report rape and other sexual assaults without fear of intimidating cross-examination, and the possibility of being found the guilty one, it would be, they believed, a result of the campaigning that began in that year.

In 1977 a Queensland member of parliament, Rosemary Kyburz, urged women to carry a letter opener or some other weapon on the grounds that even a manslaughter charge would be less humiliating than giving evidence in a rape case.[1] Ruby was inclined to agree. She was horrified at the court room ordeal to which victims in rape cases were subjected.

In her earliest years in Adelaide Ruby's greatest joy was to go home to Blackford. It was a long train journey, involving a change at Wolseley, and again at Naracoorte where a narrow-gauge spur line ran off to Kingston. From here the passengers jolted along in a petrol-driven rail car known locally as the Seaweed Express. She was not able to do it very often, and she would look forward to it for weeks, buying presents to take home for all the family. Irene recalls that 'it was always like Christmas when Ruby came home'.

Ruby would find her mother and Irene making cakes and jellies for the family party they would always have for her. The whole atmosphere of home wove a spell of warmth and laughter, of security and happiness. She longed to get married.

Part of the joy of going home was seeing her little son, John. To Ruby he was always a much-loved son, but to him Ethel was his mother. Part of wanting to get married was her desire to make a home for John and be truly his mother.

Ethel Ahang had a stroke. She made a good recovery, and with the help of her husband and children kept her active place in the centre of her household even though she walked with a calliper, and had lost the use of her left arm. But she tired more easily than when Ruby had lived at home, and Ruby wanted to relieve her of the responsibility of John.

One weekend when she was at home her father brought a young man, Bill Hammond, down to Blackford. He was a young widower. His wife had died of cancer, leaving him with two young children who his mother was caring for in Adelaide. He was working in Kingston, finding it a lonely place, and he accepted Arthur Ahang's invitation with pleasure.

He was instantly attracted to Ruby. In those days she was earning a wage that enabled her to dress well. Her hair was permed, she wore the high heels she loved and she was very much the sophisticated young working girl. Combined with this, when she was at home she radiated happiness and a sense of security.

To her he was a handsome, attentive man; each of them saw in the other a person with problems that they might share and jointly solve.

Ruby revelled in being engaged, and preparing for the traditional wedding that was so important a tribal rite in Caucasian societies.

Her father gave her away. Irene was her bridesmaid, Bill's daughter, Meredith, and Sylvie Ann Haman were flower girls and Bill's brother, Frank, was best man. Both families gathered for a wedding that, on the day, seemed full of hope and promise. In the photographs Ruby looked radiant.

Ruby and Bill settled into a house in Prospect with the three children. Ruby was not sure when it was that the marriage began to go wrong. There were probably tensions from the very beginning because, as she could see later, neither of them understood sufficiently the problems of the three children, all of whom had to adjust to a great change. Leaving Blackford was a wrench for John that Ruby did not appreciate until years later. The other two children, having lost their mother, now had to cope with another change and try to accept a new person in her place.

When difficulties arose Ruby and Bill did their best to deal with them, but all too often they would have different ideas of what was best. They applied for a Housing Trust house, hoping that a bigger place would make things easier.

While they were waiting for this Bill took a job at Iron Knob, and they all went to live in a caravan. Ruby was good at coping with the household difficulties of such a situation, and the children enjoyed the novelty of it, but it was very close quarters for a family with problems. The tensions within the family were beginning to degenerate into outright quarrels between her and Bill, but there were good times in between.

Back L–R: Mr and Mrs Hammond, Bill Hammond, Ruby Hammond, Arthur Ahang, Irene Ahang, Frank Hammond. Front L–R: Sylvie Ann Haman, Meredith Hammond, Ethel Ahang.

They were delighted when news came that they had been allotted a Housing Trust home at Angle Park. Feeling more confident of the future they decided to have a child of their own.

In 1962 Sandra was born. She was a beautiful child, and Ruby remembered with great joy receiving into her arms this little girl whom she would not have to surrender to the care of someone else, as she had with John.

The baby, delightful though she was, did not resolve the basic problems Ruby and Bill were facing. Their quarrels did not cease and their marriage began to move into a period of serious unhappiness for them both.

It was at this time that Dr Fay Gale came to see her. Dr Gale knew a great deal about what was going on in the Aboriginal community. She was the daughter of a Methodist minister and his wife, who were among the minority of people in Adelaide who knew about, and were concerned about, the substandard conditions in which many Aboriginal people were living. Dr Gale was a lecturer in the geography department of the University of Adelaide whose doctorate had been for a thesis on urban Aborigines. Her later work in this field made her a national authority on problems of the Aboriginal poor. In 1990 she became the Vice-Chancellor of the University of Western Australia.

Ruby was very grateful to her. In later years she saw this visit as the turning point, imperceptible at first, at which her life began to move towards something better. Dr Gale asked Geoff Pope to go and see Ruby. He was a young Congregational minister, who was being drawn into social work.

About this time Ruby, in desperation, gathered up the children and left Bill. It was Geoff Pope who helped them sort the situation into one in which Ruby moved back into the house with the children, and Bill left.

In some ways it was easier without him, in some ways harder. Ruby found coping with the four children to be almost overwhelming.

Then grief was added to her misery. Her mother became ill again. This time cancer was diagnosed, inoperable and terminal. Ethel came down to Adelaide so that she could be closer to the hospital. Irene had married Terry Allan the year before, and was living in Rosewater, an Adelaide suburb. When she was not in hospital Ethel stayed with Irene, who was glad to have the chance of caring for the mother who had cared so lovingly for all of them.

Ruby was pleased to have Irene so close, and the sisters fell into the habit of visiting each other at least once a week.

Ruby found another friend. Bill's brother, Frank, was concerned about his sister-in-law, and began calling in to see if he could help her. Ruby had always been on very good terms with her mother-in-law, and she too was helpful.

In spite of this, the situation was fast becoming too much for Ruby. She was not well herself, although the doctors could not diagnose any illness.

Geoff Pope advised her to let Bill's two children go back to him. This caused her days of uncertainty. She wanted to do what was best for the children, what was best for everybody, and in the end she accepted Geoff Pope's advice.

Her mother died, and this brought anxiety as well as grief. It upset John deeply, and Ruby's brothers and sisters turned to her as they had always done.

Ruby worried greatly about John. She knew that leaving Blackford presented him with problems that were too great for a seven-year-old boy to handle. She tried to be honest with him, and to help him continually to a better understanding of his own personality.

She felt she must go back to work, and found a kindly couple who undertook with delight to look after Sandra. They had no children of their own, and at first Ruby thought she had found the ideal situation. They adored Sandra and, although Ruby never doubted that she was well cared for, she began to fear that they wanted to adopt Sandra.

Ruby found herself turning more and more to Frank for support. Bill decided to divorce her, naming Frank as co-respondent. She wanted to make a counter-claim charging cruelty, but Frank persuaded her not to.

About this time Dr Gale introduced Ruby to Gladys Elphick. Perhaps the best-known Aboriginal woman in South Australia, Gladys Elphick grew up at Point Pearce Mission before the first world war, and lived there until 1939 when, a widow with two grown-up sons, she decided it would be best for her family if she came to Adelaide.

Gladys said of this change in her life, 'Point Pearce wasn't a bad place when I was young, but we lived a terribly sheltered life there. I had no idea there was so much sin in the world, and when I came to Adelaide in 1939 I was really shocked. I could hardly believe some of the dreadful things I came across, but now nothing shocks me any more.'

The years in Adelaide acquiring this experience instilled in Gladys Elphick a very deep concern for Aboriginal people, and a troubled desire to do something about the poor conditions and the hopelessness and despair in which some of them were living.

In Adelaide there were a number of people who were troubled by the fact that there were Aboriginal Australians living in a style of poverty matched only in the most backward areas of Asia, Africa and Latin America. These concerned people made up a minute part of the total population, but they were an important part of the Aboriginal story. Ruby was to meet many of these people through Gladys Elphick. Some of them she would get to know well.

An outstanding figure among them was Dr Charles Duguid, a dour Scottish Presbyterian who was also an eminent Adelaide surgeon. During the 1930s he had heard, quite by chance, stories of cruelty and injustice to Aborigines that he found hard to believe. In 1934 and 1935 he made journeys into the outback to see for himself. His experiences on these occasions left him with a lifelong dedication to the Aboriginal cause.

In 1937 he persuaded the Presbyterian Church to set up a mission at Ernabella in the Musgrave Ranges. A year or so later his wife, Phyllis Duguid, and Mary Eaton, president of the Women's Christian Temperance Union, visited the mission. On their return they helped to form a League for the Protection and Advancement of Aboriginal and Half-caste Women and Children. After the war this developed into the Aborigines Advancement League, a well-organised and continuing body. In 1958 the league led in forming, with similar bodies in other states, the Federal Council for Aboriginal Advancement.

Another man whom Ruby was to meet was Laurie Bryan. He had come much later to active involvement in the Aboriginal cause, but in a rather similar way. In 1954 he had discovered by chance the terrible conditions in which Aborigines were living in Port Augusta. Like Dr Duguid he returned to Adelaide with a concern that involved him in Aboriginal welfare for the rest of his life.

Bryan began by joining the Advancement League. Dr and Mrs Duguid were abroad, but the outcome would probably have been much the same even if they had been in Adelaide. Although the league was not specifically a Christian organisation, Dr Duguid had attracted to it mainly Christian men and women, many of them Presbyterians. He was a man used to dealing with people in high places, and this was the way the league operated. They ran a hostel for Aboriginal girls in Millswood, and did other practical work, and it was all done 'through the proper channels'. Many of their achievements were due to the personal contacts Dr Duguid had with state and federal members of parliament.

Laurie Bryan was a more down to earth man. He was a

manufacturers' agent, and he had no hesitation in contacting members of parliament when he thought it necessary, but he was less of a stickler for etiquette than Dr Duguid.

Bryan came back to Adelaide wanting to do something practical, and he found the league's way of doing things frustrating. He interested other people in helping, and found that offers of help had to be scrutinised by the executive before they could be accepted. The final straw came when he organised working people who were prepared to give time out of their weekends, but on the Sunday they were asked to stop work by a Presbyterian member of the executive who objected to this 'violation of the Sabbath'.

Laurie Bryan resigned from the league and founded the Aboriginal Progress Association. He had considered that the Advancement League, which was overwhelmingly non-Aboriginal in membership, was not giving the Aborigines a platform of their own. He gathered together as many of the better-educated Aborigines as he could find, and the Progress Association always had a predominantly Aboriginal membership, although Laurie Bryan and Eugene Lumbers, a well-known South Australian freelance writer, were its leaders.

One of the association's achievements was the Aboriginal Education Foundation, which helped Aborigines to secondary and tertiary education long before government grants were available to them. The foundation has since helped many Aboriginal children to have preschool education.

Gladys Elphick was a member of the Progress Association, but she was not very happy in it. She felt that it was dominated by men, and that the two non-Aboriginal men were the real decision makers.

Gladys recognised that valuable work was being done, especially as she felt that education was a major part of the answer to the Aboriginal problem, but she was sure that

Aboriginal women could do more for their own people than they were getting a chance to do.

What worried her were those who were desperately poor, and the many needy families for whom some help would have been available if only they had known where to turn. It seemed to her that the Progress Association was not reaching them.

She saw able women among the Aborigines in the association, and was especially impressed by Lois O'Donoghue, Faith Coulthard (who became Faith Thomas), Maud Tongarie, and Margaret Lawrie. All these women were nurses training at the Royal Adelaide Hospital. They had all been 'Colebrook girls', and all of them had battled to get their opportunity in nursing, the first profession to open its reluctant doors to Aboriginal women.

In Aboriginal circles one often hears it said of one of their leaders that she was 'a Colebrook girl' or, not quite so often, that he was 'a Colebrook boy'.

It means that they were part-Aboriginal children taken from their mothers in tribal situations and put into the Colebrook Home[2] to be 'assimilated' into the white community. Lois O'Donoghue says that not one of these separations would have been made without intense grief to the mother, and shock, loneliness and heartache to the child.

Some of the children were ten or eleven before the authorities caught up with them. When police patrols came into the outback, mothers would hide their half-caste children under bushes, in tree-trunks and little rock shelters. Sometimes the mothers would be persuaded that it was in the child's best interest to let them go into the new world that had come to their country. Other times the children were snatched away and carried screaming from their grief-stricken mothers.

The children spoke no English and were often terrified.

Ruby knew of one little boy who was ten when he was taken to Colebrook, and his little boy's mind was gripped with the fear that the children were being taken away to be eaten.

Underlying this child-snatching exercise was the belief that half-castes were not readily accepted into the tribe, and that the white society offered them their best chance for survival and their best hope for the future. Aborigines are cynical about this thinking. There would not be one half-caste Aborigine in Australia who would feel they have been easily or readily accepted into the white community; and whether life is better in a materialistic, individualistic society than in a tribal situation is nowadays a matter of opinion and debate among whites as well as blacks.

Colebrook was not the only institution of this sort in South Australia but it was an important one. Started in Oodnadatta in 1926 by the interdenominational United Aborigines Mission, it was later moved to Quorn, and then to Eden Hills in Adelaide. It was one of the best places of this sort in Australia.

Its great strength stemmed from the long, devoted and constant service of Sister Ruby Hyde and Sister Delia Rutter. They were not nursing sisters, but Christian women who found service to their faith in working for these Aboriginal children. They gave unbroken years of service from 1926 to 1952 to Colebrook.

Unfortunately neither of these devout women had any real knowledge of the Aboriginal people, of their lives before 1788, of the ruthless dispossession of their land or of their struggle to preserve their spirituality and their culture. They saw Christianity as the only fountainhead of virtue, and they devoted their lives to saving these little souls for their church.

Lois O'Donoghue, who became chairperson of the Aboriginal and Torres Strait Islander Commission, is critical of any institutional life for children, and critical of the concept of Colebrook, but she recognises that within the thinking of the times it was a good place, and she is grateful to the two women who served it with such devotion.

Faith Coulthard had an easier start at Colebrook than Lois O'Donoghue. She was so young when she arrived that she had no earlier memories. She was born at Nepabunna, ninety kilometres from Leigh Creek. Her mother, despairing of keeping her alive because she was premature, devotedly walked the long distance to the Leigh Creek railway station with the little four-pound baby, and travelled by train to Oodnadatta. She had heard that there were two women there who looked after half-caste children.

She set off within days of her baby's birth and arrived at Colebrook when the unnamed infant was only two weeks old. Miss Hyde and Miss Rutter were astounded that the frail child had survived even two weeks. It was a miracle. They took her lovingly into their care, naming her 'Faith'. Other Colebrook children claimed that Faith was one of the 'pets', but it is little wonder that she was.

Faith survived to become a Patrol Sister for the Public Health Department, operating over a vast area of the outback near Quorn, caring for the health of people, black and white, on outback stations, little settlements and fettlers' camps. Sometimes Faith had to win over the white people, but she never failed at this. She was an experienced, capable, utterly reliable nursing sister, and was resourceful, lively and good humoured.

At Colebrook Miss Hyde and Miss Rutter succeeded in creating a family atmosphere, even though they had in all 170 children. It was a home for boys and girls together, and so truly sibling were the children's feelings towards each other that there have been only two marriages among them.

The children were encouraged to forget their past. Neither at Colebrook nor at school did they learn anything significant of Aboriginal life, and talking of tribal life among themselves was frowned upon.

Nevertheless every one of them knew that he or she was an Aborigine. Subtle and not-so-subtle racism taught them that they were somehow different, and that there were people who considered themselves to be superior to Aborigines. This was often bewildering because, at each of their schools, they met white children who were neither as well behaved nor as good at their school work as some of them were, and on the whole the Aboriginal children were better at sport.

They were intensely interested in this Aboriginality that made them different. When new children arrived at Colebrook, all of them half-castes from the same northern areas that the first inmates had come from, they were eagerly welcomed for the news they could bring.

After lights-out in the Colebrook dormitories they would be plied with questions about still-remembered relations, and about the lives of those who remained behind. These sessions had the added excitement of being clandestine, and the forbidden news kept the children vitally aware of their backgrounds.

When the time came to leave Colebrook they could go back to their own people if they wished. Some of them did choose to do this, and many of the others went back just to search out their mothers and establish contact with them.

Life at Colebrook was spartan. The children did the bulk of the work on a well-disciplined roster system, and the older children shared in looking after the younger ones. The 'home' was dependent on the Church and other charity for its income and, especially during the depression, it was often difficult to make ends meet. Their clothes were mostly second-hand, and there were no luxuries of any sort.

Sometimes Miss Hyde and Miss Rutter would gather the children together and tell them there was not enough to eat.

'But we will pray,' said Miss Hyde, 'and the Lord will provide.'

The little group would sit reverently and pray. Not all the Colebrook children have grown up to be practising Christians, but they tend to acknowledge the power of prayer.

It never failed, they say. Before long the baker would knock at the door with a tray of loaves of which he had burnt the crusts, or the greengrocer would arrive with fruit and vegetables that would not keep much longer, or the butcher would bring them some meat.

The fact that they subsisted to a large extent on food that richer people would not buy did not worry them. It was all wholesome and their values were very soundly based.

The Colebrook children went to school, and indeed they went through high school to leaving standard, but it was never considered that they might go on to higher education, or professional jobs.

The girls would spend two years after leaving school helping with the domestic work at Colebrook, and would then be sent out to work as domestics in private homes.

'This,' said Lois O'Donoghue, 'served two purposes. It provided the only employment they thought us capable of, and gave us a roof over our heads.'

The boys were sent to stations and farming properties.

Lois was determined that she would seek something better. She decided that she wanted to be a nurse.

None of the training hospitals in Adelaide accepted Aboriginal girls, but Lois did not want to go to another state, and she wanted to break the barrier that kept Aboriginal girls from nursing training in South Australia. She went to see the Minister for Health, the attorney general, and the premier, who was then Mr Playford. They all received her in a kindly way, but they would not undertake to allow Aboriginal girls to train at the Royal Adelaide Hospital.

She applied again and again to the hospital itself. Other Colebrook girls wanted to be nurses too. On one occasion four of them made an appointment and presented themselves to Matron Scrymgour together.

They had learnt that you must dress neatly, stand up when the matron came into the room, stand with your hands behind your back, speak only when spoken to, and speak politely.

They prepared for all this and sat in a mute row outside the matron's office, expecting to be invited in. She did not invite them in, but came out to talk to them in the passage. The four girls leapt to their feet and stood in a silent row with their hands clasped behind their backs.

'What do you want?' asked the matron.

Lois, who spoke for them, told her they wanted to be accepted as trainees.

The matron offered them no hope. She urged them to 'go back' and nurse among their own people in Alice Springs. Apart from the fact that none of them had come from Alice Springs, this would have meant untrained nursing. She was urging them to become 'nursing aides'. This was seen as the proper role for Aborigines.

At about this time Dr Duguid was growing concerned about the lack of opportunities for Aborigines to speak for themselves. He organised a meeting in the town hall at which most of the speakers were Aboriginal. It was the first time ever that an Aborigine spoke in the Adelaide Town Hall.

The meeting was well organised and, although it was a cold wet night in August 1953, the town hall was crowded. Ivy Mitchell, a Colebrook girl who was one of the speakers, told the audience of the hopeless struggle that educated Aboriginal girls were having to be accepted for nursing training.

Some of the problems raised at the meeting were taken up by the *Advertiser*, and this was one of them. It did not result in Lois and Faith being immediately accepted into the Royal Adelaide Hospital, but they learnt that if they worked for a time in country hospitals they would be able to transfer to a major training hospital.

Lois went to the Southern Districts Hospital in Victor Harbor with Grace Lester, Nellie Lester's sister. Faith Coulthard went to Murray Bridge, and Margaret Lawrie to Angaston. They all worked conscientiously in these hospitals and won transfers to the Royal Adelaide. All of them finished their training, and they have all held important administrative positions.

Because they were Aboriginal they had to be better than other nurses to succeed, and they had the added stress of patients with racial prejudices to contend with.

'Don't put your black hands on me,' women patients would cry, but each of the Aboriginal nurses had won the respect of the matron and, with her support, they worked through these humiliations.

In half a lifetime these women spanned the great gulf between native life and acceptance into responsible positions as fully-qualified professional nursing sisters. They are part of the history of their people. They deserve to be part of its legends.

It was while these women were still young nurses that Gladys Elphick began talking to them about her feeling that Aborigines, including the women, should be acting more decisively in their own affairs. She wanted them to project a better and more positive Aboriginal image. There were many Aboriginal people living lives of achievement and social success, but publicity of every sort seemed to focus on those who were failing.

The women fell into a habit of meeting regularly, and

worked out a philosophy and a plan that emerged as the Council of Aboriginal Women, one of the landmarks of progress in the history of Aborigines in South Australia.

Gladys Elphick had a heart attack not long before Ruby met her but, indomitable as she was, she carried on making her plans. Ruby remembered that they all used to meet in 'Aunty Glad's' bedroom, crowding in, with some of them sitting on the bed.

Natascha MacNamara was drawn into the group. It was at Gladys Elphick's house that Ruby first met Natascha.

This group of young women gave Ruby a new concept of Aboriginal achievement. At the same time she discovered that there were Aboriginal people living in Adelaide in soul-destroying poverty, and she heard of them by name so that they became real people, and not just an abstract problem. She began to see that she might help them in practical ways, and that this would be some repayment for the help that had been given to her.

With a new hopefulness and a new confidence her health improved, and it was without anxiety that she presented herself for a routine smear test. She was called back for more tests – positive, negative, positive, negative, positive, positive. Ruby had cancer of the cervix.

It had been a period of tormenting uncertainty as she went back and forth for tests, and now she had this shattering news. She had just seen her mother die of cancer, and she could not bear the thought of her children seeing her suffer in the same way. Ruby was frightened and bewildered, but her doctors were incredibly kind. She remembered with gratitude the patience with which they explained it all to her, and the honesty with which they told her about the possible outcome. There was a chance that she would be all right, and she went into hospital with a sense of confidence in them.

It was not an easy operation, and afterwards there were complications that kept her in hospital for eighteen days. Blessings come in strange disguises, and for Ruby these eighteen days proved to be a profound experience from which she emerged with enhanced maturity.

It was some time before the doctors could tell her that the operation had been a success, and in that time she came to terms with the prospect of dying. She learnt that life is not to be taken for granted, and from then on she accepted every day as a gift to be lived to the full.

Looking back over her life she saw that guilt had become a millstone round her neck. She felt guilty about John, and the problems he was facing, for which she felt she was to blame. She felt guilty about the failure of her marriage, and about whether or not she had done enough for her mother.

During those eighteen days Ruby came to terms with this guilt. The only thing she would have been unable to forgive in herself would have been something done deliberately to hurt someone else, and this she had never done.

As her guilts melted away she discovered that resentments melted with them. She saw that neither she nor Bill was 'to blame' for the failure of their marriage and that, indeed, seeking for someone to blame is only a shifting of guilt. She never blamed anyone for anything again.

She liked to refer to herself as 'non-judgmental'. In the years that followed this operation Ruby spent many hours with people in all types of trouble, some of them in situations that were often described as being 'their own fault'. Ruby never saw it like that. She never judged people, never blamed them. She saw their troubles set in the whole panorama of their lives. A person in trouble was, for Ruby, a person in need of help. Everything else was irrelevant.

In hospital she also thought about her Aboriginality. She had been vaguely ashamed of being Aboriginal, and yet when she thought of all the people she had known she could see quite clearly that Aboriginal people were in no way inferior to white people. The doctors and nurses around her had special skills, but they had also had special opportunities. They did not seem basically to be kinder, or wiser, than people like her father, her mother, her Uncle Milton, or her new friend Gladys Elphick. It was only in the absurdly superficial detail of skin colouring that they were different. If you were blind you would not know who was Aboriginal and who was not.

Ruby could see that she would never be a whole person while she denied part of herself. She made up her mind that as soon as she could she would seek out her mother's family, and learn more of her Aboriginal background.

The long hours in hospital were the beginning of a new maturity, but when she first went home she was still very unsure of herself, finding it difficult to make decisions and doubting her own judgment. Nevertheless she went home with a new peace of mind, and found herself able to accept and return the love that Frank was offering her. They were married. This time she was making no mistake, and the whole situation was easier.

John had chosen to go back and live with Arthur Ahang, whom he had regarded as 'Dad' in his earliest years. There was only Sandra, whom Frank adopted, and Bruce, who was born a year later in 1967. Ruby was deeply grateful that the operation left her able to have Bruce. He was born by caesarean section, but for Ruby her pregnancy was happy and the birth easy.

The operation had been a success. Whether it was to be a total success, offering her the whole of her life, only time would tell. There was no present cause for alarm, and Ruby accepted this gratefully. She settled into her new life with Frank and the two children. It was a brief period of domesticity, in which she took Sandra to kindergarten and went to mothers' meetings, urging other mothers to come too.

She often thought of the meetings in Aunty Glad's house, and Irene would mind the children for her so that she could continue to go to them. The concerned and caring group of women who she met there raised her self-esteem, and she began to see that the work they were drawing her into was more important to her than anything else she might be doing.

FOUR

THE COUNCIL OF ABORIGINAL WOMEN

there was
a real need
for us

BY THE END OF 1966 GLADYS ELPHICK AND HER FRIENDS had formed the Council of Aboriginal Women in South Australia. Thanks to Natascha MacNamara it was registered and incorporated, and they set out to do everything in a business-like way. Ruby Hammond was drawn more and more into the work.

The council's primary aim was to create a group of Aborigines who would directly help their own people in the areas of greatest need. It was the first group of this kind in Australia, set up entirely on their own initiative.

'There was a real need for us,' Gladys Elphick said. 'We wanted to show people, and to show the government, that we could do things for ourselves. They couldn't seem to accept us as intelligent adults. Even Dr Duguid who was such a true friend, saw us as "his children".'

They made an early decision to regard as Aboriginal 'any person who identifies as, and is identified by others, as Aboriginal'. They wanted to help in the solution of social problems felt by a group of people, rather than to engage in precise argument about the degree of ancestry of particular people. This wise, humane definition has since been adopted not only by Aboriginal groups throughout Australia, but also by the Australian government.

The council's early discussions had developed a clear idea of the need to foster Aboriginal distinctiveness, emphasise Aboriginal achievement, and assert Aboriginal self-determination.

The group began by doing social work from Gladys Elphick's house. They went about it in a very positive way, and at the same time established the council formally by drawing up a constitution and having it incorporated. Natascha MacNamara played a leading role in this. She was the council's first vice-president, and its treasurer. Natascha was the source of much of the early organisation, and one of the authors of the constitution. She helped the council expand into education, and established the early administration procedures.

The Director of Aboriginal Welfare, Mr C.J. Millar, was impressed with what they were doing, and lent them his office for evening meetings. They were grateful for the faith in them shown by the Department of Aboriginal Affairs, and pleasantly surprised. One of their earlier complaints had been that the department was overprotective, and would not let Aborigines manage their own affairs. The council found that Mr Millar and his officers were always helpful, but never interfering.

For the immediate future they had three aims. They wanted a centre where Aborigines could meet each other, and feel they belonged; they wanted to raise enough money to engage a qualified social worker so that they could seek out and help more effectively the Aborigines who so badly needed it; and they wanted to improve the image of Aborigines in the wider community.

Political activity was never a primary aim of Gladys

Elphick but the 1960s was a time when this was hard to avoid. It was the decade that saw the beginning of 'struggle' on their own behalf by the Aboriginal people.

In 1911 South Australia's first legislation directly relating to Aborigines had been designed 'to make provision for the better protection and control of Aborigines and half-caste inhabitants'. This may have been the stated aim of the legislation, but in fact it outlined the duties of the Chief Protector in a way that developed into what Commissioner Elliott Johnston QC, in his overview of the Royal Commission into Aboriginal Deaths in Custody, described as '... pin-pricking domination, abuse of personal power, utter paternalism, open contempt and total indifference ...'[1]

The act was slightly amended in 1939, when assimilation rather than integration became the order of the day. It introduced the 'Limited Exemption' clause, which gave Aborigines the certificates they resented and called their 'dog licences', but which did give limited freedom, and some protection from losing their children. In 1958 the consorting section was repealed.

In Canberra a federal Liberal Party government was in power, and with the persuasion of W.C. Wentworth, the Minister for Social Welfare, they included an Aboriginal question in a referendum planned for May 1967. The question sought to amend the constitution to enable all Aborigines to be counted in the national census, and to give the federal government the authority to legislate for Aborigines. Prior to this, Aboriginal Affairs had been only a state responsibility.

There was tremendous enthusiasm for the referendum among Aboriginal people throughout Australia, and campaigning for it dominated the early months of 1967 for the Council of Aboriginal Women.

For Ruby it was a case of being thrown in at the deep end.

She had no experience in organising other people, but she must have had a natural talent for she found an early leadership role in sending the women out into the community to hand out 'Vote Yes' stickers. They were down at the airport on Mondays and Fridays when members of parliament were travelling to and from Canberra, and at public and committee meetings all over town.

This was Ruby's first demonstration of her ability to encourage others, a skill that was to be of great value to her. 'Of course you can do it, dear,' she was to say to dozens of young women.

Muriel Van Der Byl remembers what must have been one of Ruby's first occasions of this.

'I want you to go down and speak to the Seamen's Union at Port Adelaide,' she said to Muriel near the beginning of the campaign.

'I couldn't possibly do that, not on my own,' said Muriel.

'Of course you can, you are young and pretty. They are a friendly group. I've fixed it up with their secretary, Ron Giffard. He'll look after you. Of course you can do it dear.'

And, of course, she could. 'I was terribly nervous,' she recalls. 'I was expecting about twenty men, and that was bad enough, but when I got to the hall there were about 400 of them there. If Ron hadn't been looking after me, as Ruby had promised, I would just have run away.'

But Ron Giffard was escorting her in, and introducing her as someone they must listen to because she had something important to say. Muriel was so nervous that she stood with her feet apart so that her knees wouldn't knock together, but she knew she did have something important to say, and she gathered the strength to say it.

The thunderous applause promised her 400 Yes votes, and the donations endorsed this. 'I can't remember how much it was,' says Muriel, 'but it ran into hundreds of dollars.'

She has spoken in public many times since but she has never again needed to stand with her feet apart to stop her knees from knocking together.

The Yes vote to this question was 90.8 per cent, overwhelmingly the biggest Yes vote to any referendum question in Australian history. It left Ruby with a conviction that stayed with her for the rest of her life, that non-Aboriginal people of Australia were on their side, if only they could be told the facts.

Campaigning for the referendum convinced the Council of Aboriginal Women that public speaking was a skill they needed to learn more about. Faith Coulthard, who believed in starting at the top, got in touch with Dr Harry Penny who was then principal of the Adelaide Teachers' Training College.

'We want to know how to stand up in front of a group of people and speak to them,' she told him. 'We want to speak for ourselves instead of letting the men do it for us all the time.'

Dr Penny was impressed by her and the aims of the group. He offered to take the classes himself. He had expected half a dozen women, but to his surprise about twenty came along, and stayed for the whole course. He was surprised too at the range of their ages. Mrs Elphick was then in her sixties, and the youngest were still in their teens. Ruby Hammond, who went to almost all the classes, was thirty.

At first they were very diffident, but he began by telling them how to stand, how to look at an audience, how to open a meeting, and how to respond when they were introduced. Then he divided them into groups and let them practice.

'I really enjoyed those classes,' Dr Penny said afterwards. 'The women were keen and responsive, and they had a wonderful sense of humour. The classes really went with a swing.' When he retired and left Adelaide for a period in New Guinea, John Chalkner and Musgrave Horner of the Teachers' College carried the classes on.

Before long the women had a group of speakers who were accepting invitations to speak to clubs and church fellowships. As they became known invitations to speak came from a great variety of groups, including schools, Rotary clubs, and professional organisations. During 1969 they spoke to sixty-five groups on aspects of Aboriginal affairs.

It was a rewarding experience. For many of their listeners it was their first contact with an Aboriginal person, and there is no doubt at all that the women made a significant contribution to their aim of improving the image of Aborigines in the wider community. At first they were nervous, but by 1969 each one of them was a capable public speaker.

Now that they had their aims so well defined, and were making such visible efforts, other people came to their aid. Dr Gale, who had been a constant friend, won the interest of Mr J.A. Crawford of Commercial Motor Vehicles. He arranged for the council to receive $10,000 from the CMV Foundation. The grant was specifically to pay the salary of a social worker for three years, which enabled them to achieve their second aim.

They knew that the qualifications they were seeking would be found only in a non-Aboriginal. He (or she) was to be their employee and this made it easier to accept because, if it had been possible, they would have preferred to have an Aborigine.

Perhaps it was perceptive of their interviewing panel, or perhaps it was good fortune, but they managed to engage a man who proved absolutely right for their needs. He was Eddie (Edwin) Le Sueur, a highly qualified young Englishman who had been working among the very poor in a Liverpool dockyard area.

Gladys Elphick, who was president of the council, said that three factors won Le Sueur the job – he was young, twenty-eight; he was very well qualified; and he had experience of working in areas of great poverty.

Le Sueur was a man who carried his virtues modestly, but at the same time inspired confidence. He was not driven by ambition, but he cared about his career, and it was generous-minded of him to accept so quickly that the women who employed him were reaching out for the time when they could manage without him.

The state government gave them premises at 248 Pirie Street. It was an old, shabby building, and Eddie Le Sueur became very critical of it. In a report made in March 1970,[2] he described it as 'structurally unsound and depressingly decorated', and said the layout created difficulties for both clients and staff.

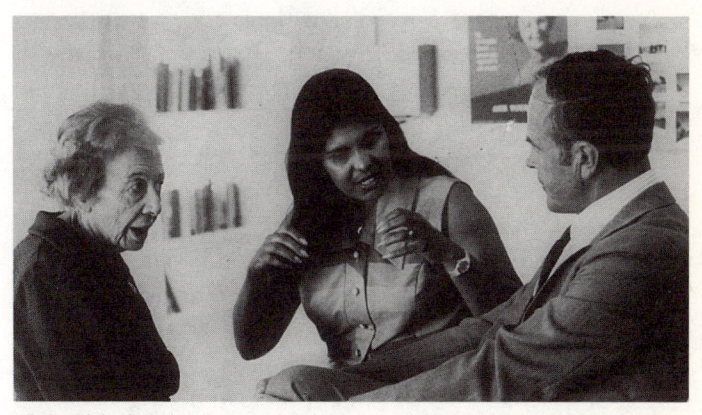

Gladys Elphick, Ruby Hammond and Stewart Cockburn of the *Advertiser*, at 248 Pirie Street.

This was true enough, but in 1968 it was a dream come true. On the ground floor there was a reception area, one large and two small rooms, and a kitchen where tea and coffee were on tap all day long. Upstairs were three more rooms.

They managed to furnish it all with gifts from friends and helpful organisations, and before long the Aboriginal community was using it in just the way the little group around Aunty Glad's bed had hoped they would.

A second-hand-clothing store was set up, with articles coming in from church groups and other people in the community. It was decided to sell the clothes cheaply, but not to give them away. It was not a money-making venture, but the council had a mistrust of handouts.

A considerable amount of voluntary social work was done, and Ruby played an increasing part in this. A major problem for Aborigines had been their lack of knowledge of the social agencies that might help them. Ruby began to learn about the agencies within government departments and the many voluntary agencies that could help, and often she would just go down herself and do what she could to solve their problems.

Aborigines began to learn that the place to turn to was 248 Pirie Street. It sometimes seemed that the phone rang all day long, and there was a steady stream of people coming through the door.

Gladys Elphick said, 'We did social work of every type you could think of. You name it, we did it.'

Inevitably they looked after alcoholics because so many Aborigines were living in the poverty and hopelessness that can underlie a desperate person turning to drink to shut out what cannot be endured. It is a problem that develops wherever serious poverty and deprivation exist.

To Ruby, alcoholics were simply people in need of help, and she always despaired about the number of social workers and people in voluntary agencies who treated them with disgust.

In March 1969, a grant from the Office of Aboriginal Affairs enabled the council to employ a secretary. Cherie Watkins, a member of the council who had been helping voluntarily, was appointed.

In July a further grant was made for the employment of an Aboriginal field officer. The position was advertised and called for 'a person who would be required to undertake social work with individual Aborigines and with groups of Aborigines in the metropolitan area under the supervision of a social worker ...'

There were a number of applicants, and the Department of Labour and National Service assisted with the assessment of them. Ruby applied for the job, and got it.

The Women's Council was reaching the peak of its development. Not only were they doing extensive social work, but they were keenly interested in education. They had regular English classes going, and sewing classes which proved to be very popular social occasions, as well as increasing the sewing skills of the women.

In June 1969, John Morley, a senior art lecturer at Western Teachers' College, offered to give art classes, and these were successful beyond all expectations. Aborigines came along in family groups, and bus loads came up from Port Adelaide.

They brought their children, not all of whom were as interested in the classes as the older people, and minding them became a problem. John Morley had to persuade the principal that this great influx of people of all ages into the place on Wednesday nights was justified. In the end the college allowed them to use the gymnasium for the children. Ruby remembered with some regret that she and Aunty Glad did not go to many of the classes. They were the ones who looked after the children.

By the end of the year there were more than 100 people in the classes, which included jewellery-making, enamelling and pottery, as well as painting. It was exciting for John Morley, who had thought that perhaps fifteen people might come along.

Some of the group showed great skill, and at the end of six months they were able to give an exhibition in the Llewellyn Galleries. More than 120 paintings were displayed, and there was an impressive opening ceremony performed by the then State Minister for Aboriginal Affairs, Mr Robin Millhouse.

More than $700 was raised from the sale of paintings and other art works, with half the money going to the newly formed Aboriginal Art Co-operative to develop economic and artistic opportunities for Aboriginal people.

In 1971 John Morley started going each week to Point Pearce for similar classes, and they too managed an exhibition. It was opened in the Maitland and District Hall on 28 May by the new Minister for Aboriginal Affairs, Mr L.J. King.

This all took a great toll on John Morley, whose only reward was the appreciation of the Aboriginal people. Among his colleagues he was criticised for neglecting his other work. He resigned and went to live in England. The classes stopped.

Ruby felt that Morley was one of the most generous of all their early helpers, and she continued to keep in touch with him.

Other people were helping too. Helen Caterer, a journalist on the *Sunday Mail*, was a good friend who gave them sympathetic publicity. The *Sunday Mail* had a Blanket Fund for helping needy people in the winter, and Helen Caterer made sure that the council was included on the list of agencies through which blankets were distributed. Many church and service groups helped the council with gifts and donations.

Aborigines always have friends in the non-Aboriginal community. They find them in every walk of life, among politicians, police, academics, government officials and other people they encounter. The trouble is that these friends are only a tiny minority of the whole population, the majority of whom hold some degree of prejudice against them. In the

1990s overt racism is against the law, and there is much less prejudice than there was in the 1970s, but racism is still a problem that must be solved if reconciliation is to become a reality. Ruby was fond of saying, 'It's only ignorance, and ignorance can be cured,' but in fact it is more than ignorance; it is a complex, involving a reluctance to recognise land as other than a source of wealth, and an unconscious desire on the part of too many people to feel superior to someone else. More than education is needed to change these attitudes.

Eddie Le Sueur was growing aware that the needs of the Aboriginal people went far beyond anything a social worker could supply. He came to see more and more of the subtle, continuous prejudice to which they were so unjustly subjected. The whole society in which they lived tended to see and notice Aborigines in situations of inferiority.

Aboriginal families found their greatest support in Aboriginal groups. There was a gulf between Aboriginal and non-Aboriginal people which had been created by white Australians, and would only be bridged if Australian people could come to a far greater understanding of the facts than they were showing signs of doing.

Eddie saw prejudice as a direct cause of Aboriginal problems. In his annual report written in March 1970, he said:

> In relation to white society the Aborigine is inferior and inadequate; this means that the Aboriginal child is deprived of an adequate model with whom he can identify. He is a member of a subcultural group that is subject to hostile prejudice and rejection from white peers and adults. This leads to conflict and confusion over identity.
>
> It is felt that the disturbance of the identity process among many Aborigines results in personality difficulties, and many of the 'problems' (e.g. alcohol, unemployment) are

symptomatic of this disturbance; and that the picture of instability, inconsistency and insecurity presented by many Aborigines is a result of this conflict and uncertainty.

Eddie saw the prejudice against Aborigines as presenting them with greater problems than those besetting any other minority group. Ruby agreed with this, but she also recognised the common problems that Aborigines shared with other minorities. She wanted to see an integrated multi-racial society in Australia where cultural differences were not just tolerated, but really valued. She believed that in such a society, Aboriginal culture would be especially valued because of its deep involvement with the land that is the basis of the life of all Australians.

Ruby was now working full time, and indeed more than full time, for she was often called out at night. Although social work was her main responsibility she still shared in many other tasks. She was one of the organisers of the sewing classes, and she helped establish the successful Boomerang basketball team. As a member of the council she took part in formal meetings with a chairman, an agenda, minutes, and decisions made by motions moved and seconded, gaining knowledge that was to stand her in good stead when she moved into the world of meetings arranged by government departments.

Each week she had discussions with Eddie Le Sueur, who helped her to a better understanding of social work. She was still not anxious for too much formal education, but learning by experience she accepted eagerly and gratefully.

Frank proved wonderfully sympathetic, so that combining marriage and a career was as easy as it ever can be. Irene was also a great help, especially in looking after the children at times when Ruby had to be away from home. Irene and Terry also had two children – Vicki, who was five weeks younger than Sandra, and Wayne, who was five months younger than Bruce. There were five years between Ruby and Irene, and this coincidence of numbers was a part of the bond between them. There was a close friendship between Sandra and Vicki, and between Bruce and Wayne.

The council wanted to expand into a more comprehensive centre for adults, and a homework centre for children. Education was always at the front of their thinking, and they encouraged mothers to send their children to school.

They wanted more sporting facilities, more recreational space, a better social centre, and a health centre. The council was beginning to think in terms of a modern community centre.

Early in 1969 they submitted their ideas to the Select Committee of the Legislative Council on the Welfare of Aboriginal Children. In the report, tabled on 22 July 1969, the committee agreed that such a centre should be established in Adelaide, and that the council would be competent to run it. The committee recommended that the government contribute half of the capital cost on a dollar for dollar basis, and give financial assistance in the early years of operation.

With all the other work the council was doing, the task of raising half the cost of a centre such as they were envisaging was hopelessly beyond them. It was difficult for them to raise the money they needed to run the services they had already established. Fund raising diverted them from what they saw as the real work of direct service to the Aboriginal people in the state, and it often seemed to take more time and effort than the results justified.

Their dreams of an Aboriginal community centre did not materialise. They did not stop dreaming, but Gladys Elphick thought sadly, and unfortunately truly, that it would not come in her lifetime. She had battled hard for her people, and by 1980 she was beginning to feel that others must take up the torch.

'They will,' she was saying, 'but it is a tremendous task. If only people would listen to us we could make better progress.'

She died in 1988, aged eighty-four, and it was not until December 1994 that the Aboriginal Community Centre moved into a building that promised to be adequate. It is still in Wakefield Street, 182–190. Its outer wall of black glass is framed by a narrow mural designed by Max Mansell and symbolising Pride and Achievement. The heavy glass doors, set in an arch of Aboriginal colours, open into a spacious foyer. A glass case that runs almost the full length of the opposite wall displays bark paintings, totem relics, artefacts and crafts that will not have to be moved out to make space for office equipment. Upstairs there are offices and meeting rooms for all their needs. Women old enough to remember Aunty Glad think of her often as they go through these double doors.

The receptionists answering the phone say it is 'Nunkuwarrin Yunti here'. This means 'working together', and seems to make the whole place theirs and not an off-shoot of some government department.

A design symbolising 'working together' has been set into the floor. It acknowledges multicultural Australia – the groups 'working together' are painted black, white, red and yellow. For those of us who understand it this design symbolises the almost incredible generosity with which the indigenous people of Australia are willing to accept reconciliation.

The year 1970 was a busy one. The annual report tells of help given to eighty Aboriginal families and individuals for problems relating to housing, employment, lack of funds, and family difficulties. There were more than 600 visits made to clients, and Ruby made many of these.

There was so much travelling to do that they began to feel they needed a car for the council. 'What about a mini-bus?' someone said.

Their old friends at Commercial Motor Vehicles came again to their assistance. They had a scheme for selling cars at a ten per cent reduction to charitable organisations, and undertook to donate half the cost of a mini-bus bought under this scheme.

This was such a generous offer that the council set about eagerly to find ways of raising the $1,500 they would need. The Minister for Aboriginal Affairs, Mr L.J. King, launched an appeal for them in November 1970, and they were able to take delivery of the bus four months later.

During the year Ruby did a course in Education for the Handicapped Child at Western Teachers' College, and achieved a credit. The following January Leila Rankine, who had been a stalwart voluntary worker since the council's inception, went to Canberra for a six-week residential seminar on The Culture, Identity and Future of the Aborigine. Each participant was expected to bring information about the situation of Aborigines in their home area. Leila Rankine obtained top distinction.

Eddie Le Sueur was often amazed at the level of tolerance and goodwill that prevailed among the council members. Forty was the average number of women actively involved in the work while he was on their staff. They carried out difficult, often frustrating, tasks in inadequate premises and with inadequate funds. Inevitably there was friction at times, but the small extent of it was in itself one of the council's achievements.

Following a period of difficulties Natascha MacNamara resigned from the council in July 1970. Leila Rankine became vice-president in her stead. Cherie Watkins, their secretary, also left. She had completed the Group Work certificate course at the Institute of Technology, and she wanted to accept an opportunity to join the Department of Social Welfare and Aboriginal Affairs as a trainee in the in-service training course. Problems were developing. They could all see the need for more staff to do the work that was crying out to be done.

The building that had seemed so wonderful in 1968 was now seen by all of them to be substandard, especially when compared with buildings from which other social welfare agencies were working. The office furniture, which was second-hand anyway, was pathetically insufficient. The place was so overcrowded it was difficult to carry out interviews. There was nowhere to park, and the only lavatory was a men's toilet, shared by staff and clients, male and female.

Eddie Le Sueur prepared a fifteen-page report that included eight pages devoted to 'Suggested Remedies'. As a result the premises were renovated – the walls were painted and the floor coverings renewed – but more than this was needed.

Despite these difficulties 1971 was another year of achievement. The mini-bus gave a wonderful lift to their spirits. It was in constant use for group activities, taking people to hospital, collecting and delivering clothing and furniture, and helping individual families in need. It ran a shuttle service for the annual children's Christmas party in the Bonython Parklands. It was taken on several trips to Point McLeay and Point Pearce; and it was used to take groups of people to funerals. The Aboriginal community was so close-knit that funerals sometimes brought hundreds of people together.

In the December 1971 annual report there is warm praise for Ruby who was accepting an increasing amount of executive responsibility, as well as continuing with her social welfare work. It added, 'Mrs Hammond's strength is derived not only from her personal quality and growth, but also from the support and guidance of the Council and its executive.' Throughout its existence the Women's Council showed a remarkable capacity for teamwork.

A feature of 1971 was an increasing demand for legal assistance. The feeling was growing within the Aboriginal community that the disproportionate percentage of Aborigines in prison at any one time was symptomatic of the Aborigines' position in society, and of white attitudes towards them. Their crimes were the universal reactions to poverty – drunkenness, resisting arrest, vagrancy. There was a growing desire among Aborigines for their people to have legal representation.

In 1971 the Aboriginal Legal Rights Movement was set up in Adelaide, and was based upon work being done in Sydney. It was a voluntary organisation, and the council helped with a lot of the early field work. For Ruby this was a continuation of work she had already been doing.

In 1972 the money to employ Eddie Le Sueur ran out. He left feeling the time had come for him to leave, that the task he had been employed to do had been done, and that the women could manage without him.

Perhaps because it was dealing with issues of social need, the council was more successful in appealing to the public than was the Aboriginal Progress Association, which was a more political body, concerning itself with land rights, protest against police harassment, and other civil issues.

The council was not indifferent to political matters. Their experience in helping Aboriginal people to find accommodation led them to believe that this was an area in which there was widespread discrimination. The Progress Association was seeking an incident to use as a test case under the 1966 South Australian anti-discrimination legislation.[3]

Ruby and other council members hoped to use one of the

incidents of discrimination that they so often encountered, but their experience was that it tended to be too underhand to sustain a court action.

Often there would be a perceptible change when an owner or agent discovered that a prospective tenant was an Aborigine. They became evasive, and offered reasons for delay. Covert discrimination of this sort is humiliating, but it is hard to establish in a court of law.

The council supported the Progress Association when they were circulating petitions, and they joined in demonstrations, particularly the marches on National Aborigines Day, the second Friday in each July.

They worked in support of an Australia-wide campaign to persuade people with accounts at the Commonwealth Bank to transfer them to other banks as a protest against the Queensland 'Trust Fund'. This was a Queensland scheme whereby certain Aboriginal wages were paid into a 'Trust Fund', and Aborigines had to make out a case to receive money from their own wages. The Commonwealth Bank handled the account.

Another issue in which the council was involved was the South Australian Tent Embassy.[4] On 13 July 1972, while the original Tent Embassy was still outside Parliament House in Canberra, four Aborigines put up two tents on the lawns in Brougham Place, North Adelaide. They set them up under a massive birch tree, against which they propped a professionally prepared sign with 'Aboriginal Embassy' written on a board painted to resemble the Aboriginal flag. Beside it was a sign saying 'We Demand Land and Social Rights for our People'.

Above the sign, on a short pole, their flag was flying. This flag, chosen in 1972 by the Federal Council for the Advancement of Aborigines and Torres Strait Islanders, shows a yellow sun, symbolising life, on a background which is half red, for the land, and half black, for the people.

There were eventually four tents, and the embassy remained there for three months, during which Ruby Hammond visited it almost every day.

Adelaide's homeless Aborigines began to find it an easy place for a night's refuge, and itinerant Aborigines used it too. Sometimes as many as thirty people slept there.

It attracted a great deal of hostile criticism from white people, which prompted one of the embassy staff to say despairingly to a reporter from the *Advertiser*, 'You white people forget how you killed us by giving us poisoned flour to eat, how you shot us and starved us, and pushed us over cliffs. How serious is our "offensive behaviour" here compared with all the white man's injustice to us over 200 years?'

Occasionally nearby residents complained of the noise or the nuisance, and there were clashes with the police. There were arrests for drunkenness and offensive language, but the embassy staff were never ordered to leave the area. They were breaking neither laws of the land nor city council regulations, and special legislation would have been needed to remove them.

The South Australian Aboriginal community had mixed feelings about it. The leader was Colin MacDonald, a young Aborigine from Alice Springs whom some South Australians saw as an interloper.

Members of the Women's Council were divided about whether to support the embassy or not. Gladys Elphick considered it undignified, and thought it did the Aboriginal cause more harm than good. Ruby, on the other hand, believed that Aborigines would get nowhere without visible, audible protest. She saw the Tent Embassy as telling Australians they had reduced the original inhabitants to squatters on their own land, to foreigners in their own country, but that nevertheless they were a people with their own flag, their own culture and dignity, and a determination to be heard. She believed that the Tent Embassy would ultimately be seen as a dramatically successful statement.

The 'blacks camp' quality of the South Australian embassy, which was so distressing to some Aborigines, did not worry Ruby. She saw it as part of the statement. At the same time she was concerned about the health and welfare of those who were camping there. She frequently took food up to them and helped them to tidy the place; and she regularly gave advice to Aborigines who just dropped in.

Early in October one of the tents was burnt down. An Aborigine from Point McLeay was charged with 'wilfully destroying a tent'. He said he had done it because he thought 'city Aborigines' were bringing discredit to 'true Aborigines' by camping there.

This was the beginning of the end. The Women's Council decided that they would remove the embassy. Gladys Elphick, Ruby Hammond, and four other members packed up the tents and the camping stoves, the refrigerator and the bedding, and loaded them into a trailer.

The embassy staff accepted their verdict. Colin MacDonald stood cheerfully in the background playing 'Home Sweet Home' and 'The Last Rose of Summer' on his mouth organ while the women did all the work. He offered no resistance, and the *Advertiser* said 'he seemed relieved at their initiative'.

It was a triumph for the Women's Council because it meant that the Aboriginal people themselves had coped with a situation that was becoming untenable.

Political activities, however, were never the mainstream of the council's work. Even the part they played in the Tent Embassy episode was largely social work.

Eventually the Progress Association broke up, but in its place the Aboriginal Cultural Centre was established. This group sponsored the Nunga football team, and tried to play a similar role to the Women's Council.

The cultural centre ran into financial difficulties, and asked if they could amalgamate with the council. It had been one of the council's triumphs that they had co-operated well with all the other Aboriginal organisations – the cultural centre, the Education Foundation, the Aged Persons' Trust. There was a very friendly amalgamation. The council had been so well established that there was no question of the men taking over. Gladys Elphick was the first president, and women continued to play a leading role.

The Tent Embassy at Brougham Place, North Adelaide, after the fire. (*Advertiser*)

'It's a change from the old days when women were so much in the background,' Gladys Elphick said with no little satisfaction.

Although it was not at all apparent to Aborigines who were living below the poverty line, and not very apparent to others, it was a time of change.

The 1967 referendum did not immediately have far-reaching results. Land rights was the burning issue among Aborigines, and although an Office of Aboriginal Affairs was set up, the wheels of government turned very slowly indeed. By 1972 Mr Peter Howson was Minister for Environment, Aboriginal Affairs and the Arts.

Following the dismantling of the Aboriginal Tent Embassy he had promised to accept an elected Aboriginal Consultative Council, and the budget provided a larger sum for Aboriginal Affairs than ever before.

Of this, $20,000 came to Adelaide for an Aboriginal legal service. This relieved the council of some of its responsibilities, but at the same time left it feeling subtly undermined. It had drawn its first support, in pre-referendum days, from the State Department of Aboriginal Affairs, and the federal government had not given the council a great deal of recognition.

The setting up of a subsidised legal service meant that new premises must be found. The Pirie Street building out of which it first operated had become hopelessly inadequate. With delight they heard they were to be given bigger, better premises – 128 Wakefield Street.

The building was a great improvement, and early in 1974 the council moved in with the highest hopes. The ground floor was to be for the legal service, except for one large room which was used to display the magnificent collection of bark paintings and totem relics that the cultural centre had gathered together under the guidance of John Morley.

The museum staff helped them set it up, and for a little while it was exciting evidence of the artistic achievements of Aborigines. The room was just on the left as you entered the building, and some of it could be seen through the glass doors, so that everyone who came there was aware of it. Upstairs the council set up its offices, its social rooms, and a tiny health centre.

Before long it was apparent that history had repeated itself. The building, which had seemed so wonderful in 1974, was soon seen by all of them to be substandard, especially when compared with other social agencies' buildings.

The legal service, distressingly overcrowded, was forced to put a photocopying machine in the art room, and gradually the beautiful and irreplaceable art works were pushed into a crowded and disorganised corner.

Upstairs there was carpet on the floor, modern filing cabinets and an electric typewriter, but when people were interviewed, typists and other clerical staff had to move out of their shared offices and find work in other parts of the building. One of the typists worked permanently in the corridor. The lavatories were an improvement on those at Pirie Street, but you had to go outside to get to them. There was a lane where cars could be parked but it was so narrow that those who used it were required to hang their keys in Ruby's office because only the last in could move without others backing out.

Their dream of a comprehensive social, health and education centre with sporting and recreational facilities seemed not closer but further away. In Wakefield Street there was a little alcove with a sink and an electric kettle where tea and coffee were made, but it was a pathetic echo of the kitchen at Pirie Street which, for all its shabbiness and ancient gas stove, at least provided an atmosphere of welcome, and room for a few people to gather and relax together.

Gladys Elphick did not lose hope to the point where she gave up trying, but she became discouraged. In 1975, at the department's request, the council submitted a three-year education program. Education was always important to Aunty Glad, and she put in many hours helping to compile it.

The program was firmly based on what Gladys saw as the needs of her people, especially the women. It included dress-making and hair-dressing with an idea that promising pupils could go on to the Institute of Technology or the Hair Dressing Trade School.

'If it is set up in the centre, or somewhere where Aborigines can go together and be among their own people, they will come,' she said. 'They don't want to go on their own to white training courses because they fear, and have reason to fear, that they won't be accepted as equals. If they had some training with us first, and got a little confidence, they would go on, but the Education Department can't seem to understand this.

'They ask us "Why don't you have an English class?", but that's not what we want. I wasn't planning school classes, more a "use your fingers" type of thing. But it is so often the way – they ask you for your suggestions, but then it is their own ideas they want to put into practice.'

Her program was based on raising the expectations of those who took part. It was aimed at producing people who could then help others to self-improvement; and at breaking the cycle whereby ignorance of the possibilities and hesitancy about pursuing them in matters of self-education was passing from one generation to another. The program was not accepted.

'We are trying to help ourselves, but we get knocked back on it all the time,' Gladys Elphick said. 'They don't want our ideas. They want to do things their way, not ours, and that's most of the trouble.'

Who were 'they'? '"They" were almost every member of the government departments, and non-governmental organisations that seek to help Aborigines,' she said.

She was not alone in this view. Among the published reports of the Australian Government Commission of Inquiry into Poverty (1975) was one on 'Poverty Among Aboriginal Families in Adelaide', by Fay Gale and Joan

Binnion of the University of Adelaide.[5] Speaking of government policies they said:

> Some programmes are still decided for the people and are directed more at overcoming observed problems such as housing than at raising self-respect. If all of the money being spent on Aboriginal welfare went direct to the families concerned there would be no Aboriginal poor in Australia. Many see the present bounty of the commonwealth as an extension of the 'hand-out' or ration system of earlier years. Self-respect cannot be so easily bought. Yet we believe it must be re-established if the Aboriginal family is to survive. Welfare programs must therefore evaluate their policies in the light of such factors.

CHAPTER FIVE

THE WISDOM PEOPLE

deep basic
values and
certainties

EVERY ABORIGINAL PERSON IN AUSTRALIA HAS TO FACE the problem of discrimination, the bewildering tendency of some white people, many white people, to regard them as inferior without discovering one thing about them beyond the fact of their darker skins.

The Australian anthropologist, Andrew Abbie, has said, 'The important thing is that neither white nor coloured has any warrant to read more into colour difference than difference of colour.'[1] This is a basic truth, but there are still people clinging to an outworn theory of superiority. As long as this continues there will be a need for each Aboriginal person to come to terms with his or her Aboriginality.

For Ruby Hammond this began when she met Gladys Elphick, and found herself part of the group which built up the Council of Aboriginal Women. It reached fulfilment when she travelled to the far north of South Australia and met the Marree Aborigines, all of whom had some link with the people from whom her grandmother Ruby Ellis had come.

The original Aboriginal groups were scattered because

cattle stations had eaten out the land on which they once lived, and they worked as stockmen or domestics, or lived on pensions; and they intermarried with the people of the mid-north, especially the Afghan camel-drivers. All of them were fully Aboriginal in their attitude towards life, and the land on which all life depends. Ruby saw them as her family.

The work she did with the council brought her into contact with Aborigines from all over the state, and from time to time she would hear of Ernie Ellis, 'the old fella' in the north. 'Ellis' is not a common Aboriginal name, and it was from the country north of Marree that her Aboriginal grandmother had come. She felt more and more certain that this man was her mother's brother. She decided to write to him, asking if she could come and see him.

Ernie Ellis did not read or write, but a reply came from Miriam Dadleh – 'Yes, you can come.'

Ruby had heard of Miriam Dadleh, a leader among the Aboriginal women in Marree. She wrote back to say she would come during the Labor Day holiday weekend in October 1971. Taking the children with them, she and Frank set out on the Friday afternoon after they had finished work for the long drive up through Port Augusta, Hawker and Leigh Creek. It was more than 600 kilometres to the little township of Marree on the flat, arid, stony ground at the beginning of the Birdsville track.

At Hawker they stopped for a few hours and slept in the car until dawn, to arrive in daylight. As they neared Marree the sandy country, with its tufts of grey, spiky grass, and its few stunted trees veiled in dust, was unlike anything Ruby had seen before. It was all utterly strange, and it added to her feeling of excitement and awareness.

At last they came to the big notice that warns travellers to advise the police if they plan to travel beyond Marree. They turned left, crossed the railway line, and entered the main street. It is a little settlement where until 1980 the standard gauge railway linked with the narrow gauge that ran on to Oodnadatta and Alice Springs. The coming and going of the trains were the big events of the week.

Little railway cottages stretched in a line on their right, and on the left the hotel dominated the scene. It was a typical outback 'pub', a massive two-storey stone rectangle with a high iron balcony supported on pillars and covered over with the same galvanised iron as the roof. Everything but the stonework and the roof was painted dark brown. It showed the dust less starkly than other colours.

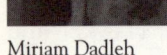

Miriam Dadleh

Marree Hotel, 1971

Even the hotel looked small under the enormous sky. It was a dome of total blue, deeply intense above them and fading to a paler shade on the horizon, which they could see in a great circle. A flock of white parrots flew overhead, screeching to be looked at, but there was no cloud to be seen. In the brilliant sunlight the wide clay roads looked golden brown. For Ruby there was always an enchanted blue and gold quality about Marree.

They drove slowly up the street.

'Which way?' asked Frank.

Ruby had no idea but with sudden confidence she said, 'Turn right.'

This took them across the railway line again. She knew that it was 'on the other side of the line' that Aborigines lived. In the distance was a scattering of shanties.

'It will be one of those,' she said.

'Which one?'

'This one.'

It was not Miriam Dadleh's house, but it was the house she was in, and it was she who came to the door; a strong, serene, cheerful woman, her dark skin lined from a lifetime of living, and her black hair streaked with grey.

'Ruby!' she exclaimed.

'It's me, it's me,' said Ruby. Miriam Dadleh was an emotional woman, and as they embraced Ruby felt tears on her warm cheek.

Ruby had enough European culture to say 'perhaps it was a coincidence' that led her to that particular door, but she had enough Aboriginality to believe it was something more profound, leading her home.

It was the beginning of an unforgettable weekend. News that Ruby Hammond, granddaughter of Ruby Ellis, had arrived spread like wildfire, and soon a crowd of relations and friends had gathered to meet her. The little house was too small to accommodate them, and there was an excited episode of greeting and laughter outside. They all wanted to meet Ruby, and Frank, Sandra and Bruce.

Ruby wanted to find Uncle Ernie, and soon they were all setting off for the reserve. Everyone came out to welcome them, the old uncles and aunties, the cousins, the children; but it was Uncle Ernie whom she was most eager to meet.

He, too, was eager to meet her. He had waited all through the previous day, watching for each cloud of dust that signalled a car coming across the plains; and now she was here, Ruby, the daughter of his dead sister, named for his own mother. It was his blood coming home. He was a big, grey-haired man, too proud to weep, but she was conscious of his emotion as he embraced her.

Miriam had reassured Ruby that Ernie Ellis was indeed the long-lost brother of whom her mother had talked so long ago. He was Ethel's full brother, brought up with her in Adelaide, but he had returned to Marree when he was still a boy and had been welcomed back by his people. He had worked as a stockman to make a living when he first arrived, but had been drawn into the remnants of Aboriginal life that survived in the mid-north. When his Aboriginal duties demanded it, he would leave his other work as all committed Aborigines do.

This was not a lazy taking of a holiday, but a commitment to responsibilities not explained to the white boss because, almost without exception, the station owners and managers of the inland had neither the knowledge nor the sympathy to comprehend them. The term 'walkabout' is a white man's phrase. Ernie Ellis was an initiated elder, able to carry out the initiation ceremonies of the Arabunna people.

'So much for the theory that the Aborigines won't accept you if you have a European father,' said Ruby. 'If you are at one with them they will accept you as such. There is no difference. No white community accepts so totally people of mixed racial inheritance.'

Ernie had forgotten all that he had learnt at the Sturt Street school, so that he could no longer read or write, but he could read the land. He had learnt all the ancient skills of the Aborigines who live off the land, and he had acquired the serenity of those who live close to it.

Ruby was related to Miriam too. Ruby's grandmother was cousin to Miriam's mother. Later Ruby was to discover that

THE WISDOM PEOPLE

Miriam knew all the complex relationships of the Aboriginal and Afghan people of the mid-north, seeing them like a road map. Her father had been an Afghan cameleer, and as a child she had travelled with him.

She was the great lady of the Marree people, the one they turned to for advice and help and comfort. Uncle Ernie was the elder who gave them guidance and leadership. There is a phrase for men and women such as these. They are 'the wisdom people'. They are unpretentious, and they have deep basic values that have built serenity and sweetness into their characters. From the first moment of meeting them Ruby felt total confidence in them.

In a material sense they are poor people with none of the trappings of success about them. Miriam, in her cheap cotton dress, her apron and her slippers, her hair pushed under a scarf to protect it from the dust, would not have impressed anyone who measured people by prosperity. Ruby, who never did that anyway, was on that weekend in an exceptionally perceptive mood. Recognition of the essential quality of Miriam Dadleh and her uncle came to her quickly, and brought her own self-acceptance to full flowering. This was Aboriginality and she was proud to embrace it totally.

'It was a beautiful weekend,' said Ruby afterwards. 'Everyone was so happy, so warm. We were all holding hands, putting our arms around one another.'

All weekend they spent talking, with Ruby's kinfolk coming and going, and the women preparing food. At night there was a camp fire, and all the family sat around, the old people telling stories of the past, the children listening quietly. When they nodded off to sleep their mothers would carry them gently off to bed.

Food was cooking in the ashes, and as it cooked they would eat it. There was no sense of time. There was no sense of noise or bustle, but there was a great deal of laughter. It was a quiet, clear night in which their voices carried, and they could all hear each other easily.

The great sky that curved over them was lined with dark blue velvet and studded with brilliant stars. It was another vast sky like those Ruby remembered from Blackford, but this was the most brilliant sky she had ever seen.

She talked with Aunty Maude, who had many memories of wandering through the north with her parents, and sharing camp fires with the old Afghan camel-drivers; and with Aunty Alice who was blind then, but who remembered meeting Burke and Wills as they journeyed across Australia. People said Alice was 102, but none of them really knew their ages. None of them knew their birthdays. Ruby shared her birthday with Uncle Ernie. He liked to have this sharing with Ruby; but the passing of the days and the months and the years was something he accepted without looking backwards or forwards. For him life was part of the eternity of now.

Everyone seemed so relaxed, to be living in the present without any stress, or any worrying about time.

Ruby asked Uncle Ernie about the mysterious mutha puttaye she had heard her mother speak of, and the stories around the camp fire were suddenly linked with her mother's stories and the strange tales Uncle Milton had told them around the fire at Blackford.[2] Uncle Ernie said he would show them the mutha puttaye, which he called 'the old bubbla'; so next day they packed up a picnic to take to Coward Springs, and set off in the Hammond's four-wheel-drive with Bruce, Sandra, Uncle Ernie and two of the aunties.

'It's just a little way up the track,' Aunty Miriam had said, so it was fortunate that Frank thought to fill up the car with petrol. It was 140 kilometres across the same sort of desert landscape that had fascinated Ruby the day before.

'It could have been just as it was that day for a thousand years,' Ruby said later. 'It was untouched, unspoiled, and all day we did not see any of the disgusting litter that tourists leave. It was wonderful.'

Nowadays the track is well marked with signs of the white man's coming. Beer bottles and cans crop up like the wild daisy, and here and there are cars that, travelling too fast, have rolled over into the desert beyond the tow-truck's reach; but back in 1971 there was less of this, and if it was there Ruby did not see it.

They drove north-west through flat, grey-brown, dry country with the sun shining down to the east of them on the dazzling salt pan of Lake Eyre. It was country where cattle grazed, but to Ruby it seemed to belong to the eagle and the lizard. It was her first awareness of eagles in her destiny. With her relations pointing out the features of the land, she began to see how, to her mother's people, it had once been a great natural larder. They knew where to find the edible seeds, the lily roots and the wild cucumbers. They all knew where the sweet water was, and Aunty Miriam knew the medicinal plants.

'There are bush turkey around here,' said Uncle Ernie as they drove through a sandy waste dotted sparsely with salt bush.

'Where?'

'Look, over there. You can see their necks pushing up from the bushes like sticks.'

Ruby looked. The ones Uncle Ernie spotted would move, but the ones Ruby saw first turned out to be only sticks.

This country, north of Marree, was veined with tracks linking the widely scattered station homesteads with the known water, and with Marree, Oodnadatta, Birdsville, and the world beyond them. The tracks were visible enough, and time was bringing traffic to the area so that wind and water were less likely to obliterate them than they once were. As long as they were on the tracks the going was easy, but near

Coward Springs they turned off into trackless country. In the distance was a rise that looked like a small version of Ayers Rock and, as they drew closer, Ruby saw that there were many little elevations rising above the plain. This is limestone country, and water springs up in many of these mounds and trickles down, leaving long white stains.

They drove up to one of these hillocks and walked to the top. It was a flat area, and within it was a pool, about three metres across. A coarse grass grew sparsely around the edge and along the little channel that flowed from it, the only green in sight.

The pool was faintly rippled. 'I wonder if old mutha puttaye will rise,' the old-timers said.

Uncle Ernie squatted down and began patting the sand, talking to the water in Arabunna.

Mutha puttaye – still, and in turmoil (Coward Springs, SA).

Suddenly what looked like the shoulder of some enormous thick-skinned grey animal came up from the water, and two arms seemed to be pushing up and thrashing about as though some creature was desperate to escape from unseen clutches below.

It moved wildly across the pool towards Bruce, who turned and raced down the hill as his grandmother had done fifty years earlier.

'Come back, come back,' called Uncle Ernie. 'It is just old mutha puttaye come up to say "hullo".'

Ruby had also turned to race down to the car, but she had gone for her camera.

When she got back the pool was still.

'Mutha puttaye doesn't want his photo taken,' they said, but Ruby sat patiently and Uncle Ernie called up the 'old grey man' again, and he came bubbling up, less wildly this time, and it was almost as though he posed for her.

Ruby went back to 'the old bubbla' on other visits, and she learnt that it did not need Uncle Ernie's calling up, which he did so dramatically on that first day. The mutha puttaye will rise for anyone who stands by the pool. Sometimes it seems to be angrily protesting at intruders, and at other times desperately pleading for help. Ruby knew it was a natural phenomenon, readily explained away by a knowledgeable scientist, but she had no desire to hear about it. It never failed to carry her back to the eerie fireside nights at Blackford with Uncle Milton telling his frightening tales of the minka bird which, in turn, took her into the earliest Dreaming of her ancestors, and the beginnings of life itself.

For Uncle Ernie and her other Marree relations it was part of the total mystery of the land that gave them food and shelter, and from which all life came. They had no sense of 'owning' the land. It was part of them, and they were part of it.

The mutha puttaye subsided, and they all went back to the reserve.

The next day Ruby and Frank went with Uncle Ernie and Aunty Miriam to Lake Eyre, leaving the children at the reserve with the new friends they were making so quickly among their cousins.

'It was so easy to leave your children with your Aboriginal relations,' said Ruby afterwards, 'because everyone in the group feels responsibility and concern for every child among them. They don't think, as so many people seem to, that children 'belong' to their parents and to no one else. They are not hostile to other people's children, as so many people are. The love they have for their own children extends out to all the other children. They love them as they do their own and, if they need to, they reprimand them as they would their own.' There are people among whom this is true within the family, but among Aborigines it applies to a greater extended family.

Ruby very quickly became part of the Marree community. As she walked down the street the old people came to their doors and called out 'nana, nana', the Arabunna phrase for 'granddaughter, granddaughter'.

Sandra and Bruce thought it sounded like 'nanna', a word they had heard for 'grandmother', but they were quickly learning new words and new meanings. They too became part of this complex family group, and Frank was drawn in with equal acceptance. He loved and valued these people, and it set a seal upon their marriage.

The Hammonds went back once a year, and on one occasion took Irene with them. Ruby could easily forget that she had not known the Marree people all her life, and they felt the same way about her. She was one of them.

It had been in the 1920s that Ernie Ellis had returned to the north, more than eighty years after the first settlers had pushed their way up there. The old Aboriginal life was difficult then, and became more so. In those days the people who still lived off the land moved about in family groups – father and mother and the children, grandparents, and perhaps an aunty. They built humpies for themselves where there was water and food, moving on before they exhausted it. Techniques for harvesting in a way that preserved the food for the next season were skills known to every Aborigine in outback Australia.

Care of the land was sacred to them. They preserved the sources of food and water within their care because they were aware of responsibility not only to each other and to their children, but to all the generations that would come after them. They saw themselves as part of the total environment, and they knew how to live by the rhythms of day and night, and of the changing seasons. All this they passed on to their children, teaching them to value the land, and to respect and cherish it.

Ruby's Aunty Maude Corporal, who was living on the reserve, was an Aborigine whose beginnings were in that sort of family. When she was born her mother had lain on a bed of dried grasses that the women had prepared for her, making ready the ashes with which to cleanse the baby.

In those days Maude's name was Mawunka Yanindah. She spoke no English, and her lessons were the skills of harvesting from the land, cooking in a camp fire, and the women's songs. The girls were brought up by the women, the boys by the men, and she knew all the rites of the women.

Later on her parents got a horse and buggy, and collected a few wild goats that they drove along with them. She remembered Marree when it was Hergott Springs, and just a railway siding.

'It was greener in those days,' she used to say, 'or it seemed that way.'

Mawunka Yanindah went to work for a station family who gave her the name of Maude Lenny (Corporal was her married name), and taught her to speak English and to keep house in the European way.

Miriam Dadleh did not live on the reserve. Her house was built of sheets of galvanised iron over a dirt floor, but it was her own, built on land bought many years before by the Afghan camel-drivers.

The calling of these people 'Afghans' is a custom with

beginnings lost in history. It was probably a similar Australianism to 'Balts', which is what European migrants in the immediate post-second world war era were called until the merciful coining of the phrase 'new Australians'. Most of the men who handled camels in the north in the days of camel transports were Indians from the north-west area near the Afghanistan border, and one of them was Miriam Dadleh's father.

He was Nemith Khan, who landed in Port Augusta on 2 November 1892, a young man in his twenties, but in charge of a group of camels and men brought to Australia by Elder Smith, the stock and station agents, to augment their transport teams. He travelled overland with his team to Burke, and worked for the company for a few years for fifteen shillings a week. He managed to save enough to buy himself a camel in calf, from which modest beginning he built up a camel team of his own.

He established a trading business that took food and clothing, groceries and household goods to the remote stations and settlements in the country around Oodnadatta, Marree, Alice Springs, and the places just over the Queensland border.

The Hermannsburg Mission was on his route, and he must have been a handsome romantic figure to the girls at the mission school.

Sometime in the early 1900s Alison Stokes ran away to join him. She was a typical mission girl, daughter of an Aboriginal mother and a non-Aboriginal father, and she had been given a typical mission name. Unlike the New Zealand Maoris who retained their rhythmic native names, the Aborigines, who were being encouraged to become 'like white people', were given mission names or station names. Sometimes they were chosen in a kindly enough way. Aborigines with European fathers often kept their true patronymics, or children were named for the mission staff that cared for them. Station people often saddled the men with names like 'Charlie Wheelbarrow', or 'Chimney Evans', names that were an instant handicap to any of them who wanted to make their own way in white society.

Alison Stokes could read and write and cook and sew, and she took these skills and her Lutheran faith into her new nomadic life. She was a religious girl, and her husband, who was a Moslem, was religious too. His father had been a muezzin, a priest of the mosque, and it had been to escape from an oppressively religious background that young Nemith had come to Australia. He did not want a totally religious life, but until his death he remained a faithful Moslem, praying five times each day to Allah.

Each of the parents offered their children the best of what they knew, and Miriam Khan knew Lutheran hymns and Moslem prayers with equal fluency. She settled for Christianity. Miriam was a Methodist, but it was from her father that she imbibed her firm ideas of right and wrong, and her belief that we are totally responsible for our own actions, that we must accept what God provides and make the best of it.

Her schoolroom for this learning was the uncompromising Australian outback. She learnt it travelling about on her father's camels, and camping at night in all weathers. She grew up close to the land.

Alison Stokes was still in her teens when she ran away with Nemith Khan, who was more than twice her age. They were married, and she bore him six children of whom three survived – two boys, and Miriam, who was born in 1910.

Alison Khan died in the influenza epidemic of 1918, and for several years, before he married again, Nemith Khan cared for his children himself, strongly resisting authoritarian attempts to put them into homes. The children always travelled with him, and each of them learnt camel handling. They all drank camels' milk, and Miriam's youngest brother, who was reared on camels' milk, would drink it from the teat.

Their father saw that they had schooling. Their home base was Oodnadatta, where at one time a community of more than 1000 Afghans was living. The Oodnadatta primary school was the one where the children spent most time; but when they were travelling their father would stop for two or three weeks at a time at centres where there were schools, resting the camels and giving the children a chance to drink from these little outback pools of learning.

Because Alison had been Aboriginal, Nemith made a point of keeping in touch with the Aboriginal people in the area in which he travelled, and the children grew up knowing all the people of the mid-north – the Aborigines, Europeans of every nationality, the other camel-drivers, and Chinese and Indians who had been brought in to lay the thin lines of railway that linked Oodnadatta, Marree and Alice Springs.

When she was in her teens Miriam Khan went to work as a domestic on a station near Alice Springs. Here she met and married Gool Mahomet, one of the great camel riders of the north. When he died she married again, another man of Indian descent, Larl Dadleh. She had nine children, twenty-seven grandchildren and fourteen great grandchildren. Her loving heart encompassed them all. She was often surrounded by five or six children, who were never out of her sight while they were in her care. Miriam taught them to say grace, threatened to put a mop down their throats if she heard them swearing, and harried the girls inside if they were spending too much time with the boys.

She was worried by some of the younger Aborigines who neglected their children. Ruby was concerned about these people too, seeing how the culture clash had bewildered them, and poverty defeated them. Aunty Miriam was less tolerant. She was angry with them, and let them know it. She believed that those who did wrong should be punished. She was a religious woman with standards of right and wrong, and no uncertainties about which was which.

It was neglect of children, not drinking, that angered her. She was unfailingly kind to lonely Aunty Ivy, who would have liked to live in a more Aboriginal way if she still had a family to live with. On cold nights Ivy longed for a camp fire and, if all she could get to warm herself was a flagon of wine, she would creep round to a bed that stood outside Aunty Miriam's back door, and sleep there with her dog. Aunty Miriam would not send her away.

That first weekend in Marree was a glowing memory for Ruby. She delighted in the feeling of having been drawn closer to her Aboriginal inheritance, but, at the same time, she was appalled at the poor way in which her people were living.

They were the Adynyamathanha people who had once won a good livelihood from a vast area of the northern part of South Australia, but were now cramped into the reserve, living at barely subsistence level. Some of them drew pensions, some had no income at all, and shared with the others, so the standard of living was very low. There was an inadequate water supply, and there was no electricity although the houses in the town, across the railway line, all had it. Ruby could see that they had many needs, and an added reason for being glad she had come was that she would be able to help them.

Some of them needed medical help. When the flying doctor was coming a little notice in English was put up on the post office door. Not all of them could read English, not all of them could speak it, and they did not often go to the post office. They knew the flying doctor was coming when they saw the plane overhead, but by then it was too late to arrange to see him.

When Ruby spoke of this to an officer of the Department of Community Welfare he said to her, 'We haven't had any complaints.' Ruby was angry. 'Aborigines in this sort of situation have no idea of how to complain to a government department. They just mumble to themselves,' she told him.

The sister at the Marree Hospital was a wonderfully understanding friend but, as in all such hospitals, there was not enough staff to deal with all the problems. Ruby would have liked a clinic that was not too 'clinical', where the people could drift in and get herbal treatments as well as western drugs, and where mothers could learn how to deal with chest complaints and respiratory infections in their children. They needed someone who could speak their language, drive a car, and explain the bewildering mysteries of the forms they were so often asked to fill in.

Brian McIvor, the Department of Community Welfare officer who was then stationed in Leigh Creek, was another good friend, but he had to keep in touch with Aborigines in a vast outback area. Each place that had an Aboriginal community needed an Aboriginal person who understood the social welfare problems of the people, and could act as a liaison with the Departments of Aboriginal Affairs and Community Welfare. There would have been no problem in finding Aborigines who could be quickly trained for such work. Ruby felt that it was only bureaucratic attitudes that made solving Aboriginal problems so difficult.

Things improved after Ruby's first visit, partly because she was able to tell them of the benefits to which they were entitled, and help them to make their applications; and partly because of the Aboriginal housing policies of the Whitlam government. Simple Housing Trust houses, some of them with breeze-ways for the hot climate, were provided for those who were living on the reserve. Some of these houses were on the town-side of the railway line, a move that greatly improved the race relations in Marree, because inter-racial friendships were much more easily made.

Aunty Maude lived in one of these houses and looked after blind Aunty Alice. If it was cold she settled her in a chair where she could hear everyone who came and went, but what she loved best was to sit on the ground outside, turning her sightless eyes to the sun. She found it hard to keep her thin arms and legs warm. She wore jumpers and skirts but she wrapped herself in blankets too, and her dog, who never left her, huddled against her and they kept each other warm. He was an untrained mongrel but he was as valuable to Aunty Alice as any guide dog.

She would have liked a little camp fire to sit by. Perhaps she, alone among them, was homesick for her wurlie.

Aunty Maude, who watched her constantly, fearful that a snake might come round the tankstand, told her she must be content with the sun. She did not want the risk of fire.

She was also 'growing up' one of her nephews, who went to the Marree School. Maude, who never went to school herself, went to parents' meetings to learn what she should do to help her boy to the best possible education.

Sometimes she thought wistfully of the days when they all sat around the camp fire. The Aborigines were a close-knit, harmonious community in Marree, but Maude thought it was not as close as it had been in the old camp fire days. But she was glad of her house, and all the things she could keep in it. For many months after she moved in she waited for curtains to which she was entitled, tacking a blanket across the window to preserve her privacy at night time.

There are still people who think it is not important for Aboriginal tenants to get their curtains and other refinements. They used to live in humpies; what do they want with curtains? These are people who judge Aborigines without ever knowing them. Many Aboriginal women, seeking to understand European standards, longed for lace curtains, and blinds they could draw, and lampshades and tablecloths and ornaments. They wanted pretty homes and little gardens with the same longing that many other women have.

Other Aboriginal women were not interested in European trappings. Their homes were sparsely furnished, and the chief value of their curtains was the cherished privacy they offered; but even they preferred a Trust home to the shack across the railway line. It was warmer and more sheltering, and it raised their self-esteem even if it was sometimes bewildering.

Aunty Miriam had bunks in one of her three bedrooms, and was well organised to cope with visits from her large family. On her modern stove, heated with natural gas, she cooked up generous meals, consulting the *Women's Weekly* for recipes, but she could also bake a batch of johnny cakes and prepare traditional food for friends who liked it. She could manage all this and keep her home 'Europeanised'. This was what she liked, and she was a woman who was naturally successful.

Some of her other relations wanted to live in a closer-to-camping style in their Trust homes, and Ruby fought for their right to do so. People who said, 'It's no good giving them houses, they don't know what to do with them,' angered her.

'Why can't they be allowed to shut the door and live their own lives like white people do?' she would say. 'Why can't the Department look more closely at what they really want, and create housing settlements in which there is privacy for family groups around an area for communal living?'

The knowledge she gained from the Marree people helped Ruby to a better understanding of the Aborigines she met at national conferences. Often the pace of these meetings, particularly the ones called by the government, made them too intense for Aboriginal people. Ruby wished, as she knew many did, that they could all go outside and sit quietly talking around a camp fire until they came to a mutual understanding, postponing decisions for days if necessary. The meetings that the Department of Aboriginal Affairs set up made no concessions to Aboriginal pace. Like the meetings of any other government department they had an agenda to cover and must end at five o'clock, or whatever time had been chosen, so that delegates could dash to the airport, and fly off for another round of frantic meetings on the following day.

Ruby was torn sometimes at these meetings. Many urban Aborigines had learnt to play the Caucasian game as well as any government official, and were able to extract the maximum advantage for their people from the type of meeting the department had set up. Ruby could play this game too, but she was sometimes fearful of playing it too well, fearful of success and advancement lest they drew her more deeply into 'white ways' which she had grown to distrust.

She was always attracted to outback and reserve people, trusting their basic judgments and wisdom. When Wandjuk Marika, an elder of the Riratjinu people of eastern Arnhem Land came to Adelaide for National Aborigines Week in 1977, Ruby sought out every opportunity to hear him.

Ruby was attracted to the women, and cherished a memory of an evening spent talking with Mrs Jean Jimmy, of the Yupungatti group, one of the river people of Mapoon[3] on the Cape York Peninsula in Queensland.

Mapoon itself was a settlement on the horn of land that divides the bay of Port Musgrove from the Gulf of Carpentaria. A Presbyterian mission was set up there in 1891 and became a focal point for half a dozen groups that had lived since time immemorial around the rivers that flow into the gulf in that area. Before the coming of the mission there had been a bitter history of conflict with white cattlemen, who are reputed to have killed hundreds of Aborigines. The mission brought changes that induced great trust in whites by the native people.

Until the land was leased by the Queensland government in the 1950s to the Comalco and Alcoa mining companies, the question of who owned it had never troubled them. The land was manifestly theirs, although they thought not so much that the land belonged to them as that they belonged to the land.

The mining companies wanted the Aboriginal people out of Mapoon, and the Queensland government offered to move them to Thursday Island. The Presbyterian Church co-operated by closing the mission. Many of the people had become devout Christians, and feeling about the actions of the Church was very bitter.

A Mapoon elder is recorded as saying to one of the mission authorities, 'You been the shepherd, and left us the sheep without a master. What God think of you? What the Almighty God think of you?'

Jean Jimmy has accused the Church of trading the people of Mapoon for thirty pieces of silver.

The Mapoon people passionately wanted to remain in their ancestral homelands with which their laws and customs were inextricably interwoven. Thursday Island would not have appealed to them anyway. On the Torres Strait Islands they became bottom in a pecking order that gave the islanders precedence over them.

Pressures were put on them to leave. The store boats, which had once included Mapoon in their weekly run, ceased to call. They were told the flying doctor would no longer come, that Mapoon was rife with hookworm, that the water supply was drying up. A few families left, but the majority stayed in their homes. The government decided that they must be removed forcibly.

There were about 100 people involved in the round-up on the night of 15 November 1963, and Jean Jimmy was one of them. She was an articulate, mission-educated woman, who could speak and write fluent English. She has described how a boat came on that day, and anchored off Mapoon until after dark. Then, without any warning, white police came ashore and began going from house to house, telling the people to pack their suitcases, roll up their swags and come immediately because they were to be taken to Thursday Island. Some of them thought they were being arrested.

The people were walked along the beach to the mission house, and the following day they were herded onto the boat. In fact it was not Thursday Island to which they were taken but Hidden Valley, about 140 kilometres north of Mapoon, near Bamaga. It became known as New Mapoon, but it was not the ancestral lands which the people needed in order to preserve their ancient customs.

Mrs Jimmy remembered this night with the same frightening vividness with which any white Australian woman would remember a night in 1963 if police had knocked on her door and told her to pack her bags and come with them immediately because some company wanted to drill for oil, or mine for bauxite, under her house. The police were armed, although they did not use their weapons. Mrs Jimmy remembers seeing their revolvers and their handcuffs and clubs shining in the moonlight as they walked along the beach.

The story of the Mapoon people has been well recorded, and Ruby sometimes related it when she was asked to speak at meetings. She was constantly amazed at the equanimity with which her audiences could hear it.

'Can you imagine,' she would say, 'the outrage if white

people had been moved like this; and it was not something that happened in the first days of settlement. It was 1963!'

Ruby first met Mrs Jimmy at a meeting of the National Council of Aboriginal Women at the James Cook University in Townsville in 1974. She was a little, dynamic woman in her seventies with thick white hair contrasting dramatically with her very dark skin. She was a good speaker, and has written her account of life at Mapoon in both prose and poetry. She was an outstanding figure at that conference and Ruby remembered a night when a number of the delegates went to Mrs Jimmy's room. They sat round on the bed and on the floor to hear her tell her story.

It was a hot tropical night, and a big ceiling fan in the room turned slowly. They could look out across the beautiful university gardens and hear the whip birds calling outside. Mrs Jimmy smoked her pipe, and told them the dreadful story of her people's dispossession.

When they left Mapoon their houses were burnt down. Many of these houses had been recently built with new materials for which the men had saved the money they got from selling crocodile skins. The last people to leave saw it happen. The new iron was pulled down, and coconut branches put inside and set alight. Not only were the homes burnt, but all the possessions that the people had not been able to pack at such short notice were burnt too.

For these people their evacuation was an even more terrible thing than it would have been for white people. They believe that part of themselves is destroyed when a home is burnt down, or when their clothing, which still retains their 'nara', is burnt.

White people laugh at this as superstition, but it is deeply true to the Aboriginal people. Many of the Mapoon people became seriously ill after they had been moved, and they blamed it on the burning of their 'nara'. The Queensland

Department of Native Affairs should have known of these beliefs. It was all shockingly done.

When Ruby sat at the feet of people like Mrs Jimmy she was especially moved by a sense of their oneness with nature, and she longed sometimes to be able to communicate this to her non-Aboriginal friends. She did not want to embrace a totally Aboriginal life, rejecting all she had learnt to enjoy of European civilisation, but she believed that there was an ultimate answer for all people which must recognise the cherishing of the land as essential for the survival of life on earth.

Ruby was well aware of the political movements within the South Australian white community. She knew the arguments for and against the causes espoused by such groups as the Conservation Council, Friends of the Earth, and the Campaign Against Nuclear Energy, how difficult the problems seemed and how terrifying the threats. When she was among Aboriginal people it all seemed so simple. You cared for the land, and the land cared for you. You did not exhaust it with frenetic searches for energy and raw materials to make into goods that ended up as rubbish to further despoil the landscape. She wished she could pass on the Aboriginal answer. She wished more people could know of the words with which Jean Jimmy ended a tape-recorded account of the Mapoon story, which has been published.

The Mapoon people were seeking to re-establish themselves in their own lands, and Jean Jimmy said:

> You might think we are silly in coming back here to old Mapoon, but this is what we wanted all the time. If you are ship-wrecked, or if you are flying in a plane and have a forced landing, well, what do you eat? Only nature provides for human beings. If you teach your children then they won't die of starvation, and if you teach your children where water is –

this is most important. All of us must look after our children – not in the life you lead today. We came here to show our children the life that God has created, and made our ancestors to see what nature had given them. They were civilised in their own ways.

Well, we want our children to be the same – to learn where water is when there is a drought, to learn to find their bush food (and this is what you want when you are ship-wrecked or crashed in the plane); but I think that you people don't understand us very much.

I want you all to understand our feelings towards our birth land, Mapoon. We want the land because the land is most important to we Aborigines. It is sacred to us, in our customs. I think most white people don't understand us very much, but there comes a time they must understand our Aboriginal ways which we think are sacred. Looking now, we live by nature because God has made our ancestors civilised in our own way – by nature, and really and truly we live by nature.[4]

There seemed so much wisdom in this, and so much senseless folly in the 'western' way of life. Perhaps Aborigines who were in Australia before Europeans came would still be there after Europeans had destroyed themselves. Aboriginal wisdom was a source of strength for Ruby. She was intensely proud that she was linked to these people by her blood, and that it was visible beyond doubt in her dark skin.

SIX

DISCOVERING CANBERRA

the very beginnings of a national voice

THE WORK RUBY HAMMOND WAS DOING WITH THE COUNCIL of Aboriginal Women was to carry her not only into the Aboriginal Legal Rights Movement but also into the administrative world of Canberra. She was to see the very beginnings of a national voice for Aborigines within the processes of government.

On 26 January 1972, the prime minister, Mr McMahon, made a long definitive outline of the government's policy for Australian Aborigines.[1] He began with a five-point Statement of Objectives which made it clear that the government now regarded 'integration' and not 'assimilation' as the basis of their policy. Within the context of Aboriginal destiny these two words have acquired special meanings. 'Assimilation' means total absorption of Aborigines into a European way of life; 'integration' means Aborigines living equally in the community while retaining their own cultural and ethnic identity.

He promised that 'they should be encouraged and assisted to preserve their own culture, languages, traditions and arts so that these can become living elements in the diverse culture of the Australian society'.

He also stated that programs to give effect to the policy 'must take into account the expressed wishes of Aboriginal Australians themselves'.

It was the most detailed statement about Aboriginal policy ever made by an Australian prime minister, and Mr McMahon had chosen it for his Australia Day speech, delivered from the steps of Parliament House. He gave an account of expenditure on education, housing, and welfare for Aborigines, and announced a 'new form of lease' for land on Aboriginal reserves in the Northern Territory.

Undoubtedly the government hoped that Aborigines would welcome this statement, but they had failed to understand many of the needs of the Aborigines and the intensity of their feeling. However well-intentioned the new policies were, it seemed they were to continue with the paternalism of the past. Before the prime minister had finished speaking some of them had put up a beach umbrella on the lawns in front of him, and the foundations of the Aboriginal Tent Embassy had been laid.[2]

The young, knowledgeable Aborigines who contrived the Tent Embassy were dissatisfied with the prime minister's speech. Nothing in it promised real relief for the many situations in which Aboriginal children were suffering from malnutrition or for the infant mortality rate, which was the highest in the world; the 'general purpose leases' fell far short of their own concept of land rights; and they found the promise to 'take into account the expressed wishes of the Aboriginal Australians themselves' to be far too nebulous. There was no suggestion of how this would be achieved.

The government was embarrassed by the Tent Embassy,

and they refused to have dealings with it, but they took the point that some way of enabling the Aborigines to express their wishes must be found.

Between 1969 and 1972 the Council for Aboriginal Affairs had organised conferences in all states and in the Northern Territory, and set up Aboriginal Advisory Councils. Mr Howson, the Minister for the Environment, the Aborigines and the Arts, decided to send personal invitations to sixty-two Aboriginal people from these councils, and to three Torres Strait Islanders, to a meeting in Canberra on 10 and 11 August 1972. He also invited an official observer from each state.

Ruby Hammond was one of nine people invited from South Australia, and the only one from Adelaide. The others were all from the reserves. Ruby is listed in the official record of the proceedings as being from the Council of Aboriginal Women. Lois O'Donoghue was the South Australian observer. Sir Douglas Nicholls[3] was one of four delegates from Victoria, and was elected chairman.

Each state had one representative on the steering committee, and Ruby was chosen for South Australia.

The invited representatives did not include anyone who had been involved in the Tent Embassy. It was the government's claim that they did not represent a significant Aboriginal viewpoint. Paul Coe, John Newfong, Gary Foley and Dennis Walker, who had all been on the Tent Embassy staff, came uninvited to the meeting and, to the minister's surprise, the delegates asked that they be admitted. They came in at first as observers but later, because a majority of those present wanted it, they were given speaking rights.

After the minister had opened the conference he left, saying he would return the following afternoon to hear what they might want to say to him. He left a suggested agenda, which they might follow or not as they chose. He also offered them the services of officers of his department to give facts or advice, or for one to act as a secretary.

The minister spoke about a proposal for a permanent Aboriginal centre in Canberra, and asked for their views about it. It was discussion on this question that led to the meeting giving speaking rights to the 'Embassy representatives'.

Not expecting to be allowed to speak they had prepared a statement urging that the delegates 'walk out of this circus' unless the government agreed to the re-erection of the Tent Embassy.

In the end a motion was carried 'that this Conference feels it is impossible to consider or debate a centre of any sort until the black Embassy is re-established on the lawns of Parliament House. We urge the government to allow the Embassy to be re-established for the peace and goodwill of the entire Australian community'.

The meeting was an immensely important one for the Aboriginal people because it brought together Aborigines from the far north, from cities and from the reserves.

The minutes show strongly dissenting views, but thirty-eight motions were carried and it became apparent that on one question there was unanimity. They wanted reserve lands to be recognised as belonging to the Aborigines, and social and economic equality to be given to all Aborigines wherever they might be. These were not two separate matters, but two aspects of the same issue – land rights.

Aborigines see 'social and economic equality' as being what they would have attained by their own efforts if they had been given proper compensation for their land in the first years of European settlement. They demand it as a debt that is owing to them.

There was a huge agenda for a two-day meeting. It included health, housing, education, employment, legal matters, women's rights, and land rights, as well as procedural decisions. The last motion carried was 'that future conferences be of at least four days duration'.

On this occasion Ruby thought back with gratitude to the insistence by Natascha MacNamara that the Council of Aboriginal Women run their affairs in a formal way. Ruby was well able to cope with the proceedings, and she was full of admiration for the way the men and women from the reserves and the outback accepted and grasped the formalities. She knew that this way of doing things did not appeal to them, and that they regarded their own unhurried ways of discussing problems until consensus was reached as a far superior manner of making decisions.

For most of the delegates the meeting was intensely exciting. They had assembled on the afternoon of 9 August, and there had been a party provided by the department in the evening. Many new friendships were made, and old ones renewed.

Flying to Canberra at the government's expense and staying at motels was a novel experience for almost all of them, and most exciting of all was the feeling that they were people of importance with something to say to which a Minister of the Crown would be listening.

The Tent Embassy representatives were cynical about the government's intentions, and there was criticism about the way the delegates had been chosen by the department instead of by the Aboriginal community. The Northern Territory delegates complained that they had neither the time nor the prior knowledge of the agenda to discuss the issues with the people they represented, and they in particular felt disadvantaged by the speed with which the long agenda was pushed through.

Despite these misgivings the excitement lasted for most of them until they got back home. Their thirty-eight resolutions seemed an impressive statement of Aboriginal hopes and aspirations.

Disenchantment came sooner or later to most of them with the feeling that it was all making very little impact on the Department of Aboriginal Affairs. If what they had to say was not to be acted upon, why bother to bring them all to Canberra to express their views?

Some, and Ruby was among them, felt they were being used in an exercise in window dressing. It was being made to appear that Aborigines were being consulted, but in fact they were being ignored as they always had been.

Subsequently the Committee of Inquiry into the Role of the National Aboriginal Consultative Committee[4] reported that: 'In the opinion of the DAA, most of the resolutions passed by the NACC did not constitute advice which could be expected to be useful to the Minister, the government, or the Department of Aboriginal Affairs. Many were expressed in general exhortatory terms and did not lend themselves to implementation as policy or programs.'

To Ruby this seemed an excuse offered to conceal the more shameful fact that the Department of Aboriginal Affairs was not prepared to take the committee seriously.

'The committee believed that they were advising the Department through the resolutions that were so earnestly discussed and framed,' she said. 'The Department would have accepted it as advice if they had been willing to rethink their own programs in the light of what the Aboriginal people wanted.'

Most Aborigines were pleased when, in November 1972, the Labor Party came to power. In his policy speech Gough Whitlam had said:

More than any foreign aid programme, more than any international obligation which we meet or forfeit, more than any part we may play in any treatment or agreement or alliance, Australia's treatment of her Aboriginal people will be the thing upon which the rest of the world will judge Australia. Not just now, but in the greater perspective of history, and further, the Aborigines are a responsibility we cannot escape, cannot share, cannot shuffle off; and the world will not let us forget that.

A government department devoted entirely to Aboriginal affairs was set up. Gordon Bryant, a long-time vice-president of the Federal Council for the Advancement of Aborigines and Torres Strait Islanders, was the minister. Barry Dexter of the old Council of Aboriginal Affairs was the secretary, and Charles Perkins, the first Aborigine to gain a university degree, was appointed assistant secretary in charge of the department's Consultative and Liaison Branch.

The new minister decided on a new beginning, and invitations went out for another meeting of selected representatives to begin in Canberra on 18 February 1973 to form a National Aboriginal Consultative Committee. This time more people with a wider range of opinions were included. There were eighty of them. Members of the Tent Embassy staff were invited and included Dennis Walker, son of the Aboriginal poet, Oodgeroo Noonuccal (Kath Walker). At the other end of the scale was the Liberal Party's senator, Neville Bonner.[5] Aborigines from the outback, the reserves and the cities were all included. Ruby was again among them.

On the first day the press and all white observers were kept out. The meeting was held in the Academy of Science conference room, and big 'Blacks Only' notices went up on the doors.

This first day saw the achievement of one of the things for which there was near unanimous support – a firm promise of a fully elected advisory council. A twenty-seven-member steering committee to plan for the elections was elected. Ruby was pleased to be one of the chosen. Having been twice included in selections made by white departmental officers it was reassuring to be elected by the group.

Ruby with Senator Neville Bonner and Senator John McLeay.

On the second day the press and observers were allowed in. The *Australian*, 12 February 1973, had predicted that 'with such a big group representing widely differing viewpoints Mr Bryant will find it presenting him with conflicting advice in many areas'. Reports of the meeting suggest that journalists wanted to prove their colleague right.

Noel Pratt, writing in the *Advertiser*, 20 February 1973, said of the press:

They witnessed a clash between Paul Coe and chairman George Abdullah from Western Australia over whether or not Sydney Aborigines were being allowed their say; heated debate on a motion (later passed) condemning the Catholic Church for racist views, and an emotion-charged discussion on a motion from Roy Marinka of the Yirrkala in which, as well as asking for more royalties and a greater say in activities at Gove, he proposed to thank the mining company Nabalco for its operations. This latter part of the motion was later dropped.

This type of reporting seemed very superficial to Ruby Hammond. The two meetings, this one and the one in the previous August, were the beginnings of a real attempt to consult people whose denial of human rights within the Australian community was becoming an international scandal. Of course there were difficulties. It was certainly true that the delegates were representing widely differing viewpoints.

They were also representing a deprived people. Not one of the eighty Aborigines taking part would have gained his or her place in the community without a struggle against discrimination. Not all of them spoke English. Some had had very little European education, some of them none at all.

The clashes were unimportant. The positive decisions, the constructive motions passed, were what mattered. The meeting was an historic forward step, an almost incredible triumph, but not one Australian newspaper described it in these terms.

The clashes that disturbed Ruby were those between the urban and outback Aborigines, because the differences were profound and complex.

The definition of an Aborigine for the purpose of the meeting was 'a person of Aboriginal descent who identifies as an Aboriginal and is accepted as such by the community with which he or she is associated'. Any other definition would have meant an intolerable exclusion of people seeing themselves as Aboriginal. Ruby believed that all Aboriginal and part-Aboriginal people should accept this definition, and weld themselves into a united force by making the effort to understand each other's needs and viewpoints.

Once again land rights, the issue on which there was such basic united feeling, was the dominant theme.

On 8 February the Labor government, carrying out an election promise, had commissioned Mr Justice A.M. Woodward 'to inquire into and report upon ... the appropriate means to recognise and establish the traditional rights and interests of the Aborigines in and in relation to land, and to satisfy in other ways the reasonable aspirations of the Aborigines to rights in or in relation to land ...'[6]

The meeting asked that two additional commissioners, both Aborigines, be appointed to sit with Mr Justice Woodward. It also demanded that the final Land Rights Bill be subject to a review by a national elected body of Aborigines, and only go before parliament when it had their approval.

Neither the request nor the demand were granted. The great achievement of the meeting was that at last there was to be an elected national body to advise the government. Ruby and the other twenty-six members of the steering committee remained in Canberra over the weekend to make the preliminary plans for the election.

Joe McGuinness, a leader of the Queensland Aboriginal people, was elected chairman, and a sub-committee was appointed to work in co-operation with the newly appointed Consultative and Liaison Branch, with Charles Perkins as secretary, within the Department of Aboriginal Affairs.

By May 1973 they had prepared a set of proposals which

were presented to a second conference of the minister's committee. They recommended that the National Aboriginal Consultative Committee should be established by statute and should comprise eighty-two Aborigines elected for two years by the Aboriginal people at a general election. Two members should come from each of forty-one electorates throughout Australia, based on population, grouping and affinity, language and geographical features. With the help of the electoral office the boundaries of the forty-one electoral districts were defined, and work began on compiling the rolls.

The wide definition of an Aborigine or Torres Strait Islander used initially when the invitations went out was adopted for the election, and eighteen years of age was fixed as the minimum for enrolling, voting, and standing for election. Prisoners in gaol were permitted to vote for the first time in Australia.

The election was one of the most imaginative achievements in Australian history. It was held at the planned time of November 1973, in spite of great difficulties which had to be overcome. The area to be covered was immense, and included settlements that were remote and difficult of access. Not only did the electors not speak English, but there was no simple 'Aboriginal' that they spoke. Interpreters had to be found for 200 languages and dialects.

Local people were able to assist in compiling the rolls, but thousands of square kilometres of Australia's difficult outback territory had to be negotiated by the travelling polling booths which were used.

There was not a single 'election day', but a fortnight in which electoral officers travelled through the outback in combi-vans and four-wheel-drive vehicles set up as polling booths.

Only forty-one members were elected. The government did not accept the recommendation of two members for each electorate, or that the committee should be established by statute. It was to be an advisory body only.

The election was not without its critics within the Aboriginal community. To some of them it was alien and distasteful. To many of them the white man's methods seemed extraordinarily crude. It was boycotted by some of the militant Aborigines in Sydney who objected to what they saw as 'white arrangements'.

It was estimated that 60,000 Aborigines were eligible to vote. Of these 36,000 were enrolled, and 25,000 voted. In view of the difficulties it was a tremendous success.

South Australia had four electorates, and there were five candidates for the Adelaide district, the one for which Ruby might have nominated. She decided not to stand for the election. She was acquiring skills and special knowledge that were deepening her confidence to act as a social worker among her people in Adelaide. It was here, and not in Canberra, that she felt she could work most effectively.

Val Power was one of the candidates in the Adelaide electorate, and was beaten by only five votes by James (Jim) Stanley. Ruby admired both these people, and felt she would have stood little chance against them.

Jim Stanley, then aged thirty-one, was already an acknowledged leader of the Aboriginal community in South Australia. He was a field officer working with the Prisoners' Aid Association, chairman of the Aboriginal Legal Rights Movement, president of the Aboriginal Evangelical Fellowship, and a member of the advisory committee of the Task Force.

Ruby was delighted at his election, especially when, in the following October, he became president and chairman of the national body. Although she had been disillusioned by the ineffectiveness of the first two committees, she had high hopes for this new one. It met in Canberra in December.

Senator Cavanagh, who by then had replaced Gordon

Bryant as Minister for Aboriginal Affairs, welcomed them.

'It will be your task,' he told them, 'to bring to the department and the Minister the wishes, the thinking, and the aspirations of your people. If your proposals are logical and justified a government would reject them at its own peril.'

There was always an 'if'. It had a familiar ring – 'if your proposals are logical and justified ...' Logical and justified by what criteria? Aborigines whose hope was to live in dignity among those they loved, and in harmony with the land they cherished, wondered if that would be 'logical and justified'. They feared that the answer would be 'no'; that 'logical and justified' would be measured against 'progress', the white man's desire to 'get on' in the community, to be continually increasing his standard of living.

For the forty-one men and women elected the realisation of this was blurred by the pleasure of success. Whether it was what they wanted or not they were being drawn into the white man's system. Some of the critics were already saying, 'We'll have to wait and see if they work for our community and not for themselves.'

Some of the elected members were sharply aware of these dangers. They struggled to keep from being drawn too deeply into ways that were alien to many Aborigines, to defend their integrity, and to keep always in their sights the real hopes and aspirations of the people they represented. It was because Jim Stanley was so clearly one of these that he had been elected president.

The second meeting of the committee was in February 1974, but before this an incident involving Charles Perkins erupted into a major issue. In his position as a senior public servant Charles Perkins had become the best-known Aborigine in Australia.

The trouble began on 16 January when the Minister for the Northern Territory, Dr Patterson, said he feared serious violence between blacks and whites in north Australia. He blamed increasing alcohol consumption by Aborigines, and 'militant stirrers from the south who are inciting Aborigines to acts of violence'.

Charles Perkins reacted angrily to this statement. If Aboriginal violence was increasing it was because Aborigines were objecting to being treated as second-class citizens, he said. Dr Patterson, whom he described as 'a hick from the sticks',[7] was ignorant of what was going on in the Territory. Senator Cavanagh was also criticised. Perkins said that he had been moving too slowly on Aboriginal programs, and was too concerned by the 'white backlash'. The prime minister was advised to deal with both these ministers.

It came as a surprise to Charles Perkins, who was accustomed to speaking his mind, to discover that now that he was a public servant this constituted a breach of public service regulations, and specifically of Section 34(B), which prohibits an officer from commenting on the administration of his department.

Perkins was quite unrepentant. 'Ministers are not God, and should be subject to criticism,' he said. If he had breached a regulation, it was a regulation that ought to be abolished.

He claimed that the Labor Party had promised 'open government', and now were not prepared to stand by it.

'Open government means people being able to speak out on vital issues,' he said, 'and that is what I am doing.'

Since a regulation had been breached, Senator Cavanagh wanted Perkins to be charged under the act, but Barry Dexter, head of the Department of Aboriginal Affairs, wanted the matter dropped, and Dexter won the day.

There had been several days of nation-wide publicity, and Charles Perkins won a new respect from the Aboriginal people. There would hardly have been an Aborigine in Australia who would not have agreed with what he had said, and applauded him for saying it. They were well aware that Australians regarded criticising the government as a national right, and it was intolerable to them that some bureaucratic regulation should prevent their chief spokesman from exercising it.

The incident was of not much more than passing interest to most white Australians. They were, on the whole, pleased that Charles Perkins had not been charged, and inclined to think that too much fuss had been made about the whole thing.

To Aborigines it had been intensely important, and had aroused high feelings that had not subsided when the Consultative Committee met in February.

They passed a motion calling for the dismissal of Senator Cavanagh, describing him as 'ignorant of the plight of the Aboriginal people'. They resolved to change their title to National Aboriginal Congress, demanding that they be the decision-making committee of the Department of Aboriginal Affairs with control over the spending of their $117 million budget.

Senator Cavanagh replied to this by saying he had no authority to pay salaries to such a body, and if they had changed their name and their function their pay would cease from that Friday.

Senator Cavanagh bore stoically what was undoubtedly a hurt. He had genuine goodwill towards the Aboriginal people, but he believed that good government depended on people obeying the rules.

He agreed to see the committee's executive, and persuaded them that the proper method was to set out their requests and submit them to Cabinet. They accepted this, and their pay was not stopped, but it resulted in their spending a great deal of time in the ensuing weeks drawing up a constitution which the government rejected.

Within two weeks Charles Perkins was again in trouble.

He had given Barry Dexter an undertaking that he would not breach Section 34(B) of the public service regulations again. He adhered to this, but on 15 February, on a television program recorded in Western Australia, he attacked the Liberal and Country Parties, then in opposition, describing them as 'the biggest racist political parties the world has seen'.[8]

This was not a breach of Section 34(B), but he discovered that even so it was not the sort of talk in which public servants were permitted to indulge. It was seen as a breach of Section 55, which forbids 'improper conduct'.

Once again he was front-page news. He was adamant that he had not broken any public service regulation, and that 'anyone in the Aboriginal field should be able to comment on any matter involving Aborigines'. He added, referring to a suggestion for an enquiry into the Aboriginal situation in the Northern Territory, that what was needed was a Royal Commission into whites.

The government would have liked to have dealt with the matter quietly, but freedom of speech was a popular issue, and newspapers in every state gave it plenty of publicity. There were many 'letters to the editor', almost all of them supporting Perkins, and many of them recalling pre-election promises of the government to give public servants 'the civil and political liberties enjoyed by other Australians in private employment'.

Trade unions, including the Commonwealth Council of Public Service Organisations, offered to give assistance if Perkins was charged.

There were strong feelings among Aborigines. The Tent Embassy went up again on the lawns of Parliament House, and plans were made for a protest meeting on 28 February 1974, when the Queen would be opening parliament.

On the Monday of that week Mr Whitlam was reported to

have told ministers at the end of a Cabinet meeting that he hoped Perkins would not be charged with a breach of the public service regulations, although Senator Cavanagh was making no secret of the fact that he wanted such a charge to be laid. The statutory power to make the charge lay with the head of the department, Barry Dexter, and the following day he defied the prime minister and Perkins was charged.[9]

He was immediately suspended. Staff of the Department of Aboriginal Affairs held a stop-work meeting and voted overwhelmingly to strike if the charge was upheld. Mr Whitlam said that if this happened the government would advise the governor general not to take any action.

In this heated atmosphere Aborigines were converging on Canberra from other states for their protest on the Thursday. By that morning there was a crowd of more than 1000. It was a beautiful summer day and the lawns had the picnic atmosphere which Aborigines always seem to create on these occasions. There was no air of hostility towards anyone. Old friends were meeting with the greatest pleasure, the women were serving tea and sandwiches to all comers, the children were playing on the grass, and people were sitting about in groups, many of them strumming guitars.

The Aborigines had put up five extra tents, and the police put up steel barricades to keep people back from the path along which the Queen would travel. The leaders among the Aborigines were urging non-violence. Charles Perkins asked them 'to play it cool'.

'My suspension,' he said, 'is only a tiny part of the whole issue. We are here for the people who are starving and whose kids' bones are turning to chalk.'

The demonstration outside Parliament House went off without any physical incident. Placards were waved calling for 'free speech', 'land rights' and an 'end to British Imperialism in Australia'. The Queen was booed, and cheers drowned out the national anthem. It was embarrassing, especially for Mr Whitlam, but that was all.

However, not far away, in the office of the Department of Aboriginal Affairs, three Aborigines were holding the acting director, Mr F.H. Moy, and the first assistant secretary, Mr J.P.M. Long, and two other senior officers at gunpoint in Mr Moy's office. Charles Perkins was sent for and he persuaded the three men to give up their gun. He was much praised for his cool handling of the situation, and the charges against him were dropped.[10]

Robert McLeod, a twenty-six-year-old Canberra Aborigine was charged with carrying an unlicensed pistol. There were protests that a more serious charge should have been laid, but McLeod claimed he had not intended to hurt anyone, and in fact he had not done so. He had wanted to protest about Charles Perkins' suspension, and the appalling conditions under which Aborigines were living. It had all been done on the spur of the moment, and he had taken a gun 'because it would have been no good taking a spear and a boomerang'.[11]

Ruby was aware that to the white community it was no more than a passing incident. She longed for a rooftop from which to cry 'Listen! Listen! You don't listen to our words, you don't listen to our deeds. When a man says he does not want to hurt anyone, but he has to take a gun to make his point, he is getting desperate. Listen to us. Please listen to us, before we have to take a gun and use it.'

The department should have been listening to the National Aboriginal Consultative Committee, but it seemed fated to carry on advising those who did not want to be advised. During the life of the Labor government it met seven times, usually in Canberra, but also in Darwin, Townsville and Perth. A total of 153 resolutions were carried on a wide range of subjects including education, employment, housing, land rights, police and prisons, and the

Queensland Aborigines Act. Once again it was advice that was not taken.

A most generous-minded resolution recommended that 'although Aborigines are the oppressed of the oppressed, community projects for Aborigines (in housing, health, education, legal services) should serve as models for government aid to other underprivileged groups in Australian society'.

A great deal of time was spent in drawing up the constitution, which the government rejected. Increasingly the committee found itself at odds with the department, and the reasons can be found in the constitution. The committee wanted to go beyond advising the minister and the department. It wanted to formulate policies, and take action to implement them.

The department began to feel that the committee 'conceived itself more as a rival than as an assistant'; and the committee in turn felt that it was just being asked to 'rubber stamp' decisions that had already been made.

The Report of the Committee of Inquiry into the Role of National Aboriginal Consultative Committee was subsequently to say, 'The name "Consultative Committee" would, in the context of affairs of state, normally suggest a body that responds to government requests for advice on specified problems. Consultation in this sense did not occur. In the atmosphere of mutual antagonism that prevailed from the beginning, the department was reluctant to take the NACC into its confidence and hence made only token efforts to enlist its aid. The NACC, for its part, fired off demands in the form of motions and relieved its frustrations in periodic confrontations with the Minister.'

The original election was for two years but, because it was deemed desirable to have new election boundaries, the second election was postponed.

Before it could be held, the greatest constitutional crisis in

Australia's history changed the outlook for Aborigines. An atmosphere of intense hostility had developed between the government and the opposition. The opposition managed to gain control of the Senate and was threatening to reject the budget, denying the government the Supply on which it operated. The government had until 30 November to bring down the budget, but on 11 November the governor general, Sir John Kerr, took it upon himself to dismiss the prime minister and call on the leader of the opposition, Malcolm Fraser, to form an interim government.

An election was held on 8 December and the Labor Party was heavily defeated.

Aboriginal Affairs were undoubtedly more important to the new Liberal government than they had been in the 1960s, but they had not rated a mention in the new prime minister's policy speech.[12]

The new Minister for Aboriginal Affairs was Ian Viner, and one of his first actions was to appoint the committee of Inquiry. The chairman, who was the only non-Aboriginal, was Dr L.R. Hiatt, Reader in Anthropology at the University of Sydney and president of the Australian Institute of Aboriginal Studies. The three Aboriginal members were Jim Stanley, Lois O'Donoghue, and Maurice Luther, community adviser at Hooker Creek, in the Northern Territory.

The 'Summary of Main Conclusions and Recommendations' in the Inquiry Committee's report made it clear that if the National Aboriginal Consultative Committee was to be effective its role should be properly defined.

Included among the ten recommendations were that the Consultative Committee continue as an elected body, with the number of electorates being increased from forty-one to forty-six to give increased representation to those in remote areas; and that a statutory Commission for Aboriginal Development be created by 1980.

Lois O'Donoghue did not support popular elections, but submitted a long and detailed scheme for a system of delegates from local, regional and state organisations.

The report was completed in November 1976, and in May of the following year Mr Viner announced his decisions.

The National Aboriginal Consultative Committee would be replaced by a thirty-five member National Aboriginal Conference with six state branches and a ten-member executive. A Council for Aboriginal Development would also be set up. It was to have ten members, five chosen by the Aboriginal Conference and five by the minister, and this would be the body from which the government would seek formal advice. There would be a 'charter of functions and duties' to define the roles of the conference and the council.

Mr Viner referred to the Inquiry Committee's recommendation that the advisory body should develop by 1980 into a statutory body able to determine programs and priorities. He would leave this question open, he said.

Jim Stanley's first reaction to Mr Viner's announcement was highly critical. He was dismayed at the reduction in numbers from forty-one to thirty-five, as the Inquiry Committee had felt there was a real need to raise it to forty-six so that specific groups with unique interests could be represented. He saw the creation of the council, with half of its members appointed by the minister, as a 'watering down of the true voice of the Aboriginal people'. However he was determined to make the best of it, and to urge the Aborigines to accept it and make it work.

'It's better than nothing,' he said.

SEVEN

THE ABORIGINAL LEGAL SERVICE

to break down the
barriers of alienation
and distrust

THE FIELD WORK THAT RUBY DID FOR THE COUNCIL OF Aboriginal Women made her increasingly aware of the need for expert legal help for Aborigines.

In the 1960s it was not so much the arrested Aborigine who would come to the council as his wife or mother. Arrested Aborigines tended to see themselves as caught up in the hand of some inscrutable fate that pushed them inevitably into prison. There was nothing, they thought, that you could do about it.

The women in their families began turning to the women they knew would help if they could, the women in the council. A worried mother would come in and say to Ruby, 'My boy's in court on a charge of resisting arrest.'

'Resisting arrest for what?'

Very often the woman did not know because 'resisting arrest' would be the most serious of the charges that had mounted up.

In those days there was not a great deal the council could do to help, but more and more women in the families of these men were coming to them, and Ruby was having increased contact with problems involving the law. She began to perceive a situation that filled her with indignation and anger, and developed in her a streak of militancy that no personal injustice would have aroused.

Since 1963 a massive study of Aborigines in Australian society had been sponsored by the Australian Academy of Social Sciences. In the 1970s the work published included a study of Aborigines and the criminal law in Victoria, South Australia and Western Australia by Dr Elizabeth Eggleston. Entitled *Fear, Favour or Affection*,[1] it is a carefully documented objective record of facts and statistics that make it quite clear that serious problems of injustice, inequality and discrimination before the law existed for Aborigines.

In 1970 Ruby did not know the statistics. She could not have told you, for instance, that for the year ended 30 June 1966, when Aborigines formed 0.7 per cent of the total population of South Australia, they made up nineteen per cent of the prison population.

She did know, however, that the Aboriginal prison population was out of proportion to their members in the community, and that almost none of them had committed any serious crime. The majority of them were in prison for drunkenness, or offences relating to drink. And why were they drinking? Because they were unemployed, and often homeless. And what had brought them to this state? By the 1960s Ruby could perceive the answer to this question in the history of the Aboriginal people. The total injustice of it all left her groping for words.

It was in these years that Ruby first met Elliott Johnston, a well-known South Australian lawyer who happened to be a member of the Communist Party. Years before it was said of him that he would have been a Queen's Counsel if it had not been for his political views. Finally in 1970, when Don

Dunstan, who was also a lawyer, became premier, he was made one.

The Liberal Party had declared that they would never make a communist a Queen's Counsel, and there were rumblings of protest when it was done, but Johnston was also a widely respected and able barrister, and some said he would have been a judge if it were not for his political views. In 1983 he attained this eminence too, when the Labor Party was again in power.

Elliott Johnston had been the legal friend of the poor and the oppressed in South Australia since he first put up his plate. He had probably done more work for less money than any other lawyer in Australia. Elliott had been helping Aborigines since 1948, but it was beyond possibility that one lawyer could find the time to help all the unfortunates who came up in court day after day on petty charges. It was these men and women whom Ruby longed to help.

In July 1971 she heard Professor J.H. Wootten speak. Dean of the Faculty of Law at the University of New South Wales, Wootten was also president of a group set up in New South Wales to administer a voluntary legal service to help Aborigines in Sydney. He had come to Adelaide at the invitation of a group hoping to develop something similar in South Australia.

Ruby felt he put her own thoughts into words and she was grateful to hear them from a man of such standing and in such circumstances. Speaking of the frequency of arrest and imprisonment of Aborigines he said they:

> ... are the poorest of the poor, and the most disadvantaged by any measure – infant mortality, housing, services, literacy, health, education. But one soon comes to feel another, a racial dimension of the problem.

The deep distrust and apathy common among Aborigines have their roots in the terrible racial history of the last 200 years, in which Aborigines were ruthlessly dispossessed of their land and livelihood, massacred as outlaws, or shot and poisoned like vermin when they resisted, and the defeated remnants finally subjected to dispiriting paternalistic control. In all this long history they never had reason to regard the law as anything but an instrument of their oppression.

By all means let us support the extension of legal aid services for all poor people, but let us through the Aboriginal Legal Service make that special effort that is necessary to break down the barriers of alienation and distrust that stand between the Aborigines and the justice in which we like to take a pride.[2]

Like most of the great steps forward in Aboriginal history, this service had come about because of efforts made by Aborigines themselves. It was an area in which, because there were no Aboriginal lawyers, they had to seek extensive aid from non-Aboriginals, but the initial impetus came from two young, articulate Aborigines.

In every state a situation existed that was similar to the one in South Australia. About one fifth of those in prison were Aboriginal, although Aborigines made up only about one per cent of the population; and this high number in prison had a high percentage of men and women arrested for incidents arising from behaviour that did not seem wrong in their own eyes.

Alcohol would give them the courage to protest against the racial slights and insults to which they were unquestionably subjected. A fight would ensue, the police would be called and the Aborigine would be arrested. Since they saw themselves as the innocent party they would resist arrest, giving the police their views on the matter in standard barroom language. This would add resisting arrest and offensive language to the original charge of disorderly conduct.

The Aborigine, with no knowledge of how to go about getting bail, would have to appear in court after a night in the cells. They would be unrepresented and, even if the magistrate made an effort to hear their side of the story, they would have great difficulty in telling it in the atmosphere of the court. The police would very likely have advised them to plead guilty.

Experience made some Aborigines familiar with court proceedings, but even to them it remained an inexplicable ritual. Sometimes they were fined, but often they were not able to pay the fine, and so prison was inevitable.

Lawyers were aware that this was going on but, as they were busy men who were seldom directly involved, they did nothing about it. It was Aborigines who felt deeply concerned about it. In 1970 there would have been scarcely one Aborigine in Australia who did not have a deep mistrust of the law, and of the police.

In that year there were two Aboriginal law students in Sydney, Paul Coe at Sydney University, and Gary Williams at the University of New South Wales. Both of them had decided to study law because they had come to the conclusion that you 'had to fight the establishment with the establishment's weapons'. It was from efforts that they made that the Aboriginal Legal Service developed.

They found good friends at both universities with whom they began to discuss the very real problems that existed. A series of meetings followed at which the concept of the legal service began to take shape.

There was a great deal of latent goodwill in the white community, and it seemed that it would be a good idea to mobilise this. Paul Coe and Gary Williams wanted significant

Aboriginal representation in whatever committee or other body was set up, but they could see that people of standing and authority in the community, and particularly the support of the legal profession, would be needed if they were to command the respect of the government agencies with which they would have to deal.

Their only source of funds was donations, but it was decided to form a council and establish a voluntary service.

A meeting was held on 11 October 1970, in a room at the back of St Luke's Presbyterian Church, Redfern. Redfern is an inner suburb of Sydney where the population is in the lowest income bracket and there is a higher proportion of Aborigines than in any other suburb.

A council of eighteen was elected, and must have delighted Gary Williams who became vice-president, and Paul Coe, a member. They were two of seven Aboriginal members. The others included Faith Bandler, general secretary of the Federal Council for the Advancement of Aborigines and Torres Strait Islanders, Gordon Briscoe, an Aboriginal welfare worker, and Tom Williams, manager of the Foundation for Aboriginal Affairs.

Professor Wootten was elected president. Other non-Aboriginal members included Ray Loveday QC and Gordon Samuels QC, vice-presidents of the Bar Council of New South Wales; and three professors from the University of New South Wales, Garth Nettheim, Professor of Law, John Lawrence, Professor of Social Work, and John Cawte, Professor of Psychiatry.

An appeal was made through the Bar Council for barristers to give their services without fee, and a large number responded immediately. More than 150 replied in writing to have their names placed on the panel, and others orally indicated support. Since there were about 450 practising barristers in New South Wales at that time the response was remarkable. The Bar Council gave its collective support, and a temporary headquarters was established at the University of New South Wales.

It is impossible to suppose that such a result could have developed if there had not been a very real need, and an awareness within the profession that Aborigines were not being justly dealt with when they appeared, unrepresented, in court.

The Federal Minister in charge of Aboriginal Affairs, William Wentworth, heard of the service and indicated that some government help might be available. The council prepared a submission and on 16 December they learnt that a grant of $24,250 would be available in 1971.

The money was received the following April and enabled the council to rent an office in Redfern, and to employ a solicitor and two Aboriginal staff members. Voluntary work went into renovating the premises, and gifts of furniture and fittings came from local firms. Barristers and solicitors continued to give their services voluntarily.

A similar need existed in every state, and before long each state was setting up a similar service. In Adelaide the work that Elliott Johnston had been doing provided the basis. With his help an Aboriginal Legal Rights Movement was set up, operating out of the rooms of the Aboriginal council.

One of Elliott Johnston's staff was a young articled clerk, Andrew Collett. He had gone through secondary school in the 1960s when there had been heavy emphasis on science. He went on to university without any clear idea of what he wanted to do except that it should involve people rather than microbes. He began to study for a BA and found English and History to be more interesting than Science. In his second year Politics was one of his subjects. Graeme Duncan was Professor and Robert Catley was Reader in the Politics Department. They were comparatively young men who encouraged lively discussion and were tolerant of divergent views. Andrew found their lectures and tutorials to be stimulating in developing his own ideas.

He decided to study Law, and here another academic was to influence him. Mary Daunton-Fear, Lecturer in Criminology, who had a respected grasp of legal problems relating to social welfare, deepened his understanding of the complex social factors underlying crime. It was she who suggested a study of the Aboriginal crime patterns in Port Augusta as a suitable topic for a thesis. He and Adrian Graves decided to take it up.

The work, carried out in 1972, gives a detailed statistical analysis of Aboriginal and other crime patterns in 1971, and it gave Andrew Collett a basic understanding of the poverty and social pressures from which it is impossible to separate the legal problems of the Aboriginal people.

When he returned to Adelaide from Port Augusta he began to work in the office of Elliott Johnston, and was often given work that charges against Aborigines brought into the office.

In August 1972, ten months after the Aboriginal Legal Rights Movement had been formed in Adelaide, a grant of $22,000 was made by the federal government. This enabled them to employ a field officer and a secretary. Some legal work was still done voluntarily, but for many cases the service was now able to pay.

In February 1973, just after the Labor government had come to office, the prime minister, Gough Whitlam, issued a policy statement which promised legal aid for all Aborigines in all courts. It immediately granted $850,000 to the Aboriginal Legal Services for the remaining five months of the financial year. From that point the funds steadily increased until in the federal budget in 1975 they were granted $3 million. It sounded a great deal to the average tax-payer, but it was never enough to fulfil the promise of giving representation to all Aborigines in all courts.

The Adelaide service's share of this money enabled them to expand, and it was decided to employ a solicitor as executive secretary. Elliott Johnston urged Andrew Collett to apply for this, and he was the one appointed.

Ruby continued to work as a field officer. The funds of the Women's Council were running out. Aboriginal affairs were now a matter for the federal government, and there was a feeling in the community that money was being supplied for all their needs. This was pathetically far from the truth, and the council, which had relied so much on its own fund raising and the help of friends, now found itself in very straitened circumstances.

When they could no longer employ Ruby, Andrew Collett took her into his office. It was at this time that she became involved in what was undoubtedly the most significant case in the early years of the Aboriginal Legal Service – the New Exchange incident.[3]

The New Exchange was a hotel in Commercial Street, Port Adelaide, which Aborigines regularly used. It was also used by seamen.

On 26 July 1974, the licensee was Mr J.V. Hacket, a forty-two-year-old former policeman, who had taken over the hotel six weeks previously. Hacket claimed that he and his wife had tried 'to start up in the right way and get things organised', but that Aborigines had 'caused strife' every night since he had been there.

26 July was a Friday. There was certainly strife that night, and Aborigines claimed it followed mishandling of an Aboriginal woman by a seaman. The serious trouble occurred the following night. At about nine o'clock twenty seamen entered the hotel. Aborigines claimed they were armed with iron bars, forks bent into knuckle-dusters and other weapons.

In the brawl that ensued hotel windows were broken, dozens of glasses shattered, and tables and chairs smashed. Broken glass and bloodstains covered the footpaths and roads around the hotel.

Twenty-one police cars and cage cars from all over Adelaide were sent to the hotel. Seventeen arrests were made – sixteen Aborigines and one seaman. The charges were the old familiar ones the Aborigines had heard so often before – assault, disorderly behaviour, offensive language, and resisting arrest.

The seaman who was arrested had been charging at an Aborigine with a can opener when the police saw him. The rest of the seamen were escorted back to their ship.

The Aborigines in Adelaide who, thanks largely to the legal service, were beginning to get a feeling for legal justice, were united in outrage at this. They believed that the seamen were more to blame for what had happened than they were, and that the arrests reflected blatant racism on the part of the police. They considered that the arrests in any case had been mainly for incidents arising from high feeling among them after the police arrived, and that the seamen had got off scot-free for everything that had happened before they came.

On the following Monday Aborigines marched to the hotel in protest. They carried banners, some of which said 'Policemen escort seamen to ship in style', 'Black garbage in dog cars, white trash free', 'Police kick Abos like animals', and 'Potential murderers protected by the police'. The placards, prepared at spontaneous indignation meetings on the Sunday, reflected some of the Aboriginal feeling.

Mr Hacket was refusing to serve Aborigines. 'I will not serve one Aborigine in this hotel. They can sue me. They can do what they like. I will not serve one,' he said.

He meant it. Andrew Collett and Ruby Hammond went to

see him on behalf of the legal service. He served Andrew with a beer, and refused to serve Ruby.

In a sudden gut reaction to this discrimination Andrew threw his beer back across the bar.

Mr Hacket felt badly done by, and he blamed the Aborigines. The Aborigines thought this reflected a racist attitude.

The legal service protested to the Minister for Aboriginal Affairs, Senator Cavanagh. They asked for an enquiry into relations between Aborigines and the police. In September Senator Cavanagh said he would seek a Royal Commission, but would need to get support of the Cabinet.

There was no enquiry, no Royal Commission, and the hearings against the Aborigines dragged on for so long that they were still being heard more than a year later. On 29 September 1975 Mrs Val Power was convicted by Mr B.H. Burns SM in the Port Adelaide Magistrates Court of loitering outside the New Exchange Hotel on 27 July 1974.

Val Power had denied the charge and, with the backing of the legal service, she fought it up to the Supreme Court. On 28 March 1977, Mr Justice Zelling in the Supreme Court quashed the conviction, and entered a verdict of acquittal.[4]

It was a triumph not only for Val Power, and Elliott Johnston who appeared for her, but for all the Aborigines who felt they had been treated unjustly on that July night.

In his judgment Mr Justice Zelling said:

The learned special magistrate's blanket acceptance of the police evidence and blanket rejection of the evidence given by the appellant [Mrs Power] troubles me somewhat.

In dealing with the general credibility of the police witnesses he does not seem to have dealt with a powerful argument by Mr Johnston [Mr E.F. Johnston QC for Power] that Constable Connell was wrong in his answers as to how his notes had come into existence, and that there had been collaboration between Constable Hansberry and Constable Connell in the preparation of the police notes.

Equally I think that the learned special magistrate might have applied his mind to the point that every time Mr Johnston asked a question of either of these constables on a matter that was not contained in the notes, the remarkable unanimity between the two suddenly disappeared.

I cannot substitute my views on credibility for those of the learned special magistrate, nor do I intend to do so, but these matters leave me with much disquiet.

In these circumstances it is my proper duty to interfere, and I accordingly quash the conviction appealed against.

Ordinarily it would be my duty to send the matter down for another trial, but the events which gave rise to this prosecution happened in July 1974, and I cannot be confident that there could be a fair trial for the accused on these facts nearly three years later.

Accordingly I shall content myself with substituting a verdict of acquittal in place of the conviction which has been quashed.

There had been a time when Aborigines felt that when they gave evidence that was in conflict with police evidence blanket rejection of their version was almost inevitable. To have a judge of the Supreme Court say that this had troubled him brought to Aborigines everywhere a new faith in the white man's law. For some of them it was the first experience of such a faith they had ever had.

After the case Val Power said, 'A lot of Aborigines think that once the police have charged them they might as well plead guilty and get it over with, but I certainly wasn't going to admit to something I didn't do.'

There is no doubt that none of the Aborigines who

pleaded guilty to the charges arising out of the New Exchange incident saw themselves as having done anything morally wrong. They might have behaved as the police claimed they did, but they had been so provoked that they did not consider their behaviour blameworthy.

Val Power was insistent that she was not guilty in any terms. She had been waiting by a telephone box to ring Senator Cavanagh when she was arrested for loitering.

The New Exchange incident was an important one to the Aboriginal community. So many Aborigines were involved in it that by the time the weekend was over every Aborigine in Adelaide had heard about it from someone who was there, or who knew someone who was there. They were united in seeing it not only as a miscarriage of justice for sixteen of their friends, but as gross evidence of a general Aboriginal inequality before the law.

Another case which Ruby followed with intense interest, although she was not directly involved, was the trial of Sydney Williams.[5] This was the first major trial handled by the legal service in which issues of Aboriginal law were raised.

Sydney Williams, an initiated Pitjantjatjara elder, was charged with murdering his wife, Dorothy. His defence was provocation. The murder charge was dropped and he pleaded guilty to manslaughter.

His counsel was Mr Peter Waye, one of the barristers whom the legal service liked to have defending clients who were facing serious charges. In his plea he related Williams's version of the incident – that Williams and Dorothy had been drinking together, that Dorothy was very drunk, and in this condition insulted the accused, mentioning secrets which under Aboriginal law women are not supposed to know, let alone speak of, that Williams himself, drunk although not as drunk as Dorothy, was annoyed and told her to keep quiet, that she continued to insult him until Williams lost his self-control, hit her violently with a stick and a bottle and killed her.

Pitjantjatjara elders had taken up the matter and Williams was due to be punished according to their customary law. Mr Waye told the court that this would involve his being taken to sacred areas beyond the Musgrave Ranges for about a year, where he would be instructed by the elders in Aboriginal history and mysteries.

Mr Justice Wells observed that Aboriginal justice should be reinforced if possible and not replaced by European conceptions of justice, and that such notions would not represent an abdication of the role of the Supreme Court.

He sentenced Williams to two years' gaol with hard labour to be suspended upon his entering into a bond under which he agreed to be of good behaviour for two years; to return forthwith to his people and submit himself to their elders and be ruled and governed by them for one year; to obey their lawful orders and directions; to abstain from intoxicating liquor while under the control of the elders, unless permitted to drink by the elders, and then only to the extent of any permission granted.

Explaining the sentence to Williams, Mr Justice Wells said, 'I am going to send you straight back to your people and have you handed over to the Old Men. You must behave yourself for two years and not get into any trouble. You must do what the Old Men tell you to do for one year. You must not drink wine or beer unless the Old Men allow you to. If you do any bad or wrong things, or if you do not do what the Old Men tell you to do, you will go to gaol here in Adelaide for two years.'

It had not been stated in court that part of the punishment would be that Williams would be speared through the thighs with a barbed hunting spear, twice in one thigh, once in the other. This fact was elicited by the *Advertiser*. Quoting

Barry Lindner, a white adviser at the Yalata Reserve, the *Advertiser* reported that the spearing would be done with great skill to avoid hitting major arteries, and that the wounds would be dressed according to traditional methods with clay, leaves and other compounds.

Spearing is a traditional punishment, and a traditional 'pay back' method whereby Aborigines are allowed under their own law to redress certain wrongs. Under Australian law it is unlawful to spear a man under any circumstances.

If Aboriginal law imposed a sentence of death on an Aborigine, the man who carried it out could be charged with murder.

Mr Justice Wells's sentencing caused a stir among people who thought he was sending Williams back to be subjected not only to a barbaric punishment, but to an assault that under Australian law would be illegal.

The sentence was condemned by John Bennett, secretary of the Victorian Council of Civil Liberties, and by the *Australian* in an editorial on 18 May 1976. Two days later the *Age* commended Mr Justice Wells for a serious and sensitive attempt to grapple with the complex problems of relations between Aboriginal and white Australian law, but raised doubts about the invitation to an act of violence which would normally be regarded as criminal, and the implication that 'there is not only one law in the land but two'. In the federal parliament Senator Withers said he would refer the matter to the federal attorney general to see whether Mr Justice Wells had overstepped legal procedures.

Aboriginal spokesmen were divided. Sir Douglas Nicholls criticised the action as involving racial discrimination and implied that, under the law, Aborigines should not be treated differently from other Australians. On the other hand, Mr Bruce McGuiness, a leading Victorian Aborigine, welcomed the judge's decision as involving a recognition of, and respect for, Aboriginal culture. This view was shared by the Federal Minister for Aboriginal Affairs, Mr Ian Viner.

Dr Alan Ward, Reader in History at La Trobe University in Victoria, wrote in the *Legal Service Bulletin*, December 1976, in defence of Mr Justice Wells. He suggested that there were elements of 'barbarism' in long sentences to Australian gaols, and added, 'I do not believe that Mr Bennett or the *Australian* or anyone else who condones or supports a prison system, even as a necessary evil, is in any position to become mealy-mouthed about the circumscribed and carefully supervised corporal punishment of Williams. The Pitjantjatjara Aborigines, among others, no doubt have their own opinions about which punishment is more "barbaric", and their views are also entitled to respect.'

He argued that to recognise Aboriginal law was no more 'two laws in the land' than it was to recognise the powers of punishment, expressly authorised by act of parliament, of the armed forces, the merchant marine and some churches in situations entirely relevant to them.

The matter has been argued on an academic level, and not to any conclusion. The extent to which the court should consider Aboriginal laws and punishments has never been defined.

The South Australian legal service welcomed the sentence. They believed that where well-defined groups of Aboriginal elders were administering their law it should be recognised by Australian law, and that Aboriginal offences among their own people should be dealt with wholly by them.

Elliott McAdam put this view to Judge Mohr during the Royal Commission Inquiry into the Juvenile Court Act.

'Even murder?' asked the judge.

'In some cases,' said McAdam. 'In some cases this would need to be decided by a working party that would have to go into the area.'

Offences which were less clear-cut were those which were outside native customs such as theft, and illegal use of motor cars and other property. These cases could be bewildering to people accustomed to common ownership, but the legal service believed that these offences in native situations should be dealt with by the elders unless they asked for help.

The Williams case involved other matters that concerned the legal service when outback Aborigines were before the courts.

Williams did not speak English, and appeared so reluctant to answer questions put to him through an interpreter that Mr Justice Wells adjourned the court to enable counsel to find out what the difficulty was. He discovered that Williams, an initiated Pitjantjatjara, felt uneasy because the interpreter was not initiated. A new interpreter was found.

Matters of great sacredness to Williams were discussed during the trial, and he showed signs of distress because of it. Andrew Collett and Elliott McAdam had suggested that, 'To overcome these problems, and to emphasise the authority of Aboriginal law, the elders, or their legal representative (as distinct from that of the defendant) might be brought into Court in cases involving Aboriginal law. The trial judge could then seek their views on the sacredness of particular evidence, the status of the defendant within the community, and the appropriate penalty.'

The question of whether confessions were voluntary or involuntary was also raised. This was a frequent problem when Aborigines were before the law, as indeed was the whole question of interrogating them. It was no use saying to an Aborigine something like 'You do not need to answer these questions but, if you do, your answers may be taken down in writing and may be used in evidence. Do you understand that?'

The Aborigine, understanding nothing more than that a

question had been put to him by someone in authority, would say 'yes', or nod dumbly; and courts began to recognise that this could not be regarded as evidence that the Aborigine understood. This applied, of course, not only to Aborigines, but to anyone whose first language was not English, or had only limited education.

Mr Justice Forster of the Northern Territory Supreme Court dealt with this problem after he had presided over the trials of five men who were accused of murdering Paula Sweet, an Aboriginal woman.[6]

The evidence against them included confessions they were alleged to have made and which, after hearing evidence, Mr Justice Forster refused to accept. After the case he brought down judicial guidelines which were endorsed by Mr Justice Muirhead and Mr Justice Ward. They proved a significant development in criminal investigation procedures. The guidelines were offered not so much in criticism of the police, as in recognition of their problems.

The judge pointed out that Aboriginal people often do not understand English very well and that, even if they do understand the words, they may not understand the concepts which English phrases and sentences express. Even with the use of interpreters this problem is by no means solved. Police and legal English is not always translatable into Aboriginal languages.

Judge Forster recommended that instead of being asked if they understood what was being discussed they should be examined to see if they did, in fact, understand it. This procedure, he said, was already used by most experienced police officers in the Northern Territory.

Another matter which needed to be understood, he said, was that most Aboriginal people were basically courteous and polite and would answer questions in the way in which they thought the questioner wanted. Even if they were not courteous and polite there was the same reaction when they were dealing with an authority figure such as a policeman. Indeed their actions were often a mixture of natural politeness and their attitude to someone in authority. Some Aboriginal people found the standard caution quite bewildering. If they did not have to answer questions, why were the questions being asked?

The judge then laid down nine guidelines which were not unlike the Aboriginal–Police Steering Committee guidelines which the legal service in Adelaide was working out with the South Australian Police. Improved police relations were one of the achievements of the legal service, but there were still times when they felt that Aborigines were less than justly treated.

In spite of Judge Forster's guidelines there were still too many yes/no questions. The movement would have liked some form of special training for police and other civil servants so that they became skilled in testing the real understanding of the people with whom they were dealing, especially in situations where understanding was a basic need or a civil right.

In some circumstances the prisoner was entitled to have 'a friend' present, but this was not always recognised by the police. There was a police standing order that Aboriginal juveniles could not be interviewed without a third party being present, but police sometimes ignored this.

Elliott McAdam told the Royal Commission Inquiry into the Juvenile Court Acts of a case in which the police at Elizabeth had 'laughed off' an Aboriginal boy's request to telephone his father; and later, when the father had turned up, having heard of his son's arrest, the police still refused to allow him to be present while his son was questioned.

'You will have to wait,' they said, and they persisted with this even when the father said he understood there was a provision to allow him to be present while his boy was being interrogated.

The commission was told that this was not an isolated instance, and that the Aboriginal Legal Rights Movement wanted the right of a third party to be present at the police interrogation of any juvenile to be removed from police standing orders and made a statutory right.

The movement wanted to see a more extensive education of police in Aboriginal matters, especially of those who were to go into the outback. Problems which many officials were incapable of understanding could arise when they were dealing with Aborigines. The legal service was particularly troubled when these problems concerned children.

All too often, court orders for the care and control of children in Aboriginal situations were based on the nuclear family pattern, but in Aboriginal areas the parent might not be the one who was 'growing up' the child. Australian court orders seldom made allowance for Aboriginal customs, and police making enquiries often had no understanding of taboos such as those that restricted the people to whom an Aborigine might speak.

The legal service believed that police should be trained to understand and respect such restrictions before they went into the outback. It was not enough for them to know of it to the point where they could joke about a man not being able to talk with his mother-in-law; it should be a respect based on a real understanding of a complex culture that enabled a stable society to endure for thousands of years.

The Aboriginal legal service had grown in the years since 1972 when it first received a government grant, but it was never able to meet all the legal needs of the Aboriginal people.

Ruby and other members of the staff worried about the Aborigines who did not get legal advice because they lived in remote places, or on the fringe of country towns. They needed more lawyers, more field officers, more country offices. They needed a national co-ordinating body so that the services in different states could share the new knowledge they were constantly acquiring in what was such an unexplored field, and so they could carry out research without duplication. Legal education, field officer training, law reform, land rights, recognition of Aboriginal law, and Aboriginal–police relationships were all problems requiring a national approach.

The service needed an office in Canberra where they could be close to the federal members of parliament, and from which they could operate a parliamentary lobby.

They were conscious that only Aboriginal people in desperate need of legal help had been given any legal advice. There was need for a comprehensive education scheme so that Aboriginal people could learn what their rights were in relation to compensation for work injuries, industrial awards, torts claims, third party accident claims, mining rights, consumer and tenant problems.

The Legal Rights Movement in Adelaide started a legal education scheme using video tapes. Topics such as 'The Role of the Aboriginal Legal Rights Movement', 'What to do when you are arrested', 'Juvenile Offenders' and 'Alcoholism' were dealt with. Lack of finance and technical skills prevented it from growing into a really comprehensive and well-used service.

The ultimate need that Ruby Hammond saw was for Aboriginal lawyers. Sandra and Bruce, her daughter and son, both had an above-average understanding of legal matters and she would have loved either or both of them to have studied law, but neither of them did.

Ruby saw, too, a need to educate people in Aboriginal problems because she knew that in the end it was only the things that had community support that would get a meaningful share of the taxpayers' money.

She worried sometimes about being able to continue at all. The Department of Aboriginal Affairs had twice suggested that the Australian Legal Aid Office should take over the responsibility for providing legal aid to Aborigines. Both times they had met with intense opposition. People who had worked with the movement were convinced that, until there was equality between Aborigines and other Australians in the community as a whole, they would need their own legal service.

In October 1976, the department sought to curb the service. They issued 'draft guidelines' that would have excluded the legal service from representing people in proceedings under the Family Law Act, in superior and intermediate courts, in courts where duty solicitors operated, and from providing ancillary welfare services.

When changes such as this were urged it was piously suggested that they would promote equality between Aborigines and other Australians.

Aristotle had something to say that is relevant to this sort of thinking – 'It is as unjust to treat unequals equally as it is to treat equals unequally.'[7]

Ruby knew this profound statement because Elizabeth Eggleston quoted it in her book *Fear, Favour or Affection*. She wished it had been a wall motto hanging in the department's offices.

EIGHT

REACHING BEYOND THE CITY

the Aboriginal people themselves must take the initiative

THE ABORIGINAL LEGAL RIGHTS MOVEMENT OFFICE IN PORT Augusta was the culmination of a four-year effort to bring legal aid closer to Aborigines in the northern part of the state and on the reserves.

It was hoped that eventually there would be other offices in country areas, but Port Augusta was an obvious place for a first one. It was a small town at the top of Spencer Gulf at the junction of the Trans-Australian and Central Australian Railways. It is a port at the head of a gulf that has pushed up more than 300 kilometres from the open sea, so that while ships can dock there it is virtually an inland town in a harshly dry area.

Lack of water was once its major problem. In the early days water was brought by ship to Port Augusta and sold at twenty shillings for a fifty-six-gallon cask, nearly a week's wage for some people. Later, when water was discovered at Woolundunga Springs, twenty-two kilometres from the town, it was brought in by horse and cart and sold at sixpence for a small bucketful. In 1944 a pipeline to the Murray River was constructed, and Port Augusta blossomed. Big trees, especially eucalypts and tamarisks, gave it an oasis quality to people approaching it from the west. In the 1970s it was an unsophisticated town of 14,000 people. Some would tell you they hated it, but it was a vital place with its own integrity, and there were many people who loved it.

The new Aboriginal legal office was at 6 Gibson Street, away from the centre of the city, but within easy walking distance. It was a small house which the movement bought with the help of the South Australian Housing Trust. Funds from the Department of Aboriginal Affairs enabled them to transform the interior into a well-designed office that was the envy of the staff in Wakefield Street.

It was opened on 12 August 1977 by Wintinna Mick, a member of the Antikirinya people, who travelled from Oodnadatta to unveil a commemorative plaque. It was believed that he was ninety years of age.

Wintinna Mick opening the Port Augusta Aboriginal Legal Rights Movement offices, 12 August 1977. Seated: R. Hammond and B. Powell (Aboriginal Affairs Dept).

He was pleased, he said, that Aborigines were controlling their own legal service. Aboriginal law had enabled Aborigines to live for many thousands of years in Australia without destroying the land. It was right for those Aborigines living in a white man's society to live under the white man's law, but those Aborigines who still lived in their old ways should live by Aboriginal law, and it would need Aboriginal people on both sides to see that the two laws existed in harmony.

Jim Stanley, who was chairman for the ceremony, conceded that Aborigines would have to compromise in order to survive, to let go of some of their own values and accept the values of the white man's world; but he urged them to unite and speak as one people.

The other speakers at the opening were Ruby Hammond and Barry Powell, the South Australian director of the Department of Aboriginal Affairs, who was representing the minister.

The staff of the new office consisted of two Aboriginal field officers, Bruce Fielding and Joseph Hull, a secretary, a receptionist and a solicitor. The solicitor's position had been widely advertised and, to Ruby's great pleasure, the council had appointed Andrew Collett with whom she had worked so well when she had first joined the legal service staff.

To Andrew Collett there seemed a certain inevitability about it. For almost all his working life he had been involved with the Aboriginal Legal Rights Movement. His undergraduate thesis had laid the foundations for this work.

In that year, Aboriginal convictions in Port Augusta were thirty-two per cent of the total convictions although the Aboriginal population, about 600, was five per cent of the total population. The study that Andrew Collett had carried out with Adrian Graves had shown that Aboriginal crime was petty crime and was overwhelmingly related to alcohol.

Three groups of Aborigines lived in Port Augusta. About one-third of the Aboriginal population had employment, working for the railways or with one of the agencies concerned with Aboriginal welfare. These people lived in houses in the town, mainly rented houses, and on the whole aspired to white standards of living. They accounted for very few of the crime figures.

A second group lived on the Davenport Reserve, and this area had several problems. The reserve was established in 1963 because of complaints from the town about people living in the sandhills. It was supposedly intended that Davenport would prepare Aborigines for life in the town, but it had not done this. The housing was substandard, and it fell into the general pattern of reserves described by Dr Fay Gale, with overcrowding, lack of privacy and unemployment.[1]

Andrew Collett saw the Davenport Reserve as more of a poverty culture than an Aboriginal culture. Only the remnants of an Aboriginal culture could be seen, he said. There was no longer any respect for the authority of the elders or any regard for the kinship system, or the traditional norms of Aboriginal marriage. There was an increasing unwillingness for the young men to undergo initiation.

The group sharing of drink, food and chattels seemed to him to be as much a characteristic of a culture of poverty as it was a remnant of the norms of the old kinship system. This cultural vacuum had not been replaced by that of western society, but by a crude parody of both cultures.

The third group, many of whom were itinerants, lived in the sandhills and on the beaches. Port Augusta attracted itinerants, both black and white. For Aborigines from the north of the state, especially the Musgrave Ranges and the opal fields, it was the closest place to come for a large hospital, or the offices of the Departments of Aboriginal Affairs and Community Welfare.

Sometimes these people had relations or friends in Port Augusta with whom they would stay but, if not, the sandhills and the beach were the most obvious places for them to sleep. Apart from the fact that they did not have the money to stay in hotels or motels, most of these places refused them service until 1975, when the Commonwealth Discrimination Act made it an offence to refuse to accept them.

It was the people in these last two groups who figured in the Aboriginal crime statistics for Port Augusta. Almost without exception they were unemployed, with little to do and little hope of any upturn in their fortunes. They were lonely, and during the day they tended to drift into the hotels, especially the Exchange Hotel, which had a back bar that had become a sort of club for them. If they got drunk and were turned out they lay on the footpath, and even in the gutter, which aroused the distaste of the white population.

For many people in Port Augusta these drunken Aborigines were 'the Aborigines'. They seemed to know nothing of the concerned and caring Aborigines who were seeking to make a good life for their children, and who were trying to help those who were down and out. It was a continuing part of Aboriginal custom for them to help each other, and many were concerned at the way the reputation of the drinking Aborigine reflected upon them all.

Concerned Aboriginal people had set up a comprehensive scheme to give real help. The Port Augusta Woma Society[2] had been formed to help Aborigines who had a drinking problem. The society opened an Aboriginal Day Care Assessment Centre in Young Street where Danny Coulson, Mark Walker and Bruce Lang gave help to Aborigines with drink or drug problems. It was a little place in a back street where none of the Aborigines minded going. There were pool tables there, and rooms where they could rest or talk with the staff.

The atmosphere was free and easy, and counselling was not forced on those who went there, although most of them were eager to talk about their problems. The staff spent a lot of time in the parks and around the hotels, speaking with the people there, and bringing them back to the centre to sober up. The average attendance at the centre was twenty each day, and many more were contacted in the parks and hotels. The Woma Society also set up literacy classes and craft classes in the local gaol.

A day care centre was the first stage of a three-part program. The second stage was to be a rehabilitation farm at Baroota, south of Port Augusta, where Aborigines striving to conquer alcoholism would be able to get care and support while they were learning farming skills. It would be important for those who recovered there to be able to get employment when they left.

Stage three of the program was to be a halfway house in Port Augusta for people who had been through the program at Baroota, and who would be able to live there and go out to work.

Woma was convinced that the development and success of the day care centre represented good value for the funds invested in it ($37,500 in 1975/76 and $25,000 in 1976/77), but they were also convinced that it would not be of lasting value unless they received the funds necessary to carry out the whole of the program.

Around the corner from the day care centre was a social club managed by Vonnie Davies, a hard-working Aboriginal woman with a flair for administration. She and her staff served meals, looked after a library and activities room, and organised classes in craft work and painting. There were other staff members, almost all of them Aboriginal, to talk about problems and offer help.

Over the road from the centre was the Tji Tji Wiltja (the

children's house), which was a kindergarten for preschool children. Brian Butler,[2] who was one of the Aborigines to plan this complex program, saw the kindergarten as perhaps the most important part of it all. These were the children who, he hoped, would succeed at school and succeed at life, so that they would not need rescuing and supporting as they grew up.

Out at the Davenport Reserve there was an adult training centre, a cultural centre and a medical service, all run by an Aboriginal community council. The federal government Department of Aboriginal Affairs and the state government Department of Community Welfare made these undertakings possible with government grants. At the same time, the success of these places was due to the fact that Aboriginal people were in charge of them.

When Aborigines in need used the services, they saw other Aborigines in charge, making the decisions, and not just working under white people.

At the Davenport cultural centre they saw Betty Dohnt in charge. She cooked and served midday meals to raise money for materials for classes that she and other Aboriginal people organised in painting, sewing, leather work and wool spinning. Dohnt, as well as being the administrator, shared the manual work with a few women who came in each day. She was responsible to the Davenport Community Council, a group of Aborigines, one of whom, Charlie Jackson, was the manager of the whole Davenport complex.

Non-Aboriginal people helped with these ventures, but most of them understood that 'helping' meant deferring to someone else's ideas and aspirations. On the whole, the Aboriginal community found there was an immense resource of goodwill among white people, especially among those who understood what the Aborigines were trying to achieve. The racism and hostility came from people who either did not know them, or who were so prejudiced that they were not capable of knowing them. Non-Aboriginal people who worked closely with them developed real understanding, and almost invariably developed respect for them.

Pat Walsh and Joan Gaskill, who taught at the training centre, were two of these white helpers. They were Sisters of Mercy. They did not wear habits, and only the quality of their lives revealed that they were Catholic nuns.

Sister Pat originally went to teach at Davenport Reserve during school holidays as a volunteer, and later when a teaching position at Davenport was advertised, she applied and got it. She was qualified both as a music teacher and as a state primary teacher. At Davenport she taught anything the pupils wanted, supplementing her own expertise by using correspondence courses. A major part of her work was literacy classes with adults. They were eager to learn and their rate of progress made the work exciting.

Pat tried to relate all her teaching to the needs of her pupils. Lallie Lennon, an Aboriginal field officer with the Public Health Department, spoke English, Pitjantjatjara, and Arabunna but wanted help to write her reports. Her studies were directly related to this. Willy Austin, who had eight children and was a member of the Central Primary School committee, was offered a job by the school as a driving instructor if he could attain a needed standard of literacy. His lessons were related to this need.

Very few of the people in Port Augusta seemed to know about efforts by Aboriginal people to help other Aborigines in need. Part of the blame for this was due to the *Transcontinental*, the Port Augusta paper which came out every Wednesday. Its office was in Tassie Street, just down the road from the Exchange Hotel, and the editor, Ray Edwards, disliked drunken Aborigines lying about on footpaths which he had to use. Of course this was something everyone disliked, but one could react to it either by saying that the police should do something about it, the government should get these people out of town; or by seeing them as people in need and making some effort to help.

Ray Edwards had the first attitude, and during 1976 and early 1977 he used his front page and his well-placed editorial column to espouse it. On 20 April 1977, his editorial complained that the police were not sufficiently zealous in moving on the Aborigines, but he made it clear that it was not the police he was blaming. 'Rather does this paper suspect,' he said, 'that orders have come from "up above" to turn a blind eye on many of the doings by aboriginals.' (The *Transcontinental* was possibly the last paper in South Australia to continue spelling 'aboriginal' with a lower-case 'a'.)

This editorial was quoted in the state Legislative Assembly[3] and had repercussions that were still simmering in July 1977 when the Port Augusta Aborigines held a march to celebrate National Aborigines Day.

The march was planned at least in part to counteract the adverse publicity the Aborigines had been getting from the *Transcontinental*. They wanted to show the people of Port Augusta that there was a solid core of concerned, sober, responsible Aborigines in their midst. They sought permission from the city council to hold the march and to fly their flag. About 200 people took part in what was a quiet, orderly event. It included white people because the theme of National Aborigines Day was 'Bunggul' (Brotherhood).

The march was held on Friday, July 8. On the following Wednesday the Aborigines were eager to see how the *Transcontinental* had reported it.

Across the front page was the heading 'Aboriginal March was a Flop'. The report said:

Had it not been for the obvious 'conscripted' appearance of young white children, some of whom were marching without the knowledge of their parents, from Central Primary School, the march would have been a dismal failure.

The Aborigines were disappointed and angry. Ian Westley, the headmaster of the Central Primary School, was also angry. His school was within the city area where many Aborigines lived, and the percentage of Aboriginal children at his school was above the population average. He had talked to his pupils about the meaning of National Aborigines Day, and the concept of 'Bunggul'. Taking part in the march had been a social studies exercise for them, and only two parents had made protests to him.

One of them was a mother who told him that her son was too young to make up his own mind, and that until he was old enough to do this his views would be the same as hers, anti-black.

The report of the march stirred feeling in Port Augusta among both black and white people. It had been a serious attempt by the Aborigines to engender goodwill among the people of Port Augusta, and following the report the editor was openly called a racist.

A Media Action Committee was formed with black and white members. The convenor was Pat Kartinyeri, a young Aboriginal woman who was studying English at the Davenport training centre.

One of the committee's first actions was to write to the Australian Press Council complaining of the way Aboriginal news was handled by the *Transcontinental*. Pat Kartinyeri went through the paper's files back to 1969 and could not find one constructive item. There had been no reference at all to the setting up of the Davenport centre, or the complex of clubs, centres and kindergartens in Port Augusta itself.

There had been a report of an open-air service Danny Coulson had organised outside the Exchange Hotel in the winter of 1976, but it had been under the heading 'Even Billy Graham Couldn't Do It'.

The committee also started a newsletter, *Yuri Wangkanyi*, which is Pitjantjatjara for blacks talking. They hoped there would be whites listening.

The *Transcontinental* gave a generous, objective report of the opening of the Port Augusta ALRM office, only a month after the march. Perhaps it was due to a letter from the Australian Press Council, but more likely it was due to a genuinely better understanding by the editor of the problems of the Aboriginal people and their own attempts to solve them.

Edwards's editorial of 20 April and his report of the July march were both commented on in the *Advertiser*. After the march the ABC sent a camera crew to Port Augusta to put the Aboriginal point of view on television. They arranged a discussion between Ray Edwards and Sister Audrey Kinnear, an Aboriginal woman who was a senior member of the Public Health Department in Port Augusta.

Racial prejudice was without doubt a problem in Port Augusta. The most serious evidence of this was the fact that no Aboriginal person had ever been employed in the town in a position that involved over-the-counter or over-the-desk dealings with white people. There were no young Aborigines working in banks, serving in shops, or typing in offices except in government departments.

This troubled the heads of the Port Augusta schools because Aboriginal children did just as well in school as other children, in spite of the fact that many of them started their school lives with greater handicaps than most of the others.

When Graves and Collett did their survey, Aborigines

were responsible for eleven per cent of juvenile crime, a much lower percentage than the adult rate, but the percentage of traffic and property offences were higher than in the adult rate, and higher than in the past. This suggested to Ruby that Aborigines in Port Augusta were moving closer to a European lifestyle, but only in terms of its disadvantages. They were still shut off from the advantages, and racism and prejudice were the reasons.

In a situation in which young people were not being accepted into the community, it was immeasurably harder for older people who had already suffered the trauma of rejection, the frustration of unemployment, and the treacherous consolations of alcohol.

Danny Coulson, looking after the Port Augusta day centre, brought an almost incredible enthusiasm and optimism to his work with these people. He had been through the cycle of unemployment and alcoholism, but Captain Ted Gray of the Salvation Army had helped him to rediscover himself. Coulson joined the Salvation Army, and considered himself to be doing God's work. He believed God would provide for it, and miraculously God did.

He was another of those impressive Aboriginal personalities who had come from a totally Aboriginal environment to a life of service to his fellows in a Europeanised community. His earliest days were spent gathering food with the other children and the women, moving from camp site to camp site, and sleeping by the camp fires or in his parents' wiltjas. He had frightening memories of being hidden by the women when the white police came round. The women would hide the children, covering them with bushes, concealing them in places away from the beaten track. Every Aboriginal woman feared having her children taken from her, and the fears were communicated to the children.

The Ernabella Mission was established while Danny

Coulson was a child growing up in the Musgrave Ranges, and he was one of the first pupils. This mission was set up in 1937 by the Presbyterians of South Australia on the initiative of Dr Charles Duguid, and its policy was to teach in Pitjantjatjara, but the good people at the mission felt that the part-Aboriginal children should have a European education, and they set about persuading parents to let their children go to the Colebrook home, which was then at Oodnadatta. It was less drastic than the police methods, but not much less frightening for the children.

Believing it would be best for Danny, his mother hugged her sorrow to herself and let him go. Danny was not only grief-stricken, he was terrified, fearing that the children were being taken away to be eaten. He went in a party of about thirty children, of whom he was one of the oldest. He knew not one word of English, and apart from the hours he had spent in the mission school his whole experience was of native life.

Danny is one of the Colebrook boys who is grateful for the laws and the mission schools which saved the mainland Aborigines from extinction. He is more bewildered than bitter about the settlers who would have killed them off, and the people who still created a climate in which it was hard for Aborigines to survive.

When he left Colebrook, Danny, like all the other Colebrook children, had the choice of going back to his parents or trying to succeed in the white world. He chose the white world, and went to work on a station near Broken Hill. Here he encountered discrimination of a far more vicious kind than he had experienced at school.

'We had no rights of any sort,' he said later, 'and the white people made us feel inferior. I used to ask myself, why am I different? Why am I inferior? Especially as I could see that I was smarter than they were when it came to the stock work.

I knew I was just as good as them. I used to think about the station owner with his cattle and his horses, especially his horses. If he had a good horse he was proud of it, no matter what its colour was. If he could judge his horses by their real worth, why couldn't he judge his men the same way?'

Danny knew that the people of Port Augusta could be cruel and vicious, and that many did not judge Aborigines by their real worth. He was one of a group that trained a football team, and he taught them to go out to play with nothing but sport and good fellowship in their minds even though they were often treated with abuse.

A thing that puzzled Danny was the way that some of them abused 'pommies' (an Australian slang term for English migrants). 'Don't they realise they are all "pommies" themselves?' he used to ask. 'I don't like the idea of any one race feeling superior to another, but, honestly, when I see them being so vicious, and so ignorant, I find it hard not to think the Aborigines are a superior race.'

The leaders of the Aboriginal community in Port Augusta tried hard to make friends among the white people. They did have friends, but these were only a minority of the population. The town was full of people who looked at the drunken men who stumbled out of the Exchange Hotel and found some public place to sleep it off. The onlookers knew and cared nothing for what had brought the men to this pass. They looked at them with disgust and, more seriously, they looked on them as 'the Aborigines'. If you talked to them about Danny Coulson, Lois O'Donoghue, Audrey Kinnear, they said, 'Oh I know there are some good ones, there are always exceptions.'

It was from this town that the Aboriginal Legal Rights Movement was reaching out to bring the justice of English law to all the Aborigines who lived in the vast northern region of South Australia.

The work was tremendously varied. Within weeks of the opening of the new office Andrew Collett travelled to Leigh Creek to see that the rights of the Aborigines living in Copley would not be overlooked when the new town was built there. Leigh Creek was a coalfield town, 260 kilometres north of Port Augusta, set up by the South Australian Electricity Trust to develop the state's most significant deposit of coal. It had been found that in the Trust's haste they had sited the town over a valuable seam, and the town was moved eight-and-a-half kilometres to the much older settlement of Copley, where a community of Aborigines had been living for more than 100 years.

Andrew Collett journeyed on, further north, to look into a case involving a group of Aborigines working on a station property near the Queensland border. The owner paid them Queensland award wages which were significantly lower than South Australian wages.

It was not the Aborigines who were complaining. The station manager had persuaded them that because they were close to the Queensland border he had a choice, and that it was an act of generosity on his part to pay them award wages of any sort. They did not want trouble, but Andrew Collett's brief was to bring them justice.

Ceduna had become a point of tension. In February 1977 Basil Coleman was arrested at nearby Thevenard for wilful damage and assault. It was alleged that he had broken the window of a pizza bar during a disturbance that had resulted in the owner's wife sending for Detective Senior Constable Schluter who lived in Thevenard, and that Coleman had resisted arrest and assaulted Schluter.

The charge was heard the following July before Mr J.W. Lewis, SM. Coleman did not deny breaking the window, but he did deny the other charges. Indeed he claimed that, without provocation, Detective Schluter had hit him. The magistrate found that at the time of the arrest 'Detective Schluter delivered a blow to the face of Basil Coleman which caused an injury ... and that the defendant did not hit, punch or deliver blows to Schluter then or at all'.[4]

After the arrest considerable hostility towards Schluter was shown by Aborigines, and the magistrate accepted that Schluter had been assaulted, but not by Coleman. It had been late at night, Detective Schluter had been off duty, and it was the third time that week he had been called out at night.

Basil Coleman and Schluter testified to a pleasant exchange between them before the detective realised that it was Coleman who had broken the window, and the magistrate concluded that 'no one commenced disorderliness until after the arrest'. He found Coleman not guilty of assault, fined him $30 on the wilful damage charge, and awarded him costs against the South Australian Police Department.

Had the matter been left at that it is likely that the Aborigines would have been pleased, Detective Schluter would have been more careful, and the people of Ceduna not much interested; but the ALRM decided that a charge of assault should be laid against Detective Schluter. This resulted in jubilation among the Aborigines, and racial tensions in the town heightened.

There is often tension in Ceduna. It is the main township in the sparsely settled arid country on the edge of the Nullarbor Plain. The Aboriginal population fluctuates, but is proportionately higher than in Port Augusta. The white people feel isolated.

Now, it was claimed, groups of Aborigines were walking through the streets chanting 'black power' slogans, and there was a report that white residents were proposing to form a vigilante group.

In July 1978, Ruby went to Ceduna and was seriously disturbed. White people in the town were complaining about

Aborigines receiving preferential treatment. The *Advertiser* received a letter signed by 843 residents of Ceduna and Thevenard which claimed 'outrageous racial discrimination against the white population'. The phrase 'black power' was being used.

Colleen Tschuna, an Aboriginal student counsellor in Ceduna, could have been echoing Ruby when she was reported as saying, 'They wouldn't know what black power is.' Ruby agreed that this was true. The talk about 'black power' came from white people, not black people, and it came from people who wanted to stir up fear and resentment among other white people. It was trouble-making talk. It came from people who liked to be superior to someone else, and who resented equality for black people.

Ruby was accused of being a 'black power' influence, and was hurt when an Aboriginal woman called after her in the street, 'Go away you black power woman, we don't want you here.'

Ruby saw her as a woman with no real understanding of the situation who had been 'got at' by white people who wanted to sow dissension among the blacks.

'Aborigines were working for their rights in a most constructive way in every state in the commonwealth,' she said. 'White people talking about "black power" were playing a dangerous game which could only bring harm to both white and black people.'

Whatever the views of the Police Commissioner and the higher levels of his staff may have been, there was considerable resentment among police generally at the charge laid against Detective Schluter. The charge was dropped after a hearing in September at which there was only a remand until a later date.

Ruby believed that Aborigines were often roughly treated by police without cause. The decision to drop the charge, which she opposed, was urged by the solicitors in the ALRM office. The decision was pragmatic, and Ruby was not a pragmatist.

It sometimes seemed to Ruby that the further the legal service got from Adelaide the more complex its problems became.

The demoralising destruction of Aboriginal social life was rarely exposed in areas where the people were still involved in their ancient ceremonies. It came about where the basis of their lives had been eroded.

There was no part of South Australia where Aboriginal people could still harvest a livelihood on land that was traditionally theirs. There were jobs on cattle stations for some of them, and some were eligible for pensions. They could buy their food at the mission store.

The men and women in those areas had the significance taken from their lives, and very little to put in its place. Ruby claimed that this underlay the problem of their drinking. Their troubles were compounded by the roads that trade and tourism were pushing into the area, bringing materialism closer to them with very little benefit.

The Eyre Highway, which linked Adelaide with Perth, was completely sealed in 1976, and traffic along it increased dramatically.

The Aborigines at Yalata discovered that they could sell paintings, boomerangs and carvings to tourists, but the tourists proved to be strange people to them. Some of the tourists were patronising to Aborigines, some of them were rude, some of them wanted to barter for lower prices than the Aborigines thought was reasonable, some of them wanted to exchange wine and spirits for artefacts. Some of them drove by without stopping, and this was frustrating to men and women who were being introduced to the 'success is sales' syndrome of western civilisation.

From time to time on the road there were clashes between Aborigines and non-Aboriginal travellers. On an October Saturday in 1977, Aborigines from the Yalata Mission threw stones and hit cars with tree branches on a two-mile stretch of the highway.[5] They broke windscreens and windows, dented panels, damaged insect screens and broke windscreen wipers. The Aborigines had set up a road block and milled about abusing the occupants of about twenty cars until the police arrived.

Twelve Aboriginal men and women were arrested and charged with disorderly behaviour and wilful damage.

Barry Lindner, the manager of the mission, blamed the incident on wine that the Aborigines had bought at Nundroo, about fifty-six kilometres away. Four men and a woman were gaoled for fourteen days, fined, and ordered to pay compensation for damaged cars. Six other men were fined for disorderly behaviour.

How did it all start? Ruby asked.

The law was not concerned with that sort of question unless provocation was pleaded, and then it had to be provocation directly involving the unlawful behaviour.

Ruby believed the Aboriginal legal service needed to look at the social causes of Aboriginal crime even if they could not be advanced in court. She believed the service had an interpretive role to play in aiding the elders to understand Australian law and Australian jurists to understand Aboriginal law, and that neither would be credible to the other unless the social factors involved were understood.

This was an important part of the legal service work that Ruby would have liked to have known more about. In September 1977, she took advantage of a chance to go to the Ernabella Reserve in the Musgrave Ranges. Andrew Collett wanted someone to discuss questions of Aboriginal law with the elders, and an opportunity arose for Ruby to fly up in a chartered aircraft with officials of the Department of Aboriginal Affairs.

There were murmurings among the Aboriginal men in the office about whether it was proper for a woman to take part in discussions with the elders, and even Andrew Collett had misgivings.

Ruby was confident that there would be no problems. She would not discuss cultural matters, only legal matters, and she found that, in fact, she was well accepted. She explained her position in the legal service to the elders, and they agreed not to raise other than legal matters in her presence. When they were discussing questions of initiation Ruby went to see the women, who were excited to have a visit from an Aboriginal woman with so much authority.

She talked to them about ways the legal service could help women, and also about child care, education and health. There were serious health problems at Ernabella, as there were on all reserves. There was need for a clinic where women could be taught about the nutritional needs of their families, about prenatal and postnatal care of mothers, and how to treat infections that attacked not only the general health of the children but also threatened their sight and hearing. Respiratory infections that were minor matters for children of middle-class families became serious conditions that could perforate eardrums; trachoma, a highly contagious viral disease which never causes blindness in Australian cities, does so to a scandalous extent on Aboriginal reserves.

The Whitlam government had planned a clinic for Ernabella, and the people were still hoping for it. The departmental officers explained that funds would not be available.

'I was moved,' said Ruby, 'by the way they accepted this news. They were disappointed, but they did not complain, and they began immediately to discuss ways in which they could raise the standards of their health care without a clinic.'

Ruby was very glad she had visited the reserve. She planned to go again, and to take slides and other material to help explain child care needs to the women. Many women came to hear her – old women, middle-aged women, young women with children, and teen-aged girls. All except the very old understood English, and the others translated for them. Ruby was besieged with questions and she felt she handled this part of the visit better than any of the men could have done.

She took her sleeping bag as they were all to spend the night at Ernabella. It was a beautiful full-moon night and most of the party chose to sleep outside. They slept within the mission fence for protection from dingoes, but they were close to the creek bed with its magnificent gum trees.

Ruby got very little sleep, partly because of the moon. She complained the next day that you could not switch off the light at Ernabella as you could in the city, but she did not really mind. It was a chance to gaze at the brilliant outback sky she loved so well, and to listen to the night sounds of the bush.

She lay there thinking about the complex problem of bringing what is best in western civilisation to the Aboriginal people without destroying their links with the land and their understanding of the rhythms of nature.

A line from a poem she had learnt in English classes at high school came back to her – 'Getting and spending we lay waste our powers.'[6] How could Aboriginal people achieve equality with white people without falling under that curse? Ruby was a splendid optimist. She believed it would be possible if only everyone tried hard enough.

NINE

JUSTICE AND EQUALITY

but not
while racism
persists

WHEN RUBY TALKED OF THE FUTURE OF HER PEOPLE SHE was optimistic and hopeful. The ultimate in 'land rights' for her was a society in which Aboriginal people had a valid choice of living either in terms of their own past, or integrating with white society, and in which, however they chose, they would not be impoverished, they would have social equality with other Australians, and they would be in control of their own organisations and their own destiny.

She liked to believe that this would come about with accelerating speed, and without any serious black/white confrontation. This was what she liked to believe, but she had times of despair when it was difficult to do so. There would be no real equality in Australia while racism persisted, and she sometimes feared it would take generations to rid Australia of this insidious evil. The Aboriginal people suffered from racism, but it was the wider community that perpetrated it, often mindlessly, refusing to see it in themselves.

But Ruby's optimism, never far from the surface, told her things were improving. Racism was not something that laws could stamp out, but laws could be helpful. She was grateful for the South Australian Prohibition of Discrimination Act, passed by the Dunstan government in December 1966, which made it an offence to discriminate against people on the grounds of race. A bill to amend this act was introduced in 1986, and was attacked by the Liberal Party opposition. Their member for Kingston, W.E. (Ted) Chapman, was particularly vehement. He said in parliament that while some Aborigines might be good citizens, 'generally speaking, they are a lazy lot, a dirty lot, with certain undesirable practices and characteristics'.[1]

He objected to Aborigines receiving preferential treatment under some circumstances, citing a housing scheme on islands north of Darwin, and he referred to 'the sort of ultra protection that Aborigines generally receive from the police force'.

On the following morning the front page of the *Advertiser* had a heading, 'Aboriginals lazy, dirty – Lib M.P.'[2]

This type of headline, this type of news, has every Aborigine going off to work with a sense of contamination, every Aboriginal schoolchild leaving home with an added sense of uneasiness. It is the sort of headline that reinforces the racism in the community, giving impetus to slights, especially in school playgrounds.

Newspapers like this sort of story. It is controversial stuff, provoking letters to the editor and argument in the community. The issue was kept alive for several days. The *Advertiser* gave Ruby a chance to reply.[3] She felt she had to accept these opportunities, although she was aware that she was contributing to a controversy that ought not to have been started. Not to reply might suggest that there was no answer to the charges.

Speaking on behalf of the Aboriginal state conference, which was then being held, Ruby said it was ludicrous that

Mr Chapman should have made such remarks while speaking to a bill to prohibit discrimination. His statements showed that he lacked knowledge of the Aboriginal people. Far from getting preferential treatment from the police the Aboriginal people had to fight to get equal treatment. Alcohol was a problem of society generally, and Aborigines in the city square were part of Adelaide's homeless population.

The Assistant Police Commissioner, Mr E.L. Calder, also denied the charge that Aborigines received 'ultra protection' from the police.

The leader of the state opposition, David Tonkin, dissociated his party from Chapman's remarks, and later in the year a vicious attack on Aborigines by a Port Adelaide councillor was published only under a council apology, and was not developed into a controversy.

Perhaps these things meant that discrimination was beginning to clear, but it was doing so at a dangerously slow pace. Ruby wondered sometimes where the beginnings of the 'white superiority' myth could lie. It had been useful in rationalising the taking over of land from people with a different culture, and the using of native people as cheap labour, but its beginnings and its perpetuation involved attitudes of great complexity.

Aborigines were pushed off the land by settlers who wanted it for themselves, and who, because of the propaganda of the South Australian Commission, believed they were entitled to it. It was useful to think the Aborigines were 'a lesser breed' not needing much consideration, and to believe they were looked after by 'protectors' appointed by the government.[4] These protectors were the legal guardians of Aborigines and their children, and were responsible for the ruthless way children were taken from their parents and sent to institutions. They had the power to order Aboriginal adults on and off reserves, and prohibit them from whole areas, including towns. These powers were used for the benefit of the settlers, not the Aborigines. They hindered rather than helped the Aborigines to integrate with white society, and tended to legalise the actions of the settlers. The church, which took on a self-appointed role as protector, added moral sanction to the notion of white superiority, the basic philosophy of discrimination.

By the 1970s the worst crudities of these attitudes had been refined, but discrimination remained, and remains in the 1990s. It is involved in the causes of the high incidence of poverty and unemployment among Aborigines, and it is the main inhibitor of attempts to put matters right. Ruby saw discrimination as closely identified with the alcohol problems of Aborigines.

She could see a cycle of discrimination that made it impossible for many Aborigines to find education, housing and employment that measured up to community standards. Because of the hopelessness of this situation many turned to drink, and their drinking was used as a justification for continuing to deny them employment, housing and education. This cycle would not be broken without special efforts.

When Senator Cavanagh was Minister for Aboriginal Affairs he was reputed to want to restrict spending on Aboriginal welfare because he feared a 'white backlash'. It was true that preferential treatment for Aborigines brought white protests. Ruby saw it as part of the minister's job to withstand these protests, and to educate the white community to see the urgent need to bring Aborigines to a level from which they could justly be given equal treatment.

In the meantime there were Aboriginal people who desperately needed help with their drinking problems, and there was growing evidence that the best people to help them were other Aborigines.

In 1973 the Central Methodist Mission in Adelaide

decided to do something to help Aboriginal alcoholics. They began by employing Aboriginal counsellors, many of whom were alcoholics who had gained sobriety. The counsellors proved to be devoted to the work of helping their fellows. They ran an evening group which became known as the Adelaide Sobriety Group. The emphasis was on treatment, but the mission was also interested in the prevention of alcoholism, and in its after-care. An attempt was made to create an awareness of the problems amongst the Aboriginal and general community.

During 1974 country centres became aware of the work being done and asked for help in establishing groups. It was not possible to give all the country centres the help they needed, and it was decided to look more closely at the problem by bringing representatives from the country to a residential conference. Fifty delegates came and the conference looked at the need for a network of alcohol programs, which preferably would have Aboriginal management. It recommended that a policy-making body should be established to consider the best actions to take, determine priorities, seek funds, and give support and help to the local communities.

Following this recommendation the Woma Committee was formed, taking its name from a Pitjantjatjara word meaning 'bad water'. The committee was based on a report brought back from Canada by Chicka Dixon. He had heard of a Canadian plan that was dealing successfully with alcohol problems among Red Indians. He told Gough Whitlam about this and was sent to Canada to look into it. The report he brought back was of great value. In South Australia the committee was made up of delegates, many of them recovered alcoholics, from all over the state. Representatives from the Public Health Department, Department of Community Welfare, Central Methodist Mission, Alcohol and Drug

Addicts Treatment Board, and the Department of Aboriginal Affairs came as non-voting members.

The committee met for the first time in 1976, and continued to meet for two days at two-monthly intervals. Meetings were held at Adelaide, Port Augusta, Murray Bridge, Port Lincoln, Ceduna, and Coober Pedy. This enabled the committee to gain a better understanding of the communities it was trying to help, and gave the communities an idea of the help they could expect to receive.

At about this time it was announced that the House of Representatives Standing Committee on Aboriginal Affairs was to look into the question of Aboriginal alcohol problems. This news was received by the Legal Rights Movement with mixed feelings. They knew it would result in some unfavourable publicity, and they considered that there was overemphasis on the Aboriginal drinking problems in a way that condemned the Aborigines rather than looked for solutions.

Aborigines claimed that alcohol problems were not peculiar to the Aboriginal people of Australia but were embedded in the whole social structure. They believed an inquiry into Aboriginal drinking problems should be part of a Royal Commission to investigate problems associated with alcohol in Australia at all levels.

The House of Representatives committee travelled widely in making its investigations, and was in Adelaide to begin hearings on Thursday, 9 June 1977 in the conference room of the Board of Overseas Trade.[5] The room had a long massive table, and enough bookshelves to give it the look of a library, but its air was of commercial responsibility rather than legal mystique.

The committee consisted of eight members, including Gordon Bryant, the Minister for Aboriginal Affairs. The four who had travelled to Adelaide were the chairman, Phillip

Ruddick of New South Wales, and Peter Drummond of Western Australia, both of whom were members of the Liberal Party; Sam Calder of the Country Party, who was considered by most Aborigines to be a friend of the mining interests; and Les Johnson, the last of the three Labor Ministers of Aboriginal Affairs.

The first day's hearing proceeded quietly enough. The people giving evidence included seven responsible Aboriginal people discussing the problems in terms of concern and practical solutions. They were speaking to written submissions that had come in from the Woma Committee, the Education Department and the Central Methodist Mission.

The following morning the *Advertiser*'s front page headline proclaimed 'Enquiry told of Social Breakup. Drinking hinders Aboriginal Progress'. A large part of the front page and most of page seven were devoted to highlighting the worst social consequences of Aboriginal drinking. The efforts to deal with the problems were given less publicity, although they had been the main topics of discussion and were included in written submissions.

Ruby would not have minded the tragic story being told if it had led to more concern within the community, but she saw it as leading only to condemnation of Aborigines.

The Education Department's submission had described children coming to school from homes where excessive drinking was the norm as being hungry, tired and lethargic. Some schools were forced to allow children to sleep for periods during the morning because their physical condition would not allow them to work effectively. In the worst cases of hunger children had been known to scavenge in school rubbish bins and to eat orange peel. In other cases work output was seriously impaired because of empty stomachs. Often the only solution available to the child was to satisfy themself with a cool drink and potato chips. Schools sometimes did not see the very worst cases of neglect because on their worst days children tended to stay away.

All this was highlighted in the *Advertiser*,[6] but there was no reference to the fact that the submission also said:

> Attainable and satisfying goals for life must be offered to Aboriginal communities to help them regain dignity and purpose. Only in conjunction with such efforts can an effective publicity and prevention campaign against drink be mounted. Such a campaign would need to be massive in its proportions, backed up by hard-hitting audio-visual impact and administered by Aboriginal people. Schools could support the adult-oriented campaign by reinforcing the objectives with the children.

It was noted that while the emphasis of the report was on people afflicted with alcohol it was 'recognised that there are vast numbers of Aboriginal people who are not in this situation'. This was not told to the readers of the *Advertiser*, nor was the fact that:

> teaching staffs feel that until meaningful, stable employment can be offered, especially to school-leavers, there can be no hope of breaking what are now established patterns of heavy drinking. They see no point in attacking the drink problem in isolation. Until the cause of the drinking can be overcome, no amount of education or coercion to stop drinking will be successful.

The Aboriginal Community College also made a submission stressing the need of Aboriginal people for satisfying and meaningful occupations, and the need for education that would build up their confidence and restore their self-esteem.

Another need was for recreational and sporting facilities with Aboriginal recreation officers where there were large numbers of young Aboriginal people. Around Australia a number of small-scale pilot schemes were producing a small number of semi-skilled, skilled, para-professional and professional Aboriginal people. The submission recommended that the standing committee urge the government to multiply the positive effects of such programs by funding more of them in places where there was a need for them. They recommended better housing, with facilities for community activities staffed by suitably qualified Aboriginal people, and greatly increased opportunities for Aboriginal people to receive advanced training in counselling and management.

None of this appeared in either of the South Australian daily papers. Ruby felt that the reports were such a distorted account of the Thursday's hearings that she gave serious thought to the possibility of a contempt of court action. She raised this matter when, at the end of her evidence, she was asked if she had anything to add. The chairman explained that the hearings had parliamentary privilege and were open to the public. Ruby could see that there were no legal grounds for a court action.

Ruby Hammond and Elliott McAdam, who gave evidence on behalf of the Aboriginal Legal Rights Movement, were both distressed and angry about the reports when they sat down to give their own evidence. Elliott McAdam spoke first, and he began by saying that he thought the whole approach of the inquiry was wrong. He said that the problems of alcohol were related to the depressed conditions of the Aboriginal people within the whole social structure, and could not be isolated.

The chairman called him to order. He told Elliott that he was there to speak for the Aboriginal Legal Rights Movement, not to give his general views.

Elliott McAdam saw himself as an Aboriginal person with special knowledge and experience of the matters into which the committee was enquiring. Now, because of some red tape restriction, he was not able to give his views. He began again, speaking directly to the submission.

The chairman immediately turned away and spoke for several moments to his secretary, and then began to read a document.

Elliott McAdam stopped speaking, but after a long moment's silence he raised his voice and said, 'Mr Chairman, who is it I am supposed to be speaking to? I came here to give evidence which you don't want to receive and now, when I give the evidence you ask for, you are not prepared to listen. It is a waste of time my being here.' He got up and left the table.

Ruddick made no apology. Defensively, and quite tersely, he told McAdam that there were Hansard reporters taking down his remarks and he, the chairman, had other things to do besides listening to what was said. It was Peter Drummond who made the first reconciling approach by assuring Elliott McAdam that the committee did want to hear his evidence. Had the chairman apologised Elliott McAdam would have come back to the table. Thanks to Peter Drummond he contributed to further discussions, but only from the back of the room.

Ruby felt that Elliott had made a justified protest, and that he'd had no alternative to leaving the table; but it left her with the burden of a decision. Should she get up and leave the table with her colleague, or stay and give the evidence she wanted to see written into the transcript. She stayed, but the incident distressed her and contributed to an undermining of her faith in the committee.

When she left, Mr Johnson, who had known her since the days when he was minister, went out and spoke to her in the hallway. Ruby did not doubt his goodwill. She wished she could have felt as confident about the whole committee.

Ironically the incident, which impressed even the chairman, resulted in polite attention being given to everyone else who gave evidence during the afternoon. Unfortunately Ruby Hammond and Elliott McAdam were the last Aborigines to appear.

They looked forward to the report which the Standing Committee would table, although Ruby feared the press would pick it up and once again write accounts of the consequences of Aboriginal drinking without any reference to the causes or the cures.

This would be serious because the well-informed suggestions for action that were made would be included in the report. Funds would be needed to implement these suggestions and would be more readily forthcoming for projects that the community understood and supported.

Newspapers, radio and television could contribute to that understanding. Sometimes it seemed to Ruby that they perceived this and that their goodwill could be tapped. In 1977 the *Advertiser* appointed a journalist, Robert Ball, to specialise in Aboriginal matters, and while he was there the situation improved.

From time to time there are sympathetic articles, television programs and radio reports, and the number of these is increasing in the 1990s. In August 1994 the *Weekend Australian* published, over a period of four weeks, a series of excellent articles devoted to the aims of the Council for Reconciliation. It was probably the best media contribution to Aboriginal welfare in that year. Some weeks earlier, on 17 May 1994, the *Bulletin* had published a cover story on Aboriginal drinking. Written by Dennis Schulz, and headed 'Drowning in Sorrow', it concentrated on the drowning rather than the sorrow. It was not an unsympathetic tale of the 'grog culture', but it had nothing to say of the deep and complex problems that induce Aborigines to turn to alcohol. An almost full-page picture on the cover showed a drunken Aborigine lying insensible on the grass verge of a paved road. Reconciliation will need better understanding than this from the media.

TEN

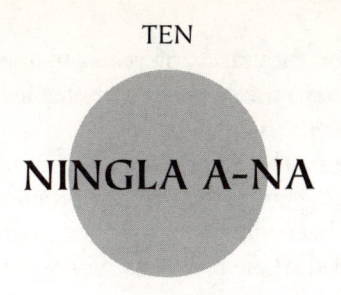

NINGLA A-NA

we are
hungry for
our land

FOR RUBY HAMMOND LAND RIGHTS WERE INDIVISIBLE from the equality and justice for which she struggled all her adult life. For her, as for all her people, it was not just a legal right they were seeking, it was a human right.

3 June 1992, a day she was to be grateful for having lived to see, offered new hope. The High Court of Australia, after a decade of legal discussion, rejected the concept of *terra nullius*, the theory that while Aborigines might have lived in Australia they were not really in possession of it. Australia's law on the impact of colonisation was redefined, and a new concept, 'native title', was introduced to the common law of Australia.[1] This was followed by another eighteen months of discussion and debate until 22 December 1993, when the Native Title Act was passed by federal parliament. Tragically Ruby was not there to share the rejoicing on that day.

The High Court decision followed the granting of their land to the people of Mer in the Torres Strait Islands. The decision has implication for Aboriginal people still living on unalienated land where Aboriginal people have lived continuously for thousands of years. It does not, as some Australians seem to think, mean a wholesale handing over of the continent to its indigenous people.

Ruby was among the Aborigines for whom the High Court decision in 1992 seemed the greatest promise for the future they had ever been given, but she knew it did not mean instant solution to their problems. She would have felt the same guarded delight at the passing of the Native Title Act. She knew how vulnerable 'unalienated lands' are to mining and pastoral interests, and how Aboriginal values are of no account to shareholders.

She recalled her office in Wakefield Street in the 1970s. Hanging on the wall was an extract from a speech by Chief Seattle[2] of the Suquamish Red Indian tribe. It hung opposite her desk, where she could see it just by raising her eyes, but she had no need to do this. She knew it by heart. It is well known to Aboriginal people, and hangs on many walls.

The speech was a reply to an appeal made by the State of Washington to the Suquamish people for the sale by treaty of their tribal land. The need for a treaty followed a US Supreme Court decision in 1823 that recognised the concept of 'native title'. This decision has been accepted and repeatedly affirmed in many common law jurisdictions in the world ever since.

It was as bewildering for Chief Seattle to understand the concept of 'selling' land as it was for the Aborigines. He said:

How can you buy or sell the sky, the warmth of the land? The idea is strange to us. If we do not own the freshness of the air and the sparkle of the water, how can you buy them?

Every part of this earth is sacred to my people. Every shining pine needle, every sandy shore, every mist in the dark woods, every clearing, every humming insect is holy in the memory and experience of my people. The sap which courses through the trees carries the memories of the red man.

The white man's dead forget the country of their birth when they go to walk among the stars. Our dead never forget this beautiful earth, for it is part of us. The perfumed flowers are our sisters; the deer, the horse, the great eagle, these are our brothers. The rocky crests, the juices in the meadows, the body heat of the pony and man – all belong to the same family ...

This shining water that moves in the streams and rivers is not just water, but the blood of our ancestors. If we sell, you must remember that it is sacred, and that each ghostly reflection in the clear water of the lakes tells of events and memories in the life of my people. The water's murmur is the voice of my father's father. The rivers are our brothers, they quench our thirst. The rivers carry our canoes and feed our children. If we sell you our land, you must remember and teach your children that the rivers are our brothers and yours, and you must henceforth give the rivers the kindness you would give any brother. There is no quiet place in the white man's cities. No place to hear the unfurling of leaves in spring or the rustle of insects' wings.

This speech is widely known to Aborigines throughout the commonwealth, and it stirs a deep response in them. If there is no comparable speech by an Aborigine it is because there was no comparable opportunity to make one. No Australian state ever offered to buy their land, and the only treaty they ever signed was with John Batman on 6 June 1835 for 600,000 acres (2500 square kilometres) of prime grazing land around Port Phillip Bay. The government refused to recognise this transaction.

Chief Seattle's speech expresses a great deal of Aboriginal feeling about the land although it does not convey the depth of their spiritual feeling.

There are Australians who have vague ideas that Aborigines have always lived in the relatively uninhabited outback parts of Australia. In fact, every part of Australian land that is confined within a fence, not only the great pastoral holdings and mining reserves, but every little suburban block, once belonged to an Aboriginal tribe. Whatever Australian homeowners may have paid for their property, they are living on land which was once taken from Aborigines without payment, without treaty, without acknowledgement of any sort.

It is not about to be handed back to them. The law will not return land 'owned' by individuals. Indeed Aborigines are not asking for the whole continent to be handed back to them. They are not wanting to drive non-Aboriginals into the sea. They are asking for the land rights they would have had if there had been real negotiation with them in 1788.

Captain James Cook's instructions from the Admiralty included a sentence that said, 'You are also, with the consent of the natives, to take possession of convenient situations in the country.'[3]

There seems to have been no thought of the possibility that the natives would not give their consent, but when the time came nobody bothered to ask.

When Captain Cook sailed by the eastern coast of Australia in 1770 he had very little contact with the natives, and certainly none that related to taking possession of land; yet on 22 August, just before the *Endeavour* turned into the open sea, he rowed ashore to a little island which retains the name of Possession he gave it. Here the Union Jack was raised, and Cook claimed all the eastern seaboard of the continent for King George III, naming it New South Wales. There is no record of any natives having been present, and certainly none of their giving consent.

Eighteen years later, in 1781, the British were defeated in

the American War of Independence, and a problem arose of where to send Britain's overcrowding prison population. Joseph Banks[4] suggested Botany Bay, and nobody had any better ideas.

It took a little time to get the First Fleet under way, but eventually, in May 1787, HMS *Sirius*, the sloop *Supply*, and nine transport and store ships set sail under the command of Captain Arthur Phillip.

The King had given him virtually absolute powers over the whole of the eastern seaboard. By the principles of common law the annexed land was vested in the Crown, and any variation had to be specifically enacted or otherwise provided for.

There was no understanding of the patterns of life that tied the Australian Aborigine to the land, and certainly none of the land's spiritual nature. The Aborigines were not seen as owning specific areas of land as they had not built up villages. It was not recognised that communities had well-defined areas they depended on for their livelihood, or that both men and women had certain duties and rituals to perform in relation to their land, and to special areas within it.

At first only a small area was occupied by the white community. It was not until 1801 that explorers began to look beyond the coast. Settlers followed them, gradually pushing the native people off the land as they went westward, and up towards the north. The settlers met with resistance, but this was never regarded as the action of landowners defending their rightful territory. It was looked upon as criminal action to be dealt with by the police. As settlers moved beyond the area where police were stationed, they treated the Aborigines in any way that suited them.

Professor Rowley tells us that 'the facts are easily enough established that homicide, rape and cruelty have been commonplace over wide areas and long periods'.[5]

The cruelty extended to callous hounding of the Aborigines away as trespassers, hunting them down, and poisoning them like vermin.

Kylie Tennant, writing of Mary Gilmore, says: 'Her grandfather Beattie on his Hunter River farm at first caused shocked complaint and comment by saying he would not hunt down black men and women with dogs and guns, but regarded such acts as murder ... the parson was sent to remonstrate with him.' Subsequently his white neighbours burned down his fences and maimed his cattle. Financially ruined, he had to leave the Hunter Valley because of his humane attitude towards the Aborigines.[6]

In Kingston, where Ruby Hammond grew up, it was widely believed that a landowner in the western ranges had killed off Aborigines by poisoning their water sources. Such wrongs do not belong only in the long-ago times of Mary Gilmore's grandfather. C.D. Rowley noted in 1970 that there were still people living who could have killed an Aborigine with impunity if not legality when they were young, and Aboriginal tribesmen who remembered such incidents.[7]

Natives who survived these onslaughts were dying of the new diseases the white man had brought, especially smallpox, tuberculosis and measles. As they were pushed off the land on which they had relied for their food, they suffered from malnutrition and starvation. Loss of the land that was the basis of their culture broke up the pattern of their lives. Rape and seduction were producing a new generation of part Aborigines. Wherever the settlers went the native population was reduced to poverty and despair.

There was always a minority of the non-Aboriginal community who felt some concern for their plight, and the state governments came under pressure to provide 'protection' for the Aborigines. This, in practice, meant that they were denied all the rights of Australian citizens. It meant the setting up of reserves where Aborigines owned no land, where all decisions relating to their lives were made by people in authority over them, and where they lived in abject poverty with little hope of education or employment.

Some of them found their way to mission stations where well-intentioned Christians did what they thought was best for them, but where they were given no more rights as individuals than on the reserves, and certainly no more title to the land. The majority of Australians never give these matters a thought, but the Aborigines know it all in the same way as the Irish know their history.

In 1957 the Federal Council for the Advancement of Aborigines and Torres Strait Islanders (FCAATSI)[8] was set up. At first it was mainly non-Aboriginal people, but Aborigines and the Islanders, growing in confidence, demanded more and more say, and after 1970 they filled all the executive positions. Each year they held a conference, which was a valuable source of energy renewal for those Aborigines struggling actively for the rights of their people. By 1969 'land rights' was clearly seen to symbolise the whole of the struggle, and the conference decided to adopt an Aboriginal term for it – 'Ningla a-Na', which is Arrente for 'we are hungry for our land'. They also adopted a flag which depicts a yellow circle, symbolising life and the sun, on a ground that is half red for the land, half black for the people. A ferment of resentment was rising in Australia, but it was marked by extraordinarily cool reason and restraint.

The first active struggle for land rights began in 1966 with a campaign that has built itself into Aboriginal legend. It began in the Northern Territory on Wave Hill Station,[9] which was part of the vast pastoral leases of the meat-packing firm presided over by Lord Vestey in England.

In August 1966, almost all the 170 Aborigines working on the station walked off in protest against their poor living conditions. They were mainly people of the Gurindji tribe.

They began by camping just across the river near Wave Hill Station, but in March 1967 they moved about thirteen kilometres to Wattie Creek, where there was a better waterhole. They settled in for what became a long and significant campaign.

Helped by Frank Hardy,[10] the author of *Power Without Glory*, they sent a petition to the governor general, Lord Casey, asking for the return of 1500 square kilometres of their land. The governor general rejected this petition, saying the government could not consider giving them land already leased, but would consider an application for vacant Crown land.

Within the white community concern for the plight of the Aborigines was mounting. Many of them were living in such appalling conditions of deprivation and poverty that it was becoming a national, and possibly an international, scandal. The federal government was powerless to act because under the constitution Aboriginal welfare was a state concern. In the referendum of May 1967 the people of Australia voted overwhelmingly to give the commonwealth power to legislate for all Aborigines anywhere in Australia.

There was little immediate result, but an Office of Aboriginal Affairs was set up, and Mr W.C. Wentworth was appointed Minister-in-Charge. 'Billy' Wentworth was regarded as a friend by the Aborigines. He did not manage to do very much for them, but they blamed this on the Country Party, part of the coalition then in power, and the powerful pastoralists' lobby in Canberra.

In 1968 Wentworth travelled through the northern reserves.[11] He visited Wattie Creek and spent some time talking with the elders of the Gurindji tribe. He returned to Canberra saying, 'We must restore to the Gurindji people the responsibility for their own destiny – a destiny we have taken from them.' If this seemed a safe sort of statement for a politician to make, pleasing the electorate without committing the government, it nevertheless disturbed the Country Party. They made it clear that they regarded the Gurindji demands as the thin edge of a very threatening wedge. We can only guess at what went on behind the scenes, but the offer made eventually to the Gurindji people was for twenty square kilometres.

In March 1968, a land rights demonstration was held in Canberra, during which hundreds of Aborigines and white supporters staged a five kilometre march to Parliament House. In July nationwide vigils were held, and a massive petition was launched by FCAATSI.

Following the demonstration in March a Sydney businessman, Alan Newbury, made a very generous protest against the inadequacy of the offer to the Gurindji. He wrote to the minister offering to pay one half of the cost of acquiring 100 square miles (269 square kilometres) of land for them. He said he thought the minister should be thinking in terms of 400 or 500 square miles to enable the Gurindji people to establish themselves on some business-like basis. Land at Wave Hill Station would not carry five beasts to the square kilometre, and twenty square kilometres was totally inadequate.

Mr Wentworth replied that funds were readily available to acquire whatever area was considered desirable, and he went on to say, 'I have personally consulted with the Gurindji people, and the area selected is in accordance with the wishes they expressed to me.'

It was patently not what they wanted, and they continued to ask for the land they believed to be theirs. They discovered that there were people who would support them. In July 1970, a Save the Gurindji Committee was formed in Sydney with more than 500 members from all political parties.

Very little progress was made. On 17 October 1972, more than five years after they sent their first petition to the governor general, the government announced that it would acquire from Vesteys some sixty-five square kilometres at Wattie Creek and lease it back to the Aborigines. The Aborigines were asking for 1400 square kilometres, and some experts believed they would need ten times as much to have an economically viable area.

Aborigines all over Australia felt a sense of involvement with the Gurindji struggle, and many of them can still sing the Gurindji song:

> *Poor bugga me, Gurindji.*
> *Me bin sit down this country*
> *Long time before Lord Vestey*
> *All about land belongin' me,*
> *O poor bugga me.*
> *Poor bugga blackfella this country.*
> *Long time work no wages we*
> *Work for good old Lord Vestey*
> *Little bit plour, chugar, tea*
> *For the Gurindji from Lord Vestey*
> *O poor bugga me.*
> *Poor bugga blackfella Gurindji*
> *Suppose we buyin' back country*
> *What you reckon proper fee?*
> *Might be plour, chugar and tea*
> *From the Gurindji to Lord Vestey?*
> *O poor bugga me.*

Another land issue that deeply concerned Aborigines was the leasing of parts of the Cape York Peninsula to overseas mining interests. Aborigines everywhere were familiar with the details, and regarded it as typical of their treatment over land issues, particularly in Queensland.

Dr H.C. Coombs, while he was chairman of the Office for Aboriginal Affairs, claimed that the terms of the lease had reduced the native community in the area to a 'depressed rabble of fringe dwellers'. Frank Stevens, a lecturer in Industrial Relations at the University of New South Wales, has written a detailed account of the leasing of this land in a paper entitled 'The Politics of Pauperisation'.[12]

Stevens relates that the land was part of a reserve which included the land of the Presbyterian Mission at Weipa on the foreshore of the best natural harbour in the area. The ease with which this lease was broken filled Aborigines throughout Australia with mistrust of agreements made on their behalf.

In July 1955 it was discovered that large quantities of bauxite were to be found within the reserve. To allow it to be developed, the Queensland government and commercial organisations involved came to an agreement with the mission authorities. By 1963 mineral leases had been granted to Comalco Pty Ltd, an international consortium representing mainly English and American capital. A great deal of lip service was paid to the rights of the Aborigines, their welfare and their entitlement to compensation. Speeches in the Queensland parliament referred to the employment opportunities the Aboriginal people would be given, and that Comalco accepted responsibility 'to help in the protection and material progress of the native population around Weipa', offering specifically to help with their education, employment and housing.

The Queensland government passed the necessary legislation to give Comalco control over the reserve. Soon afterwards an offer of $300,000, less than half the amount asked for by the mission, was accepted for rehousing the Aborigines in a new village after the original one was destroyed.

For this amount, plus five cents per ton royalty to be paid

into consolidated revenue, the company gained control of 1,485,000 acres of a native reserve of 1,600,000 acres. This created a public outcry, and finally a further 2500 acres was set aside for the Aborigines, but no form of tenure was extended to them. The company gained access to vast deposits of bauxite with only nominal haulage costs involved. State and commonwealth governments aided the 'pioneering' company with improvements then valued at $10 million.

The company prepared to negotiate a rate for Aboriginal employees that was approximately half that which they were prepared to grant European workers. Trade unions objected to this, but the company succeeded in negotiating a higher payment for 'persons other than those recruited locally'. It was, of course, the Aborigines who were recruited locally. Meals and full board were provided for the European employees, but not for Aborigines. In this and other ways, including inequalities in overtime rates, the Aborigines were in fact paid considerably less than the Europeans doing the same work.

The $300,000 was spent on sixty-two prefabricated aluminium houses which had not been designed for a humid climate. The money did not extend to including laundries or sewerage. The houses were known locally as 'the sardine tins'. By comparison Europeans were housed in louvred composite stone bungalows, with ceiling fans, gardens, footpaths, a swimming pool and shopping facilities.

Even a promise to provide a dormitory for single natives and a trade school for Aboriginal youths was not kept. Although there had been a promise in parliament that there would not be segregated schooling, the company achieved this by having two schools, one near the Aboriginal village and one in the township where the Europeans lived. There was no 'bussing' except for the very few European children who lived outside the township.

Another mining lease, this time in the Arnhem Land Reserve in the Northern Territory near the Yirrkala Methodist Mission, had consequences of historic importance. A claim by the Yirrkala tribes for the land became a test case in the Northern Territory Supreme Court.[13]

The reserve had been gazetted in 1931 and for more than thirty years the commonwealth government kept it exclusively for the Aborigines. The Aborigines believed that the land was theirs.

It was announced in April 1963 that 350 square kilometres of land near the mission had been excised for mining purposes, and leases granted to the Gove Bauxite Corporation.[14]

Two Labor Party members of the House of Representatives, Kim Beazley and Gordon Bryant, asked a series of questions about these arrangements, and especially about whether the Aborigines had been consulted and their interests protected. Mr Beazley moved 'that in the opinion of this House an Aboriginal title to the land of Aboriginal reserves should be created in the Northern Territory; a form of selection by Aboriginals of trustees to conduct affairs arising from this title should be devised; and meanwhile the safeguarding of Aboriginal rights should be ensured by discussion with spokesmen of the Aboriginals of the Gove Peninsula area'.[15]

The Labor Party was in opposition and the motion was lost. Soon afterwards the two men travelled up to Yirrkala and spent several days talking with the people. The result of this meeting was the famous Yirrkala petition on local bark parchment that Gordon Bryant presented in parliament in August 1963.[16]

By this time there was a feeling among government members that all was not well. A select committee was appointed to examine the grievances of the people, and its recommendations were tabled in parliament in September 1963.[17]

The committee recommended that the excised area should be declared a protected area in favour of the Yirrkala Aborigines; that their sacred places, waterholes and food and water supply be protected, and that building sites for the Aborigines be reserved for them. It also recommended that compensation be paid to the Aborigines for the loss of traditional occupancy of their land, and that a senate standing committee be established to which the Yirrkala Aborigines could bring their grievances for the following decade. The report was tabled without debate.

In 1965 a further lease at Gove was granted, this time to the Swiss mineral combine, Nabalco Ltd, to develop deposits worth an estimated $800 million. Kim Beazley moved in the house that the major recommendations of the 1963 report be implemented, but the Labor Party was in opposition and the motion was lost.[18]

Until the 1960s the pastoralists had been the main intruders on northern Aboriginal lands. The newer threat of the bauxite and uranium explorers seemed devastating, and a third cause for alarm was the granting to Nabalco of a lease for a wood-chip industry.

Weipa and Yirrkala were by no means the only areas affected. Among less-publicised places to suffer was Mapoon,[19] north of Weipa in Cape York Peninsula, where bauxite was mined. Six families which refused to leave were rounded up on 15 November 1963, and taken away by boat. According to Aboriginal reports it was done so abruptly that some of them left their evening meal still cooking on their stoves. Before they left their homes were burnt down.

These people did not readily accept the new life the Queensland government offered them and, in 1974, sensing a new attitude towards Aboriginal land rights, some of them began moving back.

The people of Australia, seeing articles occasionally in

their newspapers on these matters, and even sometimes reading them, began to feel vaguely that something ought to be done. Among Aborigines the feeling was growing strongly that if anything was to be done they would have to do it themselves.

It was in this atmosphere that the Methodist Commission for Aboriginal Affairs suggested to the Yirrkala Village Council that they might have a strong enough case to establish a legal claim to the lands they were occupying. The council decided to take action, and their writ was issued out of the Northern Territory Supreme Court on 13 December 1968.

Nabalco and the commonwealth government took out a summons for striking the action out. They wanted it declared frivolous. Mr Justice Blackburn disallowed the summons, and the Yirrkala case proceeded.

The commonwealth government paid the Aborigines' costs, but no government official in the Northern Territory helped them, and none gave evidence on their behalf. The solicitor general appeared for the Crown.

The hearing lasted almost a year, and finally in April 1971, Mr Justice Blackburn handed down a 262-page judgment in which he found that the Aborigines had no legal basis for their claims to the land on the Gove Peninsula. It is probably the most bitterly resented judgment in Aboriginal history.[20]

Mr Justice Blackburn found that Australia had been settled peacefully, and no doctrine of common law required a British government to recognise land rights under Aboriginal law which may have existed before 1788. The evidence seemed to him 'to show that the Aborigines have a more cogent feeling of obligation to the land than of ownership of it'.

Faith Bandler, secretary of FCAATSI, was particularly scathing about the claim that Australia had been settled peacefully. 'Australia was conquered brutally,' she said. 'The history is one of abuse, continuous horror, and callousness.'

The finding was mind-numbing to the Aborigines concerned. The land was theirs. Mr Justice Blackburn's outpouring of words was just a rationalisation of a blatant theft.

Although this finding was probably what the government wanted, it still left them with the great Australian dilemma — on the one hand white Australians do not want to sacrifice any part of their own prosperity for the Aborigines, but at the same time they wish to appear to be dealing justly with their indigenous minority.

Mr McMahon, who was then prime minister, undertook to review the government's policy. The Council for Aboriginal Affairs was invited to make an advisory submission, and on 26 January 1972, Australia Day, Mr McMahon made an important announcement.

He said that, 'The government has concluded that it is in the national interest, as well as largely in the interests of the Aborigines themselves, for mining exploration and development on Aboriginal reserves to continue.'[21]

However, the government would consult with any Aboriginal community that might be affected by such action so that their welfare could be taken into account. It had been decided to create a new form of lease which Aborigines could apply for as individuals, groups or communities. Such leases would provide for economic and social purposes including those arising from Aboriginal educational, recreational, cultural and religious activities. The Crown would reserve all mineral and forest rights.

Dr H.C. Coombs, chairman of the Council for Aboriginal Affairs, expressed disappointment. Much would depend, he said, on the spirit in which the decisions were administered. Aborigines were bitterly disappointed, feeling that once again mining and other economic interests were being put ahead of Aboriginal interests, and that there was no commitment to land rights.

Mr McMahon had not long finished speaking when three young Aborigines put up a green and white beach umbrella on the lawns of Parliament House. It was the beginning of an imaginative, ingenious, and highly successful protest – the Aboriginal Tent Embassy.

By the weekend the embassy had grown to five tents and seven people. Outside were two signs reading 'Which do you Choose – Land Rights or Bloodshed?', and 'Canberra – Meeting Place for the Wirradjuri Tribe. Now $100 million. Land Rights Now'.

It was the height of the summer holiday period. Very few politicians were in Canberra, and those who were thought it best to ignore the embassy. The press took much the same attitude until 9 February when the leader of the opposition, Gough Whitlam, and the Labor Member for the Australian Capital Territory Keppel Enderby, visited the embassy. They sat on the lawns and talked with the embassy staff and then went into the main tent. At one point Mrs Whitlam came over and joined them, and a crowd of about fifty people gathered around.

Immediately afterwards Mr Whitlam held a press conference.[22] He promised that a Labor government would reverse federal Cabinet's rejection of Aboriginal land rights, and grant Aboriginal committees full title to land. He said he would establish a fully elected Legislative Assembly in the Northern Territory that would ensure there was no discrimination against Aborigines, introduce a general civil rights bill that would guarantee the civil rights of Aborigines and other minority groups, over-rule state laws that discriminated against Aborigines, provide free legal representation for Aborigines to test their rights in court, and eliminate all differences between Aborigines and whites on matters of electoral enrolment.

By this time there was a cluster of eleven orange, green, and white tents with the striped umbrella still in the middle, and a staff of nineteen Aborigines from several states.

The postman began delivering letters to 'The Secretary, the Aboriginal Embassy', and it was becoming of interest to tourists. A Cabinet which included a Minister for the Environment, Caucasian Affairs and the Arts was formed. Michael Anderson was High Commissioner. Another minister in the Cabinet was Chicka Dixon, who was given leave by the Waterside Workers' Federation in New South Wales for 'as long as it was needed'. He was there the whole time the embassy remained. They made a determined effort not to give any grounds for eviction. Little cooking was done, the site was kept clean and tidy, and the lawns were respected by moving the tents about.

The first Aborigines in occupation were educated urban men, and efforts were made to bring Aborigines from reserves to make a more balanced representation. Michael Anderson was quoted as saying they wanted about 100 or 200 people in permanent occupancy. They were not worried about food. White men might have a bit of trouble, but they would just go up in the hills and kill a few goannas if things got tough. Support was coming from all over Australia and from overseas, so the prospects were good.

Michael Anderson also said that if Aborigines from the reserves had never been subjected to offensive discrimination they would not have to wait long at the embassy.

'We get white people pulling up and saying "go home nigger",' he said.

For six months they kept the tent staffed, and patiently explained to all comers what it was about. It was an 'Embassy' because they felt themselves to be aliens in their own land; it was a 'Tent' because so many of their people had no proper homes. A shanty of rusting sheets of used galvanised iron might have been more appropriate, but a tent fitted in well with their aim to make their point without giving offence.

Attitudes of every sort were revealed to them. There were people who came with expressions of strong support, leaving money and gifts; people who gave them casual good wishes; people who treated them as a tourist curiosity; and people who treated them to the foulest racial abuse.

The Aboriginies were grateful to talk to people who wanted to listen, but an interestingly large percentage wanted to do the talking themselves, advising them to tidy themselves up, put shoes on, mind their language, and to go about their aims in different ways.

Patiently the staff would give the details of the infant mortality rate in Alice Springs, of children on reserves retarded because of protein deficiency, of the incidence of trachoma, tuberculosis, anaemia and malnutrition among Aboriginal children, and of the homelessness of men ineligible for the dole because they had never been employed at all.

During that six months a film company became interested. They brought a camera down, and did spasmodic filming during June. They were there on 20 July to film what proved to be an historic event – the taking down of the tents.

One of the incidents they filmed involved a plump, white-haired lady who expressed some concern about the Aborigines' approach to their problems, and felt they might do better if they went about their protests in a more respectable way. Gary Foley, who was talking to her, began to inject a calculated incidence of four-letter words into his response.

'There's no need to be obscene,' the lady said.

'Fuck that load of shit,' said Gary deliberately. 'Obscenity is not words. Obscenity is children dying of malnutrition, Australian men and women living in worse poverty than in the slums of Calcutta, that's what obscenity is,' and he turned away with what seemed to be the weariness of the whole six months.

One wonders how many people who saw this film asked themselves, 'Are we really a people who find words more obscene than children dying from our neglect?'

There may have been some deliberate 'obscenity' of this sort in an effort to arouse people, but in the whole six months there was no trace of violence. The cars from which people shouted 'go home, nigger' drove on without anything being thrown at them. The most racist abuser had his say without even a threatening gesture being made at him.

The embassy staff sought to lobby members of parliament, and on 7 June, when there were rumours that an amendment to the Trespass on Commonwealth Land Ordinance was about to be promulgated, they sent a meticulously-worded petition to the Queen, explaining the status of Aborigines in Australia, and asking her to reserve the promulgation of the ordinance 'at Your Majesty's pleasure'.

They were extraordinarily patient, and their patience began to worry the government. Aboriginal land rights was not a burning issue at election time, but there were a lot of uneasy consciences on Aboriginal questions. The ordinance was first suggested on 2 March, soon after parliament resumed after the summer break. It was likely that Cabinet thought it best to do nothing. The Aborigines would get tired. They would go 'walkabout', and the whole episode would be quietly forgotten.

But six months went by without any sign of this happening. Friday, 14 July, was National Aborigines Day. Marches in support of Aboriginal land rights were held in every capital city.

The *Australian*, 15 July 1972, reported 3500 people marching in Sydney, more than 1000 in Melbourne, 2000 in

Adelaide, and 1000 in Brisbane. In Sydney they gathered in such numbers outside the town hall that traffic was halted. Violence broke out when police tried to clear the crowds, and thirteen people were arrested. There was also a brief clash with police in Brisbane. The demonstration in Canberra was cheerful and orderly, ending in a picnic singsong on the lawns. At 10 pm a working bee was held to clean up papers, candles, and other rubbish left by the demonstrators.

These had been the largest National Aborigines Day marches ever held. It had been at the FCAATSI Conference in 1957 that Pastor Doug Nicholls had suggested such a day, and it had never before generated very much publicity. Now it brought a new surge of support for the Tent Embassy. It was obvious that the embassy was not going to go away.

Three weeks earlier there had been a meeting of the Council of the South East Asia Treaty Organisation in Canberra, and the Tent Embassy had to be explained away to distinguished foreigners. Cabinet wanted to be rid of it.

Despite the Aborigines' petition to the Queen, the amendment to the Trespass on Commonwealth Land Ordinance was gazetted on the morning of Thursday, 20 July, and fifty minutes later the police moved into the tent area.

The *Australian* reported that sixty police took part. They asked the Aborigines to take down their tents and leave. The Aborigines refused. The police moved in, taking down all the outer tents and putting them in a big trailer.

News of what was happening went round Canberra like wildfire. Some students raced over, and other people came, including Stewart Harris, *The Times* correspondent. When only one tent remained about sixty people, Aborigines and their supporters, linked arms around it, and ten minutes of bitter fighting ensued. Eight people were forcibly arrested, and one Aborigine was carried away unconscious.

The tent was finally collapsed. As it went down Mr

Enderby, the Labor Member for the Australian Commonwealth Territory called through a megaphone, 'I am talking to the police. There is no tent here now. You are exceeding your authority.' Violence and bitterness had at last come to the scene.

That night the Minister for the Interior, Ralph Hunt, who had ordered the gazetting of the ordinance, went on television to deplore the violence which, he said, had been caused by 'people from outside, hell-bent on violence'. Stewart Harris ended his report to *The Times* by saying, 'I was present, and patently the Aboriginals were as determined as the "outsiders".'

Often when Aborigines actively protest against the deprivation suffered by their people their actions are excused as 'violence' caused by 'outsiders', 'stirrers', 'communists'. Educated, articulate Aborigines like Paul Coe, John Newfong, Gary Foley, and Michael Anderson, who were among the leaders of the Tent Embassy, were well aware of their own situation, and not at all subject to pressures from outside. In the film *Ningla a-Na*, Gary Foley looks under the mat for communists in a gesture of contempt for the idea.

The Aborigines countered with accusations of police violence, and Gordon Bryant supported them.

The next day four Aborigines took out a writ against the Minister of the Interior for an order making the ordinance invalid, and sought an injunction restraining any person from preventing or interfering with the re-erection of the tent. Mr Justice Fox in the ACT Supreme Court refused to grant an ex-parte injunction. This prevented the re-erection of the embassy, but permission was given to allow them to apply for an injunction in the Supreme Court on the following Tuesday.

The Aborigines decided not to wait until Tuesday. On Sunday about 100 Aborigines and as many supporters marched from the university and sat on the main road outside Parliament House, blocking the traffic. Delegations went to the Department of the Interior and the Attorney General's Department asking to be allowed to re-erect the tents until the matter could be debated in parliament. Permission was not given.

All police in Canberra were called on duty, and a special squad of 200 marched four abreast into the area to supplement those already at Parliament House.

The demonstrators moved onto the lawn and re-erected the tent, forming a tight circle around it. The police outnumbered the defenders and it took only ten minutes to overpower them again and take down the tent. This time the violence was much more intense. Eighteen arrests were made, and eight demonstrators and five police were treated at the Canberra Hospital.

Mr Howson, the Minister for Aboriginal Affairs, deplored the violence rather plaintively, saying he was making plans for a national conference of Aboriginal representatives to be held in Canberra on 10 and 11 August. Because of this he refused to meet an Aboriginal delegation.

A rumour spread in Canberra that the Aborigines were to be given Beauchamp House, a building which was about to become vacant. The *Canberra Times*, 29 July 1972, speculated that Mr Hunt had favoured this proposal, but that the prime minister had vetoed the idea.

It is likely that Cabinet preferred Mr Howson's idea of building up an Aboriginal advisory committee. It was seriously believed by many politicians that the Tent Embassy was the work of radical Aborigines, and that the government should look to a more conservative element.

It seemed to many of the Aborigines that the government simply could not see the basic issues. Later in the week a delegation was finally admitted to the office of the Minister for the Interior, and Mr Howson tried to explain to them his advisory scheme.

Roberta Sykes said afterwards, 'They spoke of articles and constitutions, and we spoke of people living in humpies and dying of malnutrition.' Roberta is a well-known black feminist in Queensland and New South Wales. She was a secretary to the Tent Embassy, and was among those arrested on Sunday, 23 July 1972. She has since won an overseas scholarship and has graduated from Harvard with a PhD.

The Aborigines were still determined to re-erect the embassy. On Sunday, 30 July, about 400 Aborigines and about 1000 supporters put it up again. A force of 250 police stood by and watched. The violence of 23 July had brought protests from all over the country. People had been horrified by what they had seen on television. This time there was no rushing in.

The tent went up, and from it the Aboriginal leaders spoke to the crowd. They kept it up for about three hours, and then they permitted the police to take it down. In the film *Ningla a-Na* the police at times seemed bewildered. When the tent went down a group of Aborigines held a sheet of canvas above their heads. Police looked at it uneasily.

'Go away,' said a young Aboriginal woman. 'We are only playing games.'

Each side saw this final day as a victory.

In August Mr Howson's meeting took place, but nothing was done to give land rights to any Aboriginal group.

In December 1972, an election brought the Labor Party to power for the first time in twenty-three years. Not all Aborigines voted Labor, but it would be safe to say that many of them did, even though educated Aborigines tended to think that in the final weighing up of Aboriginal rights against the economic advantages of mining, meat packing, tourism and the wood-chip industry, the differences between the two major political parties were only a matter of degree. However, on 2 December 1972, most Aborigines were pleased with the election results.

Mr Whitlam picked up his new responsibilities with a speed unprecedented in Australian history. He organised a two-man interim ministry of himself and his deputy, Lance Barnard, and proceeded to implement his election promises. The two ministers were sworn in on Tuesday, 5 December. The following day the abolition of national service was announced, and by the end of the week a dozen other matters had been dealt with. These included halting grants of mining leases on Aboriginal reserves.

On 8 February, just one day short of a year after his first visit to the Tent Embassy, Mr Whitlam commissioned Mr Justice Woodward to inquire into and report upon 'the appropriate means to recognise and establish the traditional rights and interests of the Aborigines in and in relation to land, and to satisfy in other ways the reasonable aspirations of the Aborigines to rights in or relation to land ...' In particular he was to examine the position in the Northern Territory.[23]

It was not quite a fulfilment of the promises of 9 February 1972, but the Aborigines, who are a patient people, hoped it would come to that eventually.

While he was making his inquiries Mr Justice Woodward won the trust of the Aboriginal people, and they awaited his report with a good deal of confidence.

It was presented on 17 July 1974. Aborigines studied it eagerly, and inevitably it disappointed them.

The report recommended that Aboriginal reserve land should be owned by Aborigines in fee simple, with Land Trusts holding land for all those having traditional interests in it. The trustees would be drawn from Aboriginal leaders in the area, and two Land Councils would direct them in administrative matters. A Land Commission, acting as an independent administrative body, would advise the government and make recommendations in relation to Aboriginal land rights.

On the troubled question of mineral rights, the report recommended that minerals and petroleum on Aboriginal land should remain the property of the Crown, but that Aborigines should have the right to prevent exploration for them. This Aboriginal power of veto should only be overriden if, in the opinion of the government, the national interest required it.

To many Aborigines the whole thing seemed unnecessarily complicated. It seemed that mineral rights had taken precedence over Aboriginal rights, and they were fearful of the government's 'escape clause', giving it the power to override decisions of Land Trusts.

The report included a section headed 'Main Principles' in which the commissioner urged autonomy for Aborigines in running their own affairs, and a considerable share of decision-making for which 'they should be free to follow their own traditional methods'.

Natascha MacNamara has claimed that these aims were not given any substance in the body of the report. In her opinion, 'Many, many Aboriginal people will see the proposed Land Rights as an authority over them rather than part of them. They already own the land, now bits of it are going to be loaned back to them.'

Another objection was to a paragraph in the report which stated, 'It is clearly most important that Aborigines should understand just what the granting of land rights means for them. This will involve a series of discussions with each community, to be arranged by the community's advisers, and no doubt co-ordinated by the Department of Aboriginal Affairs. Much of this will have to wait until decisions on the various matters covered by these recommendations have been arrived at.'

The Aboriginal people, of course, felt they should be able to understand what was proposed, and to express their views on it, before the decisions were made.

The Whitlam government introduced the Aboriginal Councils and Associations Bill to parliament on 5 November 1975, incorporating most of the recommendations of the Woodward Report. They had already appointed Mr Justice Ward as an independent interim Land Commissioner to hear claims from Aboriginal groups, and had undertaken to stand by his recommendations.

Alas for the promises of 9 February 1972. It was now too late. On 11 November 1975 the Labor government was summarily dismissed by the governor general.

The Fraser government rejected the Labor Party's bill and on 4 June 1976, presented another version, to which forty-three changes had been made. Soon afterwards the new Minister for Aboriginal Affairs, Mr Ian Viner, directed Mr Justice Ward to stop hearing claims. The stated reason was that the government believed that no claims should be heard until the passage of the bill.

Aborigines saw this as an horrendous piece of double-dealing. In April 1974, parliament, with all political parties assenting, had agreed that no new fifty-year leases should be granted until Aboriginal claims had been heard. This 'freeze' expired on 31 December 1976, so the whole intention of allowing their claims to be heard first had been nullified. The Aborigines saw themselves as having to compete against the claims of pastoral and mining companies before the Northern Territory Lands Board. They believed the Lands Board's decisions were based solely on economic grounds, and that the whole process had made a mockery of their rights.

The general feeling among Aborigines about the

Aboriginal Land Rights (Northern Territory) 1976 Act was that 'it could have been worse', and they believed it would have been if it had not been for their own campaigning.

The act undoubtedly had clauses which improved their former position, but they were dismayed by its concern for the economic needs of sections of the community which they saw as already being wealthy.

The act provided for the establishment of Aboriginal Lands Trusts to hold 'inalienable freehold title' to land in the Northern Territory which had previously been Aboriginal reserves; and for Aboriginal Land Councils to administer this land, in particular 'protecting the rights and responding to the wishes of the traditional Aboriginal owners'.

On the other hand, it no longer met a specific recommendation 'that the basic legislation should be introduced into the Australian parliament', and 'that it should be protected in such a way that its provisions cannot be eroded by the effect of any Northern Territory Ordinances'.

In March 1976, a delegation from many different parts of Australia went to Canberra to seek guarantees that this provision would be an integral part of the legislation. The Aboriginal Lands Rights Campaign claimed that a specific promise of this was given by both Mr Fraser and Mr Viner. The 1976 act broke this promise. Aborigines deeply distrusted the Northern Territory Legislative Assembly which they saw as a body catering to the pastoral, mining, and tourist interests, all of which they saw as having a record of placing economic interests above Aboriginal rights.

Other recommendations which were subject to the Northern Territory Legislative Assembly included their right to control roads passing through Aboriginal land, and to hunt, camp, and hold ceremonies on traditional land owned by pastoralists.

The right of Aborigines to veto mining developments had

been reduced. It would only apply in the initial exploration stage, and could be over-ridden 'in the national interest' if both Houses of Parliament agreed.

The act was proclaimed on Australia Day, 26 January 1977. The minister made a very high-toned speech to mark the occasion, urging the community as a whole 'to do its part by giving full value to the Aboriginal people in terms of human and cultural equality'. Unfortunately the worthy sentiments were no compensation for those parts of the Woodward Report which were not incorporated into the act.

Ruby Hammond saw as serious omissions from the act those recommendations that would have enabled the Land Commissioner to deal with claims based on need alone, rather than traditional ownership. This was particularly sad for the fringe dwellers of Alice Springs. Mr Justice Ward was looking into this matter late in 1975, and was hearing claims devised by the Arrente people to cater for the intricate demands of their social world.

The *Black News Service*[24] said of these claims:

> They had also done everything possible to avoid creating conflicts with Europeans. It was probably the most concisely formulated and adequately produced plan for development produced by Aboriginal people in the Centre. All of that effort is now being wasted because the Land Commissioner's powers over such matters have been removed. Instead we have what amounts to half a dozen blocks of land which ignore the basic principles which the Arrente owners of the Alice Springs region wish to see fulfilled.
>
> People will still be forced to camp in large numbers in the Todd River and around the fringes of the town. Whites in the town will probably start asking why they haven't been moved to the 'land claims' already granted, without understanding that Aboriginal law keeps them apart, and

that the facilities and areas provided will now be drastically reduced from the original scheme's provisions. Unless land is granted such basic services as water supplies and toilets cannot be provided. There are 1000 people in the fifteen fringe camps of Alice Springs. Only two of these camps have running water.

The Woodward Report and the legislation arising from it dealt mainly with the Northern Territory, but parts of it applied to urban Aborigines.

In the 'Main Principles' section the report said:

Cash compensation in the pockets of this generation of Aborigines is no answer to the legitimate land claims of a people with a distinct past who want to maintain their separate identity in the future.

A later paragraph spoke of 'the injustice of a compensation in cash or land made to individuals and terminating all rights of future generations'.

Ruby Hammond would have totally endorsed these sentiments so long as they were not interpreted to mean that there was to be no compensation in cash or land for this generation. 'Of course it should not be at the expense of future generations, or of the rights of the Aboriginal people as a whole; but nor should those Aborigines who were in desperate need be sacrificed for those who were not yet born,' she said.

Land was still being taken from the Aborigines. If they lived on Crown land they had nothing to sell if they chose to move. The land reverted to the Crown, or it might go to the Aboriginal Lands Trust, presumably to be kept for future generations, but this was no help to the family that was moving. They had literally nothing to replace the home they were giving up. The department would put them into a house that was of the poorest type provided by any government authority, and they would pay rent for it. If they got into arrears they could be evicted. No meaningful efforts were made to help them find employment, or to train them for work that would be available. The family, all too often, was left to manage on the dole which, in 1977, exposed the father to the recrimination of being a bludger.

Within the context of land rights, Ruby Hammond claimed that Aborigines who chose to leave a reserve or fringe situation must be given the sort of help that would enable them to achieve the life they were seeking. She saw this as involving, at least in some cases, individual grants of cash or land.

Aborigines have a different cultural heritage from European Australians, and they were developing a different set of contemporary cultural memories, a great deal of it relating to land rights.

How many people remember that on 3 November 1976, three Aborigines invaded England? They landed at Dover, erected the Aboriginal flag, played a tape recording that informed the onlookers that this was an invasion of England, and handed out gifts of beads and red cloth to the people on the beach. Aborigines remember this incident in the way Americans remember the Boston Tea Party.

On 19 March 1977, a group of Aborigines followed up this incident by entering the grounds of the British High Commissioner and erecting a sign saying, 'Under New Management'. They had intended to take over the building on the following Monday, but they were arrested and charged with trespassing.

In the early 1970s a vocal body of European Australians demonstrated, to the point at which many of them were courting arrest, to protest against South African cricket and rugby teams, which had been selected on a racial basis, playing in Australia. They included people whom the Aborigines knew as their friends, and had been seen at the Gove Peninsula meetings, but they had never before seen them so aroused.

Why didn't they protest like this about Aboriginal land rights issues? Why were they not courting arrest over the leasing of the Gove Peninsula? Ruby Hammond did not know the answers to these questions, but she knew that many Aborigines had speculated on these matters, and that some of them had a deepening mistrust of people who professed concern about the rights of black people.

When non-Aboriginal Australians talk of housing for Aborigines it is quite commonplace to hear them saying that you cannot give Aborigines good quality housing. They will just wreck it, and anyway, they don't want it. They prefer to live in shacks. Ruby could have wept with frustration at this blind cruelty. How could she answer these charges? Of course there were some who failed at housekeeping. They were poor and unprepared for city life. These people needed help, and she believed that no one who really understood their history would deny it to them. It was time to start teaching this history in schools.

During 1977 at least two television programs suggested that Aborigines were 'not ready' to take responsibility for their own properties. One of them was in the *Big Country* series. It was about Kalumburu, an isolated Roman Catholic mission run by the Benedictine Order on the King Edward River in the north of Western Australia. Head of the settlement was Father Seraphim Sanz, who had been there for forty of the seventy years since the mission was founded. The announcer spoke of seventy years of 'benevolent despotism' under which the Aborigines had led an 'idyllic existence'. They did not drink, they cultivated crops and cattle, were educated, and had full medical care.

The federal government had decreed that the settlement was to be handed over to the Aborigines in August 1977. The principal point made by this program was that the Aborigines were not ready to take control of this flourishing and economically successful cattle station. They did not want the responsibility until they were better prepared for it.

Father Sanz said he had tried to impress on the Aborigines that, after Christianity, education and hard work were the way to salvation. Education was mentioned several times, but not one moment of the program was devoted to showing that any education was given. Shots of the school showed girls playing basketball.

At no stage did the interviewer ask Father Sanz why he had not made better efforts to prepare the native people to take over the place, for he must have seen this eventuality coming. The man who was head of the council, and would be in charge when Father Sanz left, admitted that he was getting no preparation for his responsibilities.

The interviewer asked Father Sanz if the Aborigines were lazy. He replied, 'Yes, very, very lazy, or else they have not found any reason to work hard.' He did not seem to see that it had been his responsibility to help them find such reason.

This type of program dismayed Ruby. Most people viewing it tended to take it as evidence that the Aborigines were not ready to accept responsibility for their own affairs, and even that they were by nature incapable of ever doing so. Only a few people saw that the mission, however well intentioned, had actually prevented them from developing the ability to manage the cattle station. The interviewer conceded that the council leader was an excellent motor mechanic, so obviously he had ability. Why had he not been given any administrative training? And why did the interviewer not ask this and other questions that would have revealed more sharply the weakness of the mission's approach to its responsibility?

On 11 May 1977, *This Day Tonight*, another ABC program, showed what had been a flourishing property at Lake Tyrell in Victoria six years after it had been handed over to an Aboriginal group. It was completely run down. None of the equipment was working, and much of the place had been vandalised. Nothing in the program indicated whether or not any attempt had been made to prepare this group to run their property.

Ruby's reply to this was: 'Let people accept this and leave it to the Aborigines. They will see for themselves what they have done, and begin to build it up again – perhaps not in the same way as it was, but in an Aboriginal way. It is time people accepted that the rest of the world does not necessarily want to embrace their values, but may be seeking something which seems to them to be better.

'We will never learn to manage our own affairs unless we are left alone to do it. Nobody learns to do anything except by doing it. We learn to walk by walking, to write by writing, to drive a car by driving. It is the only way human beings learn anything. In every learning situation genuine help is valuable, and we want genuine help; but no help at all is better than pushing us aside and doing it for us because we don't immediately succeed.'

ELEVEN

OTHER LANDS – OTHER LIFESTYLES

from the Maria
Creek to the
Yenisey River

IN 1972 AN INVITATION CAME THROUGH THE AUSTRALIA–China Friendship Society for a delegation of Aborigines to visit China as guests of the government. Ruby was among those invited.

Going to China in 1972 was a rare excursion for any Australian. Diplomatic relations with China had been broken off in 1949 when the Chinese Communist Party came to power. By 1972 there was a movement within Australia urging recognition of the Chinese Republic, but the Liberal Party, then in government, was not responding to it.

In July 1971, the leader of the opposition, Mr Whitlam, had visited China with a group of senior Labor Party politicians. He had stated quite unequivocally that recognition of the Chinese Republic would be one of the first acts of a Labor government. When the Labor Party was elected on 2 December 1972, their outline for the Australian basis of recognition was already in existence, and the first steps towards implementing it were taken on 5 December. Recognition was announced on 25 January 1973.

In October 1972 it was already apparent that this might happen, and the Liberal Party was less ready to turn back visitors to China than they might have been two years earlier. The Australia–China Friendship Society was growing in strength, and the Aboriginal Tent Embassy had left the Liberal Party anxious to avoid clashes with the Aboriginal people.

Arrangements were made in Sydney, and Aborigines from all states were invited to join the delegation. Some of them were approached by government officials and asked not to go, but finally a party of nine was agreed upon. Ruby Hammond was the only South Australian among them. The others were Charles (Chika) Dixon, Lynette Thompson, Jerry Bostock and Terry Widders from New South Wales; Cheryl Buchanan and Lilla Watson from Queensland; Kenneth Winder from Western Australia; and an Aboriginal elder from the Northern Territory who has since died.

Despite the changing political climate there were problems that arose both from the fact that they were going to China, and also that they were Aborigines. The referendum that had been carried so enthusiastically in 1967 was seen by Australian people as conferring citizenship rights on Aborigines, but they were still legally subject to by-laws and ordinances that remained on the statute books. Under one of these Aborigines were not allowed to leave the country without permission. Jerry Bostock had served nine years in the army and there had been no problems when he was sent to Vietnam, but by 17 October the delegation had not succeeded in finalising permission to leave Australia. They were going very much at their own risk, and they met together at Mascot Airport with a good deal of uncertainty. Qantas, and several other airlines, had refused to accept their booking, but Air New Zealand had undertaken to fly them to Hong Kong.

Their luggage was searched by customs officials, and the whole event was subject to scrutiny by various government employees. Among the things they were taking was their film, *Ningla a-Na*, about Aboriginal land rights.

It had been made towards the end of the six months' life of the Tent Embassy. Its dramatic highlight was the taking down of the tent on 24 July 1972. It showed 300 police, who were all able-bodied and mostly big men, marching up in a column of four. The tent was protected by about 200 people, women as well as men, some of them Aboriginal, and others who were mainly students from the Australian National University. The type of student who was actively concerned about Aboriginal rights was apt to be actively unconcerned about dress and the general trappings of respectability. They were all totally unarmed. There were no sticks, no stones, and they gave the impression of being young, poor and defenceless.

However much one may talk of the police 'doing their duty', the sight of such a massive body of uniformed men falling upon this group to tear down a tent was truly sickening to the average non-partisan spectator. On the occasion of the filming there were eighteen arrests made, and police were shown, three and four at a time, manhandling young men and women into police wagons.

Nowadays Aborigines would assert their right to take such a film abroad with them, but in 1972 it could easily have been taken from them. Probably the officials allowed them to take it because they did not know the meaning of *Ningla a-Na* and supposed it to be a film about Aboriginal culture. In China they had many opportunities to screen it, and it was shown to thousands of people.

The flight was delayed two hours in the hope that permission would finally come. Strange men, one of them with a little matchbox camera, were moving among them or sitting stolidly in the airport seats watching them. Anti-Vietnam War stalwarts recognised familiar faces, and it was assumed they were from the Australian Security Intelligence Organisation (ASIO). Two of them eventually boarded the aircraft with them.

The two hours was a tense time for the delegation members, but it was a lively time too. Several hundred Aborigines had come to see them off, including members of the National Black Theatre, which enlivened the proceedings with street theatre type performances of political satire. In the end it was agreed that the delegation could go on to Darwin.

'Although,' said the airport officials, 'you will probably be turned back there.'

The flight had originally been going direct to Manila, but the captain, soon after takeoff, announced that they would be touching down at Darwin.

'It will be a last chance for duty-free shopping,' he said cheerily. One of the two men who had seemed so interested in the delegation got up and went to the pilot's cabin. The captain's voice came over the loud speaker.

'I am sorry,' he said, 'no one will be allowed to leave the aircraft in Darwin.'

At Darwin commonwealth police boarded the aircraft. A rumour went around the passengers that they were inspecting the air-conditioning. This seemed unlikely to the group of Aborigines, but just what they were doing was never clear.

One of them finally told Chika Dixon, the leader of the party, that they would be allowed to go on, but that there was a possibility they would be turned back in Hong Kong.

At Hong Kong airport they were met by representatives of the Chinese Travel Service, who quickly whisked them away in taxis. One of the interpreters told them that, following news of the difficulties they were having, they were to stay at a hotel owned by the Chinese Republic.

Here they had their first taste of the lack of sex discrimination that prevailed in China. Girls were among the staff who carried up their bags. This embarrassed some of the men, but the interpreter told them that it was an accepted thing.

'Chairman Mao says women hold up half the sky. In China they have equal rights, equal privileges, equal duties and equal responsibilities,' he said.

Having settled into their hotel, which was on the Kowloon side of Victoria Harbour, they went for a walk along the main street. It was night time, but Nathan Street was a blaze of light, and all the densely packed little shops that line both sides of it were open.

Suddenly there was a great noise. Two shouting groups of men ran down the street, many of them carrying knives. After them came another shouting group of armed police. In their state of uncertainty the delegation found this unnerving. They went back to the hotel.

Early next morning they caught the train for the journey through the New Territories to the border town of Lu-wu. The little group, many of whom had known intense poverty themselves, was appalled at some of the signs of poverty they saw from the train – people living in shells of cars and derelict junks, dogs with mange, and people begging.

At Lu-wu the British flag was flying, and British customs officers inspected their luggage and their passports. After what seemed an agonisingly long delay it was indicated that they could go on. A long stretch of neutral territory lay ahead of them. They must walk over this. About three-quarters of the way over was a check point. None of them felt entirely certain that they would not be turned back even there.

At the check point the soldiers were Chinese. They saluted the delegation, and there was no delay. They began to run. They stepped at last onto mainland China. The women burst into tears, and hugged each other.

'We've made it, we've made it,' they cried. They were the first Aboriginal delegation ever to step on foreign soil.

An agonisingly long delay at customs, Lu-wu, Hong Kong. (Figure masked out is an elder recently deceased.)

Here there was a railway station, a large brick building, where they were given tea. Neither then nor at any time was their luggage searched. Most visitors to China have their luggage thoroughly inspected for possible drugs, but the Aborigines were honoured guests.

Two high ranking officials had travelled from Peking to welcome them on behalf of the Chinese government. Ruby was amazed at the way the welcoming party knew them all. They had seen photographs of each of them, knew them by name, where they came from, and what work they did. Ruby's Chinese maiden name intrigued them, and she told them about her Chinese grandfather.

The two strange men who had accompanied them had crossed the border with them. Ruby assumed they were officially going to the trade fair which was in full swing in Guangzhou (Canton). They had entered the railway station with them, but at the top of the stairs Chinese soldiers had indicated that they were to go to another room. It was the last the delegation saw of them.

They set off by train for Guangzhou, travelling first class, all of them for the first time in their lives. The train was rather like the Spirit of Progress, pride of the Victorian Railways at that time, with the addition of hostesses who brought around tea and cigarettes.

The group began to relax. They commented to each other on the contrasts between one side of the border and the other. Perhaps in their tense uncertainty on the Hong Kong side they had been too ready to see signs of dirt and poverty, and perhaps now they were too ready to see only the best, but every member of the delegation was impressed by the cleanliness and tidiness of everything they saw, and a sense that if there was poverty there was no deprivation.

They were soon persuaded that there were no minorities suffering discrimination. It was an alternative lifestyle. Ruby could see that it was achieved at the cost of freedoms that were valued in Australia, but if the minority groups had suffered discrimination before the revolution, they had not known these freedoms anyway.

'What can you lose,' asked Ruby, 'if your pride, your heritage, your culture, your livelihood have all been taken from you?'

Their first stop was Guangzhou. Revolutionary music was playing at the station. There were revolutionary posters on the hoardings. There seemed to be thousands of people at the railway station.

Most of the people were getting into buses, but there were private cars waiting for the Aboriginal group. They were Japanese cars as were most of the few cars they saw. In 1972 the population of Guangzhou was three million. It was an industrial city with people working round the clock in three eight-hour shifts, their bicycles crowding the streets. The Chinese people rode on bicycles, walked, or travelled by bus. Private cars meant people of importance, and the bicycles parted in front of them to let them through. Traffic lights were manually operated from little control boxes at each set of lights. Car drivers had only to toot, and the lights went green for them.

They drew up at the Tung Feng (East Hotel). It had been an old palace, and the cars turned into a magnificent courtyard. The people working in the hotel had come out to greet them. They were lined up in single file and the Aborigines were introduced to each one individually. Many of the staff were young students learning English, for whom this type of work was a recognised part of their course. When they ascended the steps an armed guard formed a double rank presenting arms.

That evening they were taken to the Sun Yat-sen Memorial Theatre to see an exhibition of singing and dancing that had been put on to coincide with the trade fair. The theatre, which seated 5000, was full. The Australian delegation, all of whom had suffered the sort of humiliating segregation in the front seats that Ruby had experienced in Kingston, were now ushered into the front row of the circle to sit with leaders of the Chinese community.

The next day they were taken to the trade fair where the deputy director of the fair greeted them. They were taken on an exhausting day-long tour.

The fair was an annual event begun in 1957, when twenty countries were represented and 20,000 people came. In 1972 the fair had opened on 15 October, nine days before the Aboriginal visit. There were thirty countries represented, and already more than 60,000 people had visited it.

Agricultural machinery formed an important part of the display, and here, and in other sections, there were Australian exhibits. There were more Australians than usual in Guangzhou that day. None of them greeted the Aboriginal delegation in any way, but there was one moment when Ruby became very conscious of them. Some Australian men were standing by a combine harvester and apparently explaining it to two Chinese. The Chinese were wearing their national costume of blue pants and tunic. They could well have been engineers.

The Chinese moved away and, as the Aborigines passed, Ruby heard one of the Australians say, 'They grasped it all very quickly, didn't they! They are really quite intelligent.'

Ruby looked round at the speaker and his companions. With their pale faces and their well-cut suits they looked to her like typically successful Australian males. Ruby looked at them in astonishment. It was not only Aborigines they considered themselves superior to. It was also the Chinese. Perhaps it was every other race on earth. She caught the eye of Jerry Bostock who had heard it too, and bubbled into laughter.

'They don't honestly think they are as superior as all that, do they?' she said. If racism had not had such tragic consequences, she thought, it would have been truly funny.

That night they were driven to the Friendship Restaurant for a banquet. Ruby wrote in her diary, 'The Chinese people treated us like kings.'

The next day they saw 'The Institute', the famous Peasant Movement Training Institute founded in 1924 that Chairman Mao had helped to develop, and where he had lectured. It had played an important part in the development of the agrarian revolution. School children, and even preschool children, went there to learn about the early history of the revolution.

Three preschools were visiting The Institute while the Aboriginal delegation was there, and the little pupils sang and danced for them. The songs and dances were full of praise and fervour for the revolution, and the children sang them proudly and with delight. They were more disciplined than Australian children, and on the whole more charming. Ruby had been warned before leaving Australia that she would see evidence of 'brain-washing'. She wondered if this was it, and if it was very different from the old flag-saluting at the Kingston primary school. The children certainly seemed happy.

From The Institute they went on a tour of the city, and then to the Guangzhou People's Museum, where they were shown the historic contents of five floors.

Although they were tired they then asked to see the Friendship Store. There was one of these stores in each city especially for visitors, and Ruby had heard they were good places to buy gifts. There was just time for this before they had to hurry to the airport for the flight to Beijing (Peking). Ruby says in her diary, 'I was very excited as I felt that history was being made, and I was part of it.'

Chika Dixon had facetiously expressed a hope that they would be in the front of the aircraft. They were tired of being always at the back. He need have had no fear. They travelled in the best seats wherever they went.

When they touched down at Beijing they were asked to wait in the aircraft until all the other passengers had alighted. Still remembering the uncertainty of the early part of their journey they wondered uneasily what was going to happen.

The other passengers alighted through the tail of the aircraft, and when the last one had left, the front doors seemed to open automatically. A red carpet stretched down over the gangway and across the tarmac until it disappeared into the terminus. Lining it were representatives of about forty of the fifty-five minority groups that live in China. They were wearing their national costumes, although it was bitterly cold, and as the Aborigines descended they began to clap.

The head of the Chinese People's Association for Friends from Foreign Countries was there to greet them, and presented them to the minority groups.

'It was tremendously emotional,' said Ruby. 'By the time we had walked that 150 metres all the women, and some of the men, had tears in their eyes.'

In Beijing they stayed in the Beijing Hotel, which is an old palace, and Ruby was spellbound by the wonder and beauty of it all.

One of the places they visited was the Institute of National Minorities. Here the traditional culture of the minority groups, including their songs and dances, was taught to people from the original areas, and to other people too. People from the minorities could study their own languages up to tertiary level, and some of the teaching was directed at bridging the gap between the rural schools and the more advanced schools in Beijing.

An audience of 1300 students had gathered in the Great Hall to hear about the lives of the Australian Aborigines. On the dais were five or six white-draped tables at which the delegates were to sit. They showed their film, *Ningla a-Na*, and took it in turns to cover aspects of Aboriginal life, their past and their present history.

Jerry Bostock spoke last, and he ended by reciting one of his own poems, *Black Children*. At first he waited at the end of each verse for the translator, but towards the end, carried away by his own rhetoric, he moved to the front of the stage and just spoke to his audience without waiting for the translator.

'They seemed to understand,' he said. 'When I came to the last line, "Rise up Black Children", I heard the rest of the delegation getting to their feet behind me, and suddenly the whole audience began to rise and applaud. I felt we had their understanding and their sympathy.'

Ruby, one of those standing behind him, found tears in her eyes once again. 'If only people at home would listen to us like this,' she thought.

That evening they were guests of honour at a banquet attended by Chou En-lai, vice-president of the Peoples Republic of China, and representatives of most of the national minority groups.

They visited the Imperial Palace where they were ushered into a room that visitors seldom see, and given tea from a priceless golden tea-set once used by the Dowager Empress. Ruby was impressed by the careful way all the beautiful things belonging to the old imperial regimes were treasured. They were seen as the work of the common people, and valued as achievements of human endeavour.

The group went to the children's hospital, where they were given masks and gowns, and shown over many of the wards and theatres, and the acupuncture outpatients' clinic. They visited schools, kindergartens, factories, medical centres and communes. They were taken to theatres, and they often had opportunities to talk and show their film to audiences of Chinese people.

The communes fascinated them. The first one they saw was the Red Star People's Commune not far from Beijing, which had grown out of co-operative efforts dating back to 1957. Seven co-operatives had developed into one commune, and the figures for increased production recorded by Ruby are staggering – before liberation, 300 kilograms of rice to the acre; after liberation, 2208 kilograms to the acre.

Her diary, which she wrote up each night, is full of this sort of information, scrupulously recorded from material handed out wherever they went, detailing the principal industries and the output before and after liberation. It was propaganda, but it was a euphoric time for Ruby and she had no difficulty in accepting it.

The whole delegation was impressed by the air of co-operation and achievement that the communes presented. For people whose cultural heritage related to Aboriginal living, communes seemed like simple common sense.

From Beijing they flew 400 kilometres into Inner Mongolia to the city of Hohhot. Here they entered another world, a world that very few visitors to China ever saw. The Aboriginal delegation was taken there because it was part of the vast area of China peopled by minority groups. About ninety-five per cent of the total population of China was composed of Han Chinese people who spoke one or other of the dialects of China. The other five per cent was made up of about fifty-five national minorities, ethnically and linguistically different from the Chinese. Despite their relatively small numbers, the minorities were politically significant as they occupied between them almost half of the area of China, including the vitally important strategic border areas with the Soviet Union, the Mongolian People's Republic, India, Burma, Vietnam and Korea.

Because so few visitors travelled into Mongolia the Aborigines found themselves as interesting to the Mongolians as the Mongolians to them, and wherever they went crowds would gather.

In Hohhot, as in Beijing, they were honoured guests. They were taken to factories, schools, kindergartens, clinics and hospitals.

A special performance of national dancing and singing was staged at the theatre for them, and once again they were invited to speak to large audiences, and to show their film. They travelled by jeep a further 160 kilometres to Darmao, the chief town of the Darhan-Mow Mingan United Banner area. Here they were in the heart of rural Mongolia where, on the great rolling plains of the plateau, the main activity is caring for great herds of horses, sheep, cattle and camels.

The Aborigines stayed in an old stone building that was a far cry from the palatial Beijing Hotel. It was a place of great simplicity with a stone floor, whitewashed walls, and heating from a fire in the centre of the main room. It was warm, and on the whole comfortable, although Ruby's diary says 'the beds were like rocks'.

They were welcomed, as always, by the leaders of the local revolutionary committee, and here again they heard stories of achievement and progress. Darmao had scarcely existed fifty years before, but it was developing into an industrial centre with wool mills, and factories processing food and making farm implements.

Before the revolution, they were told, the Mongolians had been virtually slaves. Shao-Ci-Mar, president of the Country Women's Federation, told them of incredible poverty in a childhood dominated by landlords who demanded unpaid labour. She had seen her sisters die of starvation, and had been forced to beg in order to survive.

The Darmao Guerrilla Theatre staged a special performance for them. Like all theatre they saw in China it had a strong revolutionary impact. There was often a gaiety about the performances, and the stark, uncompromising 'message' would come as quite a shock to Ruby. She remembered a scene with an 'American'. He was chewing gum, had long pointed shoes, a cigar, and a tall hat decorated with stars and stripes. A beautiful young girl appeared. She was a soldier in the Peoples Liberation Army, but she was off duty and carrying a basket of flowers. The American saw her as a prospect for casual sex, and made an arrogant advance to her. She took a gun from her basket of flowers and shot him dead.

Even shadow puppets had the same underlying political

meanings. Ruby recalled a puppet show of a beautiful bird, standing in a pool, being tormented by a turtle. The turtle nipped at one side of the bird, which gracefully bent down and nipped back at the turtle. The turtle nipped at the other side, and the bird bent down gracefully again and nipped back. It happened a third time. The bird was no less graceful in bending down, but this time it snapped the turtle's head off.

On the way back to Hohhot the group visited a Mongolian commune where they saw herds of horses, camels, and sheep, and saw a specially staged exhibition of dazzling horsemanship. The commune had developed around seventy-eight families of 270 people belonging to three different nationalities – Mongolian, Han and Hui (who are Chinese Moslems). There appeared to be no discrimination among them.

The families lived in tents, and things like watches, bicycles and sewing machines were new to them. Schooling was only to primary level, but some children were at boarding school in Darmao, and those with ability went on to school in Hohhot. The families felt they were moving forward, and saw the commune as a transformation from bitter poverty in the past. None of the people went hungry. There was a clinic with two full-time barefoot doctors, one of whom had a knowledge of gynaecology. Ruby thought, heart-achingly, of the Aboriginal minority people camped in the Todd River area of Alice Springs, and their desperately high infant mortality rate.

The Aborigines went into the tent of the chairman of the revolutionary committee and met his family. The tent was wool-lined and very comfortable. A Mongolian feast had been prepared for them, and a whole roast lamb was borne in on a dish. The host cut it, and invited the guests to help themselves. 'You are our brothers and sisters,' he said.

They travelled back to Hohhot where a farewell banquet with officials of Inner Mongolia was awaiting them. When it

258 FLIGHT OF AN EAGLE

Above: Factory tour, Hohhot, Mongolia.
Right: Greeted by Kuo Mo-Jo for the banquet in the Great Hall.

In front of Mao's childhood home, Changsha. Ruby seated middle front. (Figure masked out is an elder recently deceased.)

was over they boarded the train to return to Beijing. Here there was another round of sight-seeing and banqueting. Ruby was impressed by the Great Hall of the People, built in 1959 to foster political development among the ordinary citizens. There was a huge meeting hall with 10,000 seats, each seat with earphones for a translation system of twelve languages. There were also 100 small meeting rooms, including one for each province, most of which were decorated with their crafts.

One evening the members of the group were guests at a banquet in the Great Hall. The invitation had come from Comrade Kuo Mo-Jo, vice-chairman of the Standing Committee of the Peoples National Congress.

On this visit they also saw the fabulous Ming Tomb, which had been unearthed in 1956, and visited the Great Wall.

The next stop was Shanghai where they saw the Industrial Exhibition, workers' residential areas, and a dozen factories, small and large. A factory where the workers were either blind, deaf-mute or otherwise physically handicapped made a great impact on Ruby. Prior to 1958 these people had all been beggars, fortune tellers or street singers. There had been early fears that accidents and inferior products would mean the factory could not succeed, but thought had gone into designing special equipment and, when Ruby saw it, there were five workshops with 538 workers of whom 178 were blind, 148 were deaf and mute, and twenty-two were otherwise handicapped. The factory was producing plastic spoons, plastic pegs, bicycle reflectors, and electrical fittings.

Throughout the journey Ruby had been interested in kindergartens and arrangements for mothers and children. It seemed to her that grandmothers played a big part in the care of children of working mothers (and most mothers went to work), but there were adequate out-of-school care centres for children who needed them. In Shanghai the Children's Cultural Palace was a centre of out-of-school activities, with forty staff members and sixty part-time instructors. The centre worked in close co-operation with the schools.

Once again there were visits to the theatre, and opportunities for the Aborigines to speak to groups of people, and to show their film.

Their journey was coming to an end. There remained only one major place on their itinerary – Changsha, the birthplace of Chairman Mao in the Hunan Province. They travelled by train to Zhuzhou, the nearest city to the little town that was then a mecca for the people of China. Mao Tse-Tung's early home and places associated with his life were then exhibition places and training centres for young communists. The group was proudly shown all of this, but Ruby found it less moving than the Darmao commune. The weather was dismal, and there were guards on the hotel doors, something she had not seen anywhere else.

From Zhuzhou it was an overnight train journey to Guangzhou, from where they returned to the border, and the flight home.

For every member of the delegation the Chinese visit had been an exciting, thought-provoking, stimulating experience, and each one of them returned home with enhanced self-confidence. They had been treated throughout the whole tour as people to be honoured and respected as representatives of the Aboriginal people of Australia. Each one of them had been able to accept this and respond to it.

They had seen people of different nationalities, some of them minority groups, and had seen with their own eyes that racial differences are a matter involving skin colour, styles of dress and special customs; but that these are only surface differences, interesting but unimportant. They had seen a different political system, and it seemed to them that it treated minority groups better than the capitalist system did.

Ruby had no political allegiances. Her loyalties were to her people, and she saw the struggle in Australia as one to get 'land rights' from whatever political party was in power.

This would be the attitude of most Aborigines. When they go to the polls many of them vote for the ALP candidates, because the Labor Party seems to them to be more concerned about Aboriginal rights than the Liberal Party, the only other party likely to gain office; but they did not join the Labor Party, and they would vote Liberal at any election if they thought the Liberal Party was offering more for their people.

On their return all the members of the delegation spoke at meetings about their fascinating experiences. At one meeting Ruby spoke of the hopeful life of the people in the Darmao commune. A Latvian woman asked her, 'Would you exchange all your beautiful freedom for life in a commune?'

Ruby looked at her for a moment in astonishment, and then she said, 'I don't think "beautiful freedom" is a phrase with much meaning for Aborigines. We have been robbed of our land; and our dignity, our culture and our livelihood were taken from us too. I think a commune system in a society that respected the rights of minorities would be wonderful for Aborigines.'

A comment which was not 'funny', although it made Ruby laugh, came from Senator Neville Bonner.[1] He predicted that well-organised and violent eruptions in Australia would result from this visit to China. The group had probably been brainwashed to come back and cause some form of violent demonstrations, he said.

If brainwashing had been what the visit to China was about it had been of an extremely subtle kind. Not one word was said to them at any stage of what they might do on their return to Australia.

Ruby joined the Socialist Party[2] when she got back. No pressure was put on her to do this, but what she saw as the nonsense of Neville Bonner's comment helped her to make this decision. Other friends tried to urge her against it. 'They'll use you,' they said, but Ruby felt this did not happen.

Four years later Ruby was able to visit the Soviet Union. The invitation came, through the Socialist Party of Australia from the communist government, for a group to study the life of national minorities in Russia.

It was a party of six of which three were Aborigines. The leader was Dr Hannah Middleton, lecturer in sociology at the University of New South Wales. She organised and led them as a working group. The Aborigines were Ruby; Mary Davis, from Koonawarra in New South Wales, a member of the Koomaditchi Aboriginal Housing Association; and Marceil Brady, of the Queensland Aboriginal Legal Service. Hannah Middleton; Kevin Manski, secretary of the Darwin Branch of the Waterside Workers' Federation; and Con O'Clerkin, a member of the Aboriginal Rights Council of New South Wales, were non-Aboriginal.

This time there were no problems about leaving Australia. The group flew out of Sydney on 21 July 1976 in a charter aircraft. It was not as comfortable as Air New Zealand but, with brief touchdowns at Singapore and Karachi, it got them safely to Moscow in the early morning of 22 July.

They were guests of the Soviet Communist Party, but at a more informal level than their status had been in China. In China they had been representing the Aboriginal people and had been treated as foreign dignitaries. In Russia they were a study group, and Ruby remembered that it was all much more fun.

At Moscow airport they were greeted with flowers. The welcoming party included four people who were to become their friends – Yuri Segeivich Ivanov and Pakhamova Helena, the guides who were to remain with them through the whole tour, and two Australians, Jim Mitchell and his wife, Marcia.

Yuri, a man in his forties, was an historian assigned to the group to help with their studies, and he was also in charge of the tour. He was a member of the international department, and the group were to discover that to have him with them was an honour. The people they met in Siberia and Georgia regarded him as a great man, and were excited at meeting him. Helena, as they all called her, was a woman in her twenties, a lecturer at the Institute of Foreign Languages.

Both of them spoke excellent English. Yuri had grown up in New Zealand and, in the overwhelmingly Anglo-Saxon community that New Zealand was in the pre-war years, his family had been aware of rejection and discrimination. He was a sensitive, kindly man, and Ruby was touched by the way he quickly realised that Mary and Marceil were the shy, inexperienced members of the group and constantly showed concern for them.

They were to visit the Khakass region in Siberia and the Abkhazian republic in Georgia, but first they were to have a week in Moscow.

Some of these first days were blurred in Ruby's memory because she fell ill with acute gastro-enteritis. She later remembered the great concern of everyone, especially Helena, and afterwards she learnt that there had been consultations about whether or not she should be put in hospital. Their aircraft touched down in Karachi and there were fears that her illness could be serious. If she had gone to hospital she would have missed the visit to Siberia where Yuri had planned a unique gesture for the Aboriginal members of the group. He wanted Ruby to be there, and it seemed as though he almost willed her to get better and come with them.

Mary and Marceil came to visit her each day to tell her about the wonderful things they had seen and done. Ruby especially regretted that she missed the Bolshoi Ballet. She hoped to go back to Moscow with Frank someday, and the Bolshoi Ballet was one of the things she dreamt of them seeing together.

Jim and Marcia Mitchell came to see her too. Jim, an

Australian journalist, and his wife were dedicated communists. Jim, who joined the party during the depression, lived for some years in the Soviet Union and nothing ever diminished his faith in Marxian socialism as the ideal way of life.

The hotel was quiet and comfortable, and everyone around Ruby encouraged her to get better. Her health improved, her spirits rose, and before they left Moscow she was well enough to visit the huge museum inside the Kremlin, and to go to the circus.

Ruby saw the Lenin mausoleum and was astounded at the queues with thousands of people lining up to pay homage to the Father of the Revolution. It was all tremendously impressive, but she was homesick, and one of her most vivid memories of Moscow was seeing a magpie in the square outside her hotel. She had thought only Australia had magpies, and she was as astonished to see it as if it had been a kangaroo.

On 27 July they left Moscow to fly the 3200 kilometres to Abakan, the capital of the Khakass Autonomous Region. These regions in the USSR were self-governing, but federated, in a similar way to the Australian states but, as there were more than 100 nationalities in the Soviet Union, there was a much greater variety of laws and customs. The Khakass region is in the heart of Siberia in fertile country through which flows the beautiful Yenisey River. Rising in the great mountains that divide the Soviet Union from Mongolia, the river winds across Siberia for 4000 kilometres into the Arctic ocean, watering cities with romantic names like Krasnoyarsk, Dudinka, Igarka and Yeniseysk.

Abakan was only 560 kilometres from the Mongolian border. Ruby thought of her friends at Hohhot, no further away than Adelaide from Perth. It seemed incredible because Hohhot was an Asian city, a place of strange sights and customs, but Abakan might have been in Australia. It was smaller than Adelaide and had quiet tree-lined suburbs that reminded Ruby of home. The group was there in summer time. The beautiful trees were in full leaf. The parks and gardens seemed very like Australian gardens, with geraniums, roses and other familiar flowers.

They stayed in a hostel where a lively young woman named Vyeena looked after them, fussing over their health, cooking enormous meals for them and worrying when she thought they were not eating enough.

When they came home each day they would find the clothes they had taken off the night before laundered and folded on their beds. Their car drivers were always on time, concerned for their comfort, and ensured that they were playing music the group liked.

'They looked after us in every possible way,' said Ruby, 'and what was so overwhelming was that they really seemed to care about us, and our welfare. Even from people who did not speak a word of English we would get the feeling that there was real friendship in their attitude towards us, and not just curiosity.'

It was different in many ways from the China visit, and one of the reasons was that Yuri and Helena were with them all the time and became part of 'the family'. In China there had been different interpreters wherever they went and, although they had been unfailingly friendly and considerate, none of the Australians formed such warm friendships with them as they did with Yuri and Helena.

Students and teachers of English were especially interested to meet them, and there always seemed to be people with the group who could tell them about the local animals, birds and plants. Ruby said, 'We were like children, wanting to know about everything.'

As in China there were almost daily visits to factories, hospitals, schools, kindergartens, collective farms, communes, and holiday camps. Ruby's diary was once again filled with statistics of production and output and progress.

They were often guests of honour at banquets given by the leaders of the communities they were visiting, but more often small groups would come to dine with them and talk informally about life in Russia, and life in Australia.

In the evening they would sit on the balcony in the long twilight, watching the passersby, and discussing what they had seen during the day, and what they thought of it all. There was much more time for this sort of relaxed talking than there had been in China, and Ruby found herself looking at life more broadly than ever before.

The group often walked to where they were going, and Ruby felt that this helped to give her a feeling of closeness to the community they were studying.

Later on, in Georgia, they were to encounter tourists from all over the world, but in Abakan they were the only 'foreigners', and it added to a feeling of being special guests. Abakan was a small city, but it was bustling with activity, and Ruby was impressed by an enormous wool factory surrounded with a complex of homes, schools, recreation centres, a medical centre, canteens and shopping facilities for 10,000 workers. There were forty different nationalities at work there, and more than half the employees were women. There were 15 million metres of cloth produced there annually, they were told, and twenty-five per cent of the wool came from Australia.

On their second-to-last day in Abakan, Ruby, Mary and Marceil were given no hint of a surprise planned especially for them. In the morning they visited a marble quarry, and the enormous Yenisey power station that is comparable with the Snowy River Scheme. They had lunch, and then they boarded a launch for a trip down the river. The launch had been gaily decorated, and there were flowers everywhere.

Although they'd had lunch there was enough food and wine on board for a banquet. An accordionist travelled with them who, they later discovered, was a nationally famous musician.

The launch travelled down the beautiful river, and then pulled into an island. It was a small island, but tall trees were growing on it, and summer flowers were bright among the grasses. They all went ashore, and Yuri gathered everyone together.

'We have all heard,' he said, 'of the struggle of the Australian Aborigines for land rights, so today we are going to present to the Aborigines of Australia a piece of land, this island, to symbolise our support for the Aboriginal people in their struggle for justice.'

Ningla a-Na Island, Yenisey River.

Turning to Ruby, Mary and Marceil, he asked them to accept the gift on behalf of their people.

Then he asked them to name the island. It was Marceil who responded to this question. She knew exactly what the island should be called. 'Ningla a-Na,' she said, without a moment's hesitation.

They told the Russians the meaning of this phrase, 'we are hungry for our land', and of the way it had been chosen as a symbol of the struggle for land rights in Australia.

Yuri declared the island to be named Ningla a-Na, and the Australians signed the deed of acceptance.

'If we had known we could have brought our flag,' said Ruby, and they all laughed, which was a good thing because the three women were close to tears.

Ruby took off her shoes and walked barefoot through the grass. She was overwhelmed with a nostalgic memory of the little island in Maria Creek, the island she never managed to set foot on. This Russian island seemed to link her to her past, and to symbolise all her hopes for the future.

They began to sing, Russian songs and Australian songs. The musician with them could pick up any tune, and accompany any song. Food and wine were brought on to the island. The first toast, as always in the Soviet Union, was to Peace and Friendship, and then they drank to the newly named island, and to the day when Aborigines would have equality, dignity and land rights in Australia.

They explored their island, and then they sat and talked and sang. The captain of the launch and some of the other Russians with them could speak no English, but it did not seem to matter.

'There are times,' said Ruby, 'when friendship does not need words, and there seemed to be understanding and sympathy between all of us.'

They travelled back to the city. It was dark when they got to their hostel, and they crept in quietly lest Vyeena should wake and want to prepare another meal.

Singing became a part of their lives, and often they would all sing together as they were walking or travelling by car. Ruby, who had a beautiful voice, felt she had never sung so well as she did in the Soviet Union. When they left, Helena inscribed a photograph to her, 'Thanks for all the lovely songs.'

Ruby taught them Aboriginal songs like Bob Randall's *My brown-skinned baby, they take him away*, the sad song of an Aboriginal mother whose child is taken from her; and she taught them the catchy country-and-western songs she had learnt from the Watson's gramophone in Kingston. In return they learnt old folk songs of the Russian steppes from Helena and the drivers.

Flowers and music, food and wine, singing and laughter were in the background of all Ruby's memories of the Soviet Union. She had, too, an overall impression of unfailing kindness. They had only to express a wish and it was granted. They went fishing one day because Hannah Middleton liked fishing. On another occasion they saw a horse and cart.

'I'd love a ride on that,' said Marceil, and within minutes they were getting on it.

'Look out, the tyres have gone flat,' called Kevin Manski as Ruby, who was no light weight, jumped on. Since the cart had no tyres there was a good deal of laughter as Helena tried to translate it for the Russians. It proved to be a very sprightly horse, and they went for quite a long ride, bumping round the paddock on the wooden wheels.

There were many, many kindnesses, but two of them Ruby especially remembered. She and Hannah had been abroad before. It was easy for them to enjoy it all, but for Mary and Marceil it was sometimes bewilderingly strange, and they were often very homesick. Mary missed her children, and their hosts discovered that she had sons who loved soccer, and that Mary, watching it with them, had become a soccer fan. So they all went to a soccer match, and one of the Soviet Union's leading teams gave Mary a ball to take home to her boys.

Marceil was a musician, and she missed the guitar she had left at home. Before they left, the Russians gave her a superb guitar such as she had once only dreamt of having.

On their last day in Siberia they visited Abazar, a mining town. They did not see any mining, but Ruby was impressed by the number of women working in the administration and control systems and in the laboratories. There were three complexes where children were cared for, and a Pioneer camp, which was a children's holiday centre with a swimming pool, recreation park and sporting ground.

'Look out, the tyres have gone flat!'

The group returned to spend that night at Abakan, and the following day they were to fly to Tashkent on the first stage of their journey to Georgia.

There was a farewell lunch, and the guests included the captain of the launch that had taken them to their island, the drivers who had taken them on excursions, and the photographer who had come to the island. The group gave these people gifts they had brought with them – a scarf with a wattle design for Vyeena, stamps and coins for her children, a kangaroo key-ring for the photographer. These people had become friends, and there was sadness in saying farewell.

Tashkent was destroyed by earthquake in 1966, and rebuilt with help from all over the Soviet Union and from abroad. Because so much of it had been rebuilt it seemed a very modern city, but parts of it were centuries old, for it had been a city on the ancient trade route from the Middle East through Samarkand. Ruby, who had never cared much for history at school, was fascinated by it.

The incredible experience of the gift of the island constantly returned to Ruby's mind, and on the flight out of Tashkent she suddenly wanted to put it into words. She found herself humming a song she had made up herself:

> *Ningla a-Na,*
> *Ningla a-Na,*
> *You are the symbol*
> *Of our future dreams.*
> *You're calling softly*
> *From the Yenisey*
> *Of the love and strength*
> *You gave so free.*
> *We shall be as one*
> *And stand together,*
> *Ningla a-Na,*
> *In solidarity.*

From Tashkent they flew to Tbilisi, the capital of Georgia. It was a centuries-old city with an ancient culture. On a hillside above it stood the most enormous statue Ruby had ever seen. Visible from miles away, it was a statue of Mother Georgia, who held a sword in one hand for her enemies, and a cask of wine in the other for her friends.

The Australian delegation was welcomed with wine. There were banquets and welcoming parties wherever they went in Georgia. Ruby was glad she was not the leader because it enabled her to avoid some of the toasts. Sometimes they began with champagne at breakfast, and Hannah, the leader, had to cope with them all. An assortment of glasses at her place at a formal dinner always reminded Ruby of Russia.

There were less formal occasions when the group met students and teachers, shepherds, factory workers, or farmers, often in their own homes; but they used to look forward to 'family' meals, when no one had been invited to meet them, and they could relax and drink tea.

In Georgia there were seventy different nationalities, and special attention was given to the development of each one. They each had a quota of students in the university intake, and their own theatres and institutes. Special efforts were made to preserve and develop all the national languages and cultures.

Wherever they went Ruby was impressed by the schools and the care lavished on children. She later remembered the magnificent Pioneer holiday camps, especially one in Georgia for miners' children. There were many nationalities among the children, but the accent everywhere was on friendship, and Ruby felt there was genuinely no trace of discrimination anywhere.

She remembered a picture of three hands on a wall of this camp. A black hand was holding a Chinese child, a white hand a black child, and a brown hand a Russian child. The concept of children of all nations moving forward to a time of peace and goodwill had become an ideal for Ruby. She was sad that there seemed less evidence of it in Australia than she found in the Soviet Union.

There was also a concern for the physically handicapped

that seemed to her to be far greater than in Australia. No physically handicapped person who had enough ability to work seemed to be without a job in Russia.

Georgia was a tea-growing area producing ninety-five per cent of the tea drunk in the Soviet Union, so there they saw many tea plantations; but each area sought to be self-supporting so there were also orchards and farms, and industries exporting to other parts of the Soviet Union and to eighty countries of the world.

Once again Ruby was impressed by the number of women employed in all kinds of work except the heaviest of manual labour. She learnt that of 400 people in the Georgian legislature, 144 were women. This was in 1972, before International Women's Year. In the House of Representatives in Canberra that year there were no women among the 125 members. In South Australia, with forty-seven members in the Legislative Assembly, there were two women (Mrs Molly Byrne and Mrs Joyce Steele).

There were times of recreation for the Australian group as well as study. In Georgia they were promised they could go sunbathing on the beach at Sukhumi, a holiday resort on the Black Sea. Having seen so much that reminded her of Australia, Ruby was anticipating golden sands. She was astonished to find that planks of wood had to be provided for the sunbathers to lie on. The beach was covered in little stones. It was like lying 'on a bag of marbles'.

Near Sukhumi they were taken by train into a mountain to an enormous limestone cave. It was Ruby's first experience of a cave, and she was truly awed. It was so vast, so quiet, so peaceful and so beautiful.

'It was like being on the moon,' she said. 'We looked down from a ledge to water and sand like a little beach on the floor of the cave, and we could see other caves leading off from the main one.'

Ruby wondered if people had ever lived there and whether, if she'd had more time, she would have found ancient bones, or indications of fire.

The cave was lighted, the lights fading behind them and lighting up ahead as they went along. It was very cold, and Helena shared her coat with Ruby.

'This kept us closely together,' Ruby said, 'with our arms round each other, a white woman and a black woman from two different continents, sharing this place that seemed to have a mystical quality. It made me realise anew how alike human people are, and for a little while I felt there were no problems in the world at all.'

Georgia seemed to Ruby to be a truly multi-racial society. She was not conscious of minorities as such, but she was aware of people living in their own groups while still being part of the whole. It seemed to her that there was no prejudice of any sort. She liked the way the extended family was an important social factor, and old people were able to stay with their families because the whole social life of the community allowed for this. People were not expected to retire until they wanted to, and they seemed to live much longer.

Ruby was aware that old people working was just one of the things she found to praise which other people sometimes condemned. Women working in the streets was another.

'Mostly they are sweeping the streets,' she said. 'I don't see what's wrong with that. We expect women to sweep the floors, the paths, and the backyards in our homes. It can't be seriously wrong to have them sweeping the streets. I know Aboriginal women who would be glad to have a job sweeping the streets for a decent wage, rather than living on the dole.'

'In fact,' she added, 'Aboriginal women are not being given nearly as many opportunities to join the workforce as cleaners as they should be. With the equipment they have nowadays it can be pleasant and dignified work, and mostly migrant women are doing it. It is good work for them, especially where they have little education and language problems. Often Aboriginal women have little education and language problems too. I don't begrudge the migrant women their opportunities; I just ask that Aboriginal women be given a chance to share in them.'

She felt that many Aboriginal women would envy Russian women their childcare facilities, especially those whose husbands were unemployed. 'They would dearly love to share in the bread-winning,' she said, 'but because of the problems of having their children looked after they cannot get work, and many of them are living below the poverty line.'

Ruby liked the way old people were allowed to work without being put under pressure. Her own father was not looking forward to his compulsory retirement.

'We hear people describing themselves as being "thrown on the scrap heap",' she said. 'I got the impression that this never happened in China or the Soviet Union.'

The Soviet Union was quite different from what she had expected. There was less austerity and uniformity. She was surprised to find that women were using cosmetics and nail polish, and that their clothes and shoes were as varied and fashionable as in Australia. Cottons were cheap and plentiful. T-shirts and jeans were coming into fashion, and imported jeans were among things that attracted queues into a shop.

People they met seemed to know all about Australia, and about the difficulties and injustices that Aborigines were suffering. 'But,' she said, 'it was not until we sang songs relating to them that they realised how close these problems were to us. When we were singing everyone listened. They were interested in the music, and in the words, which they wanted translated.'

The group did not have their film with them, and they were not called on to talk at length at big meetings, as they had been in China, but Ruby felt they succeeded in giving the people they met a closer understanding of what it was like to be an Aborigine in Australia. The Russians in their turn had shown the Australians that different nationality is no bar to friendship. When the time came to say goodbye at the Moscow airport, the farewells were deeply emotional.

After her return Ruby was asked at meetings about Russian treatment of their Jewish minority. Had the subject been as much in the news before her visit as it became afterwards she would have sought for information, but she was not aware of charges of anti-semitism against the Soviet Union. She could only say that all she had seen in Russia suggested concern for the rights of minorities.

She had not been told about persecution of the Jews, but many people went out of their way before her trip to talk to her about the evils of communism, the hoodwinking methods of propaganda and techniques of brainwashing. She would be shown, they told her, only what her hosts wanted her to see.

These warnings seemed to be redoubled as she prepared to go to the Soviet Union, but nowhere did she see anything to justify them. She had expected to see places bristling with armed police, but the only gun she saw on either trip was on the stage at Darmao.

TWELVE

'SISTER, IF YOU ONLY KNEW...'

poverty and racial discrimination are the greatest problems

IT IS HARDLY TOO MUCH TO DESCRIBE THE RESPONSE OF women throughout Australia to International Women's Year as sensational. The United Nations from time to time proclaims years as being devoted to special goals. 1977 was the 'Year of Water – the Precious Resource'; 1976 was the 'Year of the Habitat', for raising the standard of the living quarters of those who were inadequately housed; 1974 had been 'World Population Year'. These years went by almost unnoticed, but there would hardly have been a woman or a man in Australia who did not know in 1975 that it was International Women's Year.

The year was given added impetus by the Labor government, which had made improvement in the life of women a part of its election platform. The prime minister had appointed Elizabeth Reid as his special adviser on Women's Affairs, and in 1974 he asked her to set up an Australian national advisory committee for International Women's Year.

Once again it was to be not an elected committee but a group of specially chosen individuals. In addition to Elizabeth

Reid there were nine women and two men. As always in these cases there was a good deal of dissatisfaction about the choice. Ruby Hammond was the only Aborigine, and there were wide murmurs of unrest about this choice. Other Aboriginal women in South Australia and also in other states would have liked to have been chosen. Some of them let her know they thought she was selected too often by European committees.

There was no other South Australian woman chosen. Non-Aboriginal committee women in Adelaide would not have wanted Ruby to have been excluded, but they thought some other South Australian should have been invited too. Other states, including Western Australia, had more than one representative.

On the day the committee was announced Ruby received dozens of congratulatory telephone calls, many of them pointing out to her that she would have to represent the whole state. Before she had been to even one meeting she was beginning to wonder if she would be equal to it all.

It was an exciting committee to be on. The invitations went out as personal letters from the prime minister. The members were all interesting and capable women, and some of them were well known. They included Margaret Whitlam, the prime minister's wife, and Caroline Jones, at that time the best-known woman in Australian television.

The main task of the committee was to advise the prime minister on the expenditure of $2 million allocated for special International Women's Year projects. $2 million! Newspapers all over Australia wrote it up as an astounding allocation. A heading in the *Age*, a normally serious Melbourne newspaper, proclaimed '$2 Million for the Sheilas – Surprisingly it's not a Joke'. People with a tendency to measure national expenditure against their own bank accounts were staggered at this sum devoted to women's activities that, for generations, they had been conditioned to regard as unimportant. In 1975 it was a bigger sum than it seems in 1995.

Ruby Hammond and Gough Whitlam PM with Elizabeth Reid, special adviser on women's affairs, International Women's Year Committee, Canberra, 12 September 1974.

In terms of applications for the money it was not really very much at all. Almost 700 applications for funding were received, which is an average of less than $3000 for each project. It was not a large sum in terms of the demands upon it. The projects included child care centres, women's health centres, women's refuges, family planning clinics, adult education programs, rape crisis centres, and counselling centres; plans for books, plays and films relating to women's aspirations; and research projects.

Ruby Hammond was thrilled to be a part of the prime minister's committee, but before long she was feeling bewildered. The discrimination with which the year was concerned was sex discrimination. Ruby was sympathetic with the struggle women were having to gain equal employment opportunities with men, equal pay, equal opportunities at school, and an equal chance to be elected to parliament and to serve on governing and administrative bodies. She supported all this, but it was not her first priority. Compared with the scalding effects of racial discrimination it all seemed less important.

If she was to speak for Aboriginal women, then racial discrimination was what mattered. Within the Aboriginal community women do not want to set themselves against their men, but to stand side by side with them in a united struggle. This, as Ruby saw it, was what women's liberation was about anyway, but not all sections of the Women's Liberation Movement saw it in that way.

Of the United Nations slogans about the aims with which the year was launched, the one she liked best was 'an equal partnership of shared responsibility', but this was the one they never seemed to use.

Looking back Ruby wished she had arranged for more Aboriginal women to put in claims for a share of the $2 million. The money went, usefully, to support projects that had already been initiated, and were struggling for funds. Perhaps the kindergarten that Mary Williams was trying to establish in Port Adelaide would have qualified, but it was too late to organise a request

The applications that did come in for Aboriginal projects received especially sympathetic consideration, and Ruby was often able to give extra needed information or background for them.

A Women's Electoral Lobby Discrimination Action Group

in New South Wales received $1000 to produce and distribute a series of ten half-hour discussion cassette tapes on the theme of women and discrimination. Discrimination against black women and migrant women was the subject of one of the discussions.

A group of Aboriginal women received funds to establish a rest centre and meeting place for women who came to Cairns to collect pensions, receive medical attention and to shop. It was expected that this venture would become self-supporting through the sale of refreshments. A group in Jarradale, Western Australia, that received $16,500 for a communal women's centre included 'Aboriginal women who felt isolated' among their concerns; and two Queensland women were given $908 to prepare a video tape on Aboriginal women in Queensland to illustrate the difficulties of being both black and female. The James Cook University Women's Group received $11,000 for a study to identify the nature and extent of discrimination against black women in the Townsville area.

All these projects were worthwhile, and Ruby was glad to be associated with funding them, but the desperate problems of Aboriginal women were not matters of gender discrimination, and IWY committee members tended to see racial discrimination as a problem for some other group.

Pressure was put on Ruby, as the only South Australian woman on the prime minister's committee, to come to meetings of the South Australian International Women's Year Committee. She just could not find the time for this extra demand, and Natascha MacNamara did it for her. It was a generous act on Natascha's part for she had been intensely critical of Ruby's selection by the prime minister. She thought Aboriginal women should have been given a chance to choose their own representative, and she was honest enough to admit that if Aboriginal women were going to be chosen in this way, she would have liked to have been chosen herself sometimes.

The Women and Politics Conference, held in Canberra in August 1975, received a great deal of publicity, most of it critical. A group of Aboriginal women went along demanding that they be heard. Elizabeth Reid, urging that they be given a special place in the discussions, admitted that Aboriginal women had been overlooked in the planning of the conference.

One of the activities of the year was a South Pacific Regional Women's Conference, held in Suva at the end of October. The organisers asked that a delegation of six Aboriginal and Torres Strait Islander women should come, and grants were made to the Federal Council for the Advancement of Aborigines and Torres Strait Islanders, the National Council of Aboriginal and Islander Women, and the Australian South Sea Islanders United Council to enable them to send delegates. The Federal Council for the Advancement of Aborigines and Torres Strait Islanders chose Ruby as one of their delegates.

This was the one event of International Women's Year into which the problems of Aboriginal women seemed to fit naturally. The delegates came from Fiji, the Cook Islands, Tonga, Samoa, many other islands around the Pacific, and from Australia and New Zealand.

Poverty was the theme of the conference, and this included the struggle to obtain equitable standards of living in white-dominated situations. Poverty had been the personal experience of every woman present, but none of them from the other islands spoke of the sort of degrading poverty in which Aborigines were living in parts of Queensland, the Northern Territory and Western Australia. Ruby came away feeling that it was in affluent Australia that the worst poverty in the world existed.

In Suva she felt more personally involved not only in the discussions but also in the social occasions. She remembered with delight a visit to a Fijian village. It was the sort of excursion she loved.

They set off in a truck to drive into the mountains and, crowded into the back, they taught each other songs that they sang together. They came to a wide river and transferred into two canoes with outboard motors which raced each other downstream through beautiful bush country until they came to a little landing jetty. From here they had a long walk up a narrow mountain track with lush green forest on either side, and only bird calls and their own voices to break the silence.

As they neared the village, women and children came flocking down to meet them. The villages had a pedal radio network and news of their arrival had been sent up from the landing jetty.

The village was on the edge of a deep stream that flowed into the river below them. The children ran on ahead, leading the way to a part of the stream where the bank sloped gently into it, and they could take off their shoes and wash their feet.

In the great community hall a wonderful feast had been set out for them. Palm leaves had been laid down the full length of the room and covered with deliciously cooked chicken and fish and pineapple. The Fijian women waited on them, and the room seemed filled with light and colour and laughter and gaiety.

Ruby met the oldest man in the village and talked to him about land rights. It had been easier for the Fijians, he said, because they inherited directly from their fathers, and this was something white people had been able to understand. The land rights problem in Fiji concerned the Indians, some of whom belonged to families that had lived for three or four generations in Fiji but who, under the constitution, were not allowed to own land.

After lunch it was a Fijian custom to lie down and sleep, so the visitors did this too. Then there was more laughter and talk, and all too soon it was time to leave. Their hosts wanted them to stay and have a party at night, but the canoes were waiting for them at the river, and they had to say goodbye. The whole village came out to wave to them, and the children and young mothers came down the track with them.

As they were walking back great clouds gathered in the sky, and before they had gone far in the canoes there was a torrential downpour. They had to bail water out of the canoes all the time, and they got absolutely drenched. When they came to the place where they were to meet the trucks again, the Fijian girls went to the little local stalls and bought lengths of material. They took off their soppingly wet clothes and draped the material around themselves in a sort of sarong, so the visitors did this too. Ruby was very nervous about hers in case it fell off, but she got safely back to her motel.

It had been a day of laughter and singing such as she could never remember experiencing with white people.

Another International Women's Year activity that Ruby found worthwhile was the making of a film, *Sister, If You Only Knew* . . . It was funded through the Department of Aboriginal Affairs as a special activity for the year. It was an Aboriginal women's statement, and Adelaide was chosen as the city in which to make it because of the well-organised Council of Aboriginal Women. It is a forty-minute film, in colour, that is still available, and is still screened occasionally.

No doubt the film was carefully planned, but it gives an air of following four women quite casually as they go about their daily activities, stopping occasionally to talk with each of them. The four women were Gladys Elphick, Leila Rankine, Mary Williams and Ruby Hammond.

The film begins dramatically with two little children being taken from a poor Aboriginal home, and then Leila Rankine tells how close we are to the days when this happened. She herself was asked by a policeman if she had exemption certificates for her children.

On location for *Sister, If You Only Knew* ...

'The authorities could come and take them from you if you haven't, you know,' he said.

'Yes,' said Leila, 'they could – over my dead body.'

It is a moving film of four women, all of great ability, reaching out to make the best use of their talents.

In 1975, the year the film was made, Ruby was doing field work for the legal service and for the Council of Aboriginal Women. The film shows her helping a bewildered Aboriginal girl and taking food to men who have been sleeping in the park.

The title of the film was from an incident related by Gladys Elphick. Although she grew up on the Point Pearce Reserve, seeing herself as an Aborigine and identifying totally with the Aboriginal community, she could have passed as white if she had wished.

She was sitting on a bus one day next to an English migrant woman, to whom she was chatting.

'Do you like it here?' she asked.

'Oh yes,' said the English woman. 'We are very glad we came. England has been spoilt. There are so many black people there now.'

'I didn't make any comment,' said Aunty Glad, 'but I thought to myself, "Sister, if you only knew ...".'

As the title of the film the meaning of those words went, of course, far beyond the incident. For Ruby they seemed a good summing up for the whole of International Women's Year. She had met so many middle-class women, almost all of whom had been sympathetic and friendly, but it had been beyond Ruby's powers to reach them with the whole Aboriginal situation. Again and again she would think, 'Sister, if you only knew ...' But how could she tell them?

She was aware of irony in the fact that the Aborigines who were most able to speak articulately of the plight of their people, the ones who could most easily reach the authorities who might help, were the ones who were least in need.

In the north of Australia there were people living in shanties and huts for whom the cry of 'land rights' was a begging for alms, but it was not their voices which the people of Australia heard. How could people like Ruby Hammond speak for the desperately poor?

Talking to some women during International Women's Year she spoke of Nancy Young, thinking that this would remind them of the dreadful conditions in which some Aborigines lived.

Nancy Young! Who was she?

Only six years earlier Nancy Young had been charged with manslaughter on grounds of alleged failure to provide her infant daughter with adequate food or medical attention.[1] Her conviction by the Queensland Supreme Court was followed by protests from a meeting at the Sydney University Law School. A few months later there was a documentary about the case on the ABC television program, *Four Corners*. The Public Defender in Queensland found grounds for re-opening the case, and the conviction was quashed.

The documentary, entitled 'Out of Sight, Out of Mind', was screened on 30 August 1969, and for a little while thousands of Australians felt appalled that the conditions revealed to them, and events that had taken place, could be a part of the Australian scene. Very little was done about it, and by 1975 no one could remember it.

Nancy Young lived on the Cunnamulla Reserve in Queensland, close to the town sewerage outlet, crowded into one of eighteen corrugated iron shacks, ten feet by fifteen feet, with three other adults and ten children. She was striving to live on $6 a week, which was her income from child endowment and a little part-time waitressing.

In July 1968, her four-and-a-half-month-old daughter died in the Cunnamulla hospital. Four months later, when another of her children fell ill, she was charged with manslaughter.

Chief witness for the prosecution was the doctor from the hospital where Nancy had taken her desperately ill baby. Chief witness for the defence was Dr Archivides Kalogerinis, medical superintendent of the District Hospital at Collarenebri in New South Wales. Since 1957 he had been carrying out research with Aboriginal children that indicated that, because of the inadequate diet of their mothers, some Aboriginal children were born with an inbuilt vitamin C deficiency which, if not remedied, led to scurvy, severe weight loss, dehydration and death. He argued that the failure of the hospital to administer or recommend vitamin C, and Nancy's inability to buy fresh fruit at the inflated Cunnamulla prices, made the onset of scurvy inevitable.

Nancy lived with another Aborigine, Walter Turnbull, who was made to testify against her on the grounds that they were not legally married, although he doggedly referred to her throughout the trial as his wife. Nancy's counsel decided not to put her in the witness box because of the tendency of uneducated Aboriginal defendants to say what they believed 'authority figures' expected from them. The judge told the all-white, all-male jury that 'it is legitimate for you to take this failure into account as a consideration which makes it less unsafe to infer guilt than it otherwise would have been'.

The jury did as the judge appeared to expect of them, and found Nancy guilty of manslaughter.

On the evening of the verdict the ABC news program, *This Day Tonight*, screened a ten-minute account that had been prepared by one of Australia's most perceptive television reporters, the late Frank Bennett.

A public outcry sparked off by this report led to the much longer *Four Corners* documentary. This revealed the abject squalor of the reserve where Nancy Young lived, and exposed the town's racism in a series of interviews. It concluded with a table of Aboriginal infant mortality superimposed on a close-up of the child's grave, edged with toys. The table showed that the Aboriginal figure of 296 deaths per 1000 births was the highest in the world.

Nancy Young's case was dreadful evidence of white society's tendency to accuse Aboriginal mothers of neglecting their children. Care of children is a deeply inbred Aboriginal characteristic, and where Aboriginal parents were failing they were desperately in need of help.

The work of Dr Kalogerinis in revealing the complex consequences of protein deficiencies and other malnutrition among Aborigines was carried out in the face of incredible difficulties. He stuck to his findings, and by 1977 they were recognised and accepted.

It was for people like Nancy Young and her children that Ruby Hammond was pleading. It was for children dying of malnutrition, or growing up with physical or mental handicaps because of protein and other deficiencies; for people living in Australia in shacks made of rusting galvanised iron; for men and women, homeless and hungry because no one helped them to get the social benefits to which they were entitled; for children whose parents did not know how to help them accept the education that was available; for young men and women, who, having struggled to get education, were not even considered for employment because they were Aborigines; for people living in Australian cities below the poverty line.

What Ruby Hammond was asking for these people was 'land rights'. This phrase for her meant four things – the return of all remaining traditional land, preservation of Aboriginal sacred sites, land for groups in the outback in economically strong enough areas for them to be self supporting, and social and economic equality with the non-Aboriginal community.

This last demand meant standards of health, housing, education and employment equal to that of working-class Australians. Ruby was aware that it would cost the taxpayer money, but the taxpayer, who derived his wealth from the land that was taken from the Aborigines, surely owed no less than this to their descendants. Australia was one of the wealthiest nations in the world. It was not lack of money that stopped the raising of Aboriginal standards of living – it was lack of will, lack of goodwill. What needed to be done?

There was no simple answer to this question, and no one person who could give the whole of the complex answer. It was all handicapped by the fact that the ultimate answer needed to be found by the Aboriginal people themselves, and that for 200 years they had been encouraged to believe that society would impose on them whatever the government thought best, and that no one was interested in their views.

Now, suddenly, the government was asking for their views, and they were not yet ready to give them. On the other hand some of the problems were so desperate that something needed to be done at once.

Ruby did not offer her ideas as anything more than the thinking of a concerned Aborigine, contributing them to the pool of ideas from which the answer would come.

She believed that health was the most fundamental of all the Aboriginal needs. It had been the first casualty for Aborigines after the coming of the Europeans. They brought diseases to which the Aborigines had little resistance, and at the same time they took the land which gave the Aborigines their food, and their water, reducing them to abject poverty and malnutrition, and leaving them vulnerable to diseases of poverty no longer seen in the white population.

Action was desperately needed and Ruby saw with relief what she believed was the beginning of Aboriginal medical services, but it was not enough and it was not good enough.

When she spoke at meetings she advocated prenatal and post-natal care for Aboriginal mothers, and care for the many women with serious infections, especially eye, ear and chest infections. Each Aboriginal community, she said, should be helped to establish its own Aboriginal medical service.

Ruby considered health to be an area in which the

government failed to see the need to involve Aboriginal people. She was constantly urging training of Aborigines as doctors and as fully-trained nurses.

There were many health areas where help for Aboriginal people was needed, and health programs were being launched, but Ruby feared they would not succeed unless Aborigines themselves understood the programs and were able to introduce them into their own social structures. This was not a problem that government departments appeared to understand.

In the cities there was need for health clinics run by Aborigines and staffed by people of their own choosing. In the 1960s Gladys Elphick had been campaigning for clinics of this type. She and Ruby both believed it was of great importance for Aborigines to be able to bring their problems to other Aborigines, to people who knew what it was like to be 'put down' constantly because their skins were dark, to go to school from a household in which even the concept of education was not understood. They needed people who knew how frustration, lack of opportunity, and lack of work drove so many of them to seek the oblivion of alcohol; who knew how loneliness and lack of skill could make them bewildered in the jobs they did get, so that many of them walked away from them. They needed people who knew these things, not from hearsay, but because they had experienced them, or seen them first hand. It was as though most people lived on a platform onto which Aborigines had to struggle to climb before they could even begin to compete. They did not want decisions about their lives made by people who at best only dimly perceived their struggle.

Gladys Elphick started a medical clinic at the Aboriginal Community Centre at 128 Wakefield Street in October 1976. A doctor came two days a week, and the centre ran a pick-up service for people who found it difficult to get into the city. They had 539 patients in their first nine months, but Gladys dreamt of a much bigger, more efficient clinic. She wanted to see Aborigines themselves developing it, and feared that too much government assistance would swamp the direct efforts of the Aboriginal people.

She made an appeal on a radio program for $800 for the centre to buy an electro-cardiograph. The money came in within two weeks. Aunty Glad loved to work in that sort of way.

The community centre functioned from a very crowded single room upstairs at 128 Wakefield Street, above the legal office. Ruby would have liked it to have developed with a whole building to itself. It needed a coffee shop, a quiet reading room, and a bigger room with facilities for billiards and table tennis. She wanted it to be run in conjunction with a hostel for people from the country. But above all, the centre needed to be run by people like Aunty Glad who so completely understood the Aboriginal people.

Housing was the need that Ruby placed second on her list. The shortage of housing for Aborigines was so acute that it eroded their health and their living standards, and their educational and employment opportunities.

A report issued by the Aboriginal Housing Board of South Australia in August 1977 said it was not unusual for a whole family to occupy one room or a garage at someone else's house. The board had 525 applicants on its books, with more than 380 families living with other families. If the South Australian Housing Trust had enforced tenancy agreements that said only the tenant and his immediate family could occupy funded homes, the majority of the board's applicants would have been homeless or forced to live in makeshift accommodation.

Twenty per cent of their applicants had no permanent address, and were constantly moving from area to area, with disastrous effects on the lives and education of the children. Even those who had homes were often not living at the standard of the average wage-earning Australian.

Ruby believed that a fundamental part of 'land rights' was a real opportunity for every Aboriginal family to own a furnished house of the average standard of wage-earning Australians. It was not good enough just to provide houses they could rent. One solution could have been subsidies and long-term interest-free loans, with the understanding by Aborigines and non-Aborigines alike that these were not 'hand-outs' but repayment of a long overdue debt. When people received payment for land they sold it was not seen as a 'hand-out', and it should not be considered a 'hand-out' if Aborigines received belated payment for the land that had been taken from them.

Most Aboriginal people came to the cities from reserves or other Crown land where they had no individual equity in the houses in which they were living. South Australia was vesting reserve lands in a trust for the Aboriginal people. Ruby thought that this was good, but not if it was at the expense of the individual families who moved to the cities to find education and employment for their children. These families left their homes behind them, getting nothing for them. To Ruby it was as though they were being robbed for the second time.

She urged that in the outback and reserve areas the housing should be based on what the Aboriginal people wanted as a group, and real attempts made to find out what this was. One attempt to do this had already been made. Between 1971 and 1974 the Rev J.H. (Jim) Downing discussed with Aboriginal people on reserves the sort of housing settlements they would like. He had noticed that traditional camp layouts catered for extended family and totemic groupings. This was totally ignored in the European suburban-type layouts that were being given to them, and which often caused community fragmentation and breakdown.

Talking to Aboriginal people he discovered that the groupings of their camps were related to 'dreamings' or totemic groups that preserved the spatial relationships of the members of the group. The layout was, in fact, a reminder to the people of their law, and the whole proper order of things.

It took Jim Downing a long time to persuade Aboriginal people to talk, or even to think, about what they really wanted in the way of new housing. They assumed that houses provided for them would be in gridiron rows, side by side. The idea of the government asking to know what they really wanted was difficult for them to grasp.

Over a period of three years he persuaded ten groups each to produce their own layout. Each one is startlingly different from the others. The Fregon people who belonged to the dingo dreaming had a plan in the shape of a dog's paw, with groups of houses in the positions of the four toes, the clinic and school in the pad, and service buildings in the foreleg. The Indulla people produced a plan based on the tracks of the kangaroo. The Papunya people, who belonged to the honey-ant dreaming, made an imaginative design based on concentric circles. It took Jim Downing a long time to convince them that the government really would set their houses up in that way.

Ruby Hammond regarded his approach as a model for all dealings with Aboriginal people.

The ten plans that the Aboriginal communities prepared for Jim Downing were published in a booklet entitled *Aboriginal 'Dreamings' and Town Plans*.[2] Ruby would have liked it to have been a text for study in Australian schools. When it came to education she believed that educating the white community was more important than educating the Aborigines. She wanted a course of Aboriginal history culture and art to be an integral part of the state education system, a subject to be included in every year from preschool to matriculation.

The Woodward Report suggested that historical documents could be used as part of such a course and, in a ten-page appendix, set out extracts that could form a basis for 'the story behind the bald facts'.

The course could be designed to be of value to Aborigines as well as other Australians. Some Aborigines were looking for re-education in their Aboriginality. These people could be helped to go back for short periods to the reserves. If they wanted to stay for longer periods there was work they could do, and they could stay on, learning and at the same time giving of their own experience.

Special education for Aboriginal children could be provided wherever it was needed, and carried on for as long as it was needed. Grants and scholarships which were already available could be brought into the reach of every Aboriginal child.

Financial aid to help Aboriginal children stay at school was the only social welfare benefit in which Aborigines had an advantage over non-Aboriginal Australians. Other people who knew about it sometimes complained.

'I don't mind them having equality,' they said, 'but why should they have special advantages?'

Ruby saw this sort of protest as being like people racing with someone who had broken a leg and protesting because he was allowed to use a crutch.

Teachers at primary schools should be encouraged to give special help to promising Aboriginal pupils. Ruby knew that already there were many teachers who did this, but they did it on their own initiative, and not because it was the laid-down policy of the Education Department.

The Aboriginal Community College in Adelaide aimed to

give further education to people who had left school without acquiring the skills and knowledge they afterwards found they needed. People of all ages came to improve their language and number skills, study arts and crafts, and acquire technical training. The staff was understanding of the many problems that brought adults back to a school of this sort, and they gave real consideration to the needs and aspirations of the students, encouraging them to share in the decisions that had to be made.

In the 1990s the college continues very much along the same lines. Michael Gray, for many years the curriculum services manager, says that very little has changed for young Aborigines.

'Main stream systems are orientated to majority culture and do not meet the needs of minority groups,' he says. 'The college tries to help the students into main stream education while preserving great respect for their Aboriginality. Our programs are more academic than they were in the 1970s, and we have a strong continuing need to respect their basic holistic philosophy and to appreciate their history, both their recent history and their long links to their Dreaming.'

He believes there is still a great deal of latent racism in the community and a very real need for the college.

The Davenport centre at Port Augusta ran on lines very similar to the Aboriginal Community College, and there was another centre at Coober Pedy. Workshops had been organised at Ceduna and Koonibba, and a mobile teaching unit travelled to centres in the north-west of the state.

These were the sort of activities Ruby wanted to see extended, but it was feared that funds for these projects would be less in 1978 than they had been in 1977. They were the sort of schemes that needed unrestricted support. Ruby could see there was almost no end to the things such centres could teach. Aborigines were often bewildered by government documents, and such things as hire purchase agreements, tenancy agreements, Medibank, and even price lists.

During the 1977 state elections Ruby was helping at Nepabunna Reserve, where many Aborigines were voting for the first time.

'What will happen when I get inside?' she was asked again and again.

Adults and children should all be able to learn about things like this, Ruby said. It should not be left to political party campaigners. They should be learning about their civic rights, their social service entitlements, and their legal rights.

Statistics relating to education in the 1970s revealed the urgent need for help to be given. One in every 120 white Australians was at university. Only one in every 5000 Aborigines was at a university or tertiary college, and not all of them were doing recognised degree courses. Only two per cent of Aborigines attended secondary school. Of these, more would have matriculated if they had not felt that their Aboriginality would bar them from the sort of work for which they would be qualified.

These figures, poor as they were, showed some sort of improvement. A survey carried out by Fay Gale and Alison Brookman in the late 1960s revealed not one Aborigine over the age of forty-five with any secondary education.

After 1971 there were courses in Adelaide to train Aborigines as teacher aides. The first scheme was for aides in Aboriginal schools, and later a second one was started for aides in metropolitan and country schools. These courses were proving successful but, like all Aboriginal welfare schemes, they were not extensive enough to meet needs. In 1978 the South Australian Education Department introduced teacher training for Aborigines at the Torrens College of Advanced Education.

Ruby welcomed all these developments, and hoped they

would be the beginning of a rapidly accelerating education scheme. She was grateful for the growing awareness of basic Aboriginal needs that she found in people dealing with Aborigines, especially in some government departments, but realised that there was still a long way to go.

Social workers needed special training if they were to work among Aborigines. Many of them came from good homes and expensive schools. Poverty was another country, and they had no idea of its customs, its hardships, or even its language. They saw things from a different point of view, from a basis of different values, and often, it seemed to Ruby, their training had not taught them much more than how to write reports. There was a great need for more Aboriginal social workers.

There was a need too for properly staffed community hostels, and small hostels for Aborigines on remand, and for Aboriginal boys who ought not to be at the McNally Training Centre, and would be better cared for in an ordinary home where just a few boys could be looked after by a married couple.

There was a need for 'training farms' where skills could be taught to Aborigines who had been brought down to Adelaide from reserves and country centres, and found guilty of relatively minor offences.

If the worst of their health, education, housing, and welfare problems could be solved, Aborigines would be a long way towards solving their unemployment problems. One inhibiting factor remained, and this brought their plight back full circle, for this factor was discrimination, which even in 1995 underlies all their problems.

Since 1975 when the Commonwealth Racial Discrimination Act came into force, it has been an offence to deny anyone a job on grounds of race, but this is a charge which is difficult to prove, and discriminations of the past have left many Aborigines lacking the confidence to seek jobs for which they are qualified.

A report of a survey carried out in 1976 by Aboriginal Hostels Ltd indicated that about half of the Aboriginal workforce of 35,000 was unemployed. Because they were unemployed they were poor, because they were poor they were shabby and discouraged, and this exposed them to further discrimination.

How could this cycle be broken? A suggestion came from Dr C.H. Coombs.

With his long concern for Aboriginal people Dr Coombs was disappointed at how little had been achieved since the referendum. He had seen the huge Yes vote as a direction to the commonwealth government to accept responsibility for legislating for Aboriginal Australians, and to over-ride state laws that put them at a disadvantage.

In January 1972, already nearly five years beyond the referendum, the prime minister, William McMahon, made the first detailed statement of the Liberal Party's Aboriginal Policy. It revealed what some people saw as a failure to grasp the fact that social welfare policies that may not last beyond the next election were not the rights that Aborigines were seeking. State laws were not mentioned.

The Labor Party came to power in December 1972, and Aborigines hoped for better times with the Office of Aboriginal Affairs elevated to a department, the establishment of the National Aboriginal Conference, and the setting up of a commission headed by Mr Justice A.E. Woodward to investigate the restoration of rights to land to the Aboriginal people. But alas! After a time of political turmoil and an election in December 1975 the Liberals were back in power with Malcolm Fraser as prime minister. Dismantling the bill based on the Woodward Report was one of their first actions.

It was the old 'political football' syndrome, and the

Aboriginal people were beginning to think their hopes were doomed.

In 1975 the Queensland government had rushed through a bill allowing an agreement with a multinational consortium of mining companies to exploit a very large bauxite deposit at the Aurukun and Mitchell rivers. The Arukun Aborigines appealed against the agreement, taking it right up to the Privy Council, but they did not win their case. The people turned to the commonwealth government.

'The commonwealth has a constitutional obligation to Aboriginals. We will not fail them,' said Prime Minister Fraser. However, the Queensland government changed the status of the land to local government shires whose councils were virtually appointed by and directed by Queensland officials.

Dr Coombs could see what had become painfully clear to the Aborigines – that the commonwealth government could be held to its referendum mandate only if it was bound by some irrevocable instrument.

The idea of a treaty came, as solutions to Aboriginal problems often did, from an Aboriginal action.

Back in March 1972 the Larrakia tribe of the Gwalwa Daranki people had sent a petition to the McMahon government. Their land had originally covered the area now occupied by Darwin, and they were far from happy at the way it had been taken from them.

They asked the government to appoint a commission to 'go around to every tribe and work out a treaty to suit each tribe'. If the treaty was acceptable 'then all the tribe shall sign it and make it good for all time'.

It took Mr McMahon more than a year to frame a reply, and then he said it was not appropriate to negotiate with British subjects as though they were foreign powers.

Princess Margaret was to visit Australia in October 1972. Undeterred, the Larrakia people drew up a petition to be presented to her. On 20 October they took it to Government House. A police barrier prevented them from entering and the petition was torn. They sent it to the Queen with an apology for its condition. The *Northern Territory News*, 21 December 1972, reported that it had been returned to the governor general, who had sent it to the commonwealth government. No more was heard of the petition but Dr Coombs was impressed by its possibilities.

He was aware that governments will make changes only if they are what the electorate wants. If a treaty was to be made, it was up to the non-Aboriginal people to seek it.

Among those with whom he talked of his idea was Stewart Harris, who was well known in Canberra as the correspondent of *The Times* of London. In May 1977 Harris was a speaker on the ABC *Guest of Honour* program, and he spoke at length of this suggestion for a treaty.

It would be a treaty of commitment with the Aboriginal people which all major political parties should sign, he said. The treaty should agree to devote one per cent of every federal budget to Aboriginal recovery, with the money being spent by a mixed commission of Aboriginal and government representatives.

A second provision of the treaty would direct to Aboriginal recovery a fixed proportion of all annual royalties on mining, hunting, fishing and forestry throughout Australia, not just on Aboriginal land. This would acknowledge that Aborigines had a prior interest in the whole of Australia, and that the land was the spiritual source of Aboriginal welfare and happiness.

Annual royalties totalled about $180 million at that time. The Aboriginal share could be fixed at say, forty per cent, which would given them $72 million. This sum would be spent entirely at the discretion of Aboriginal representatives, and would reflect Aboriginal priorities and values.

Such a treaty would run initially for twenty years and could then be re-negotiated like most other treaties.

There was an encouraging response to this broadcast. Church groups and human rights organisations responded with enthusiasm and letters came from individuals. A group decided to form an Aboriginal Treaty Committee. Stewart Harris became the first chairman and the other members were Dr Coombs, Judith Wright, Professor C.W. Rowley, and Professor W.E.H. Stanner. They made no attempt to include Aborigines as they saw their role to be educating non-Aborigines and marshalling their support.

The campaign was publicly launched by Dr Coombs in another *Guest of Honour* program on 2 June 1979. At the same time the National Aboriginal Council was asking for a Makarrata, an Aboriginal word used in Arnhem Land, meaning an end of a dispute. They had prepared a position paper referred to as the 'twenty-four demands'. Senator Chaney, then Minister for Aboriginal Affairs, provided funding that enabled the council to discuss the paper with Aborigines around Australia.

Aboriginal opinion was divided. Many of them distrusted what seemed to them to be an over-complex suggestion, and they were especially wary of ideas fostered by a committee in which Aborigines had no say.

Ruby had mixed feelings about it. She wanted to be sure that 'spent entirely at the discretion of Aboriginal representatives' meant real responsibility for spending the money and not, as it so often seemed to be, a case of giving advice that need not be taken.

She was heartened by the thought that a treaty needed the signatures of both parties. If it would really make the responsibilities of the referendum binding on the commonwealth government, such a treaty would go a long way towards bringing about the longed-for day when Aborigines would have a dominant say in their own destiny.

This would not happen without tremendous goodwill on the part of all Australians and, since goodwill is dependent upon understanding, the greatest single need of Aboriginal Australians was for Australia as a whole to understand their problems, and the 200 years of history that had created them. The goodwill was basically there.

Ruby thought back to the 1967 referendum when ninety-one per cent of the people had voted Yes for Aborigines. Perhaps there could be a referendum for the treaty. She could hardly restrain herself from beginning to plan the campaign. She remembered the circular 'Vote Yes' stickers they'd had in 1967. Perhaps this time they could have yellow ones, edged half in red for the land, half in black for the people, so that the stickers would evoke the sun, the symbol of life from their flag.

The campaign would be a wonderful opportunity to tell the people of Australia of their hopes and aspirations, to urge them once again to 'Vote Yes, Vote Yes for Aborigines'.

THIRTEEN

NEW TASKS, NEW STRENGTHS

for the same
aim, the same
struggle

THE DREAM OF A MAKARRATA THAT WOULD BRING JUSTICE to the Aborigines was not about to come true. Towards the end of 1982 support for a treaty was waning, and in February 1984 the committee disbanded.

Long before this Ruby had seen that the idea was unrealistic. If there was to be a meaningful reconciliation between the indigenous people and the newcomers there would need to be a radical change in thinking throughout Australia.

She knew that many Aboriginal people thought the treaty suggestion was all too hurried; that a treaty of mutual understanding would need a deeply considered input from them. Non-Aboriginal Australians would have to come at last to an awareness of the complex social order, the laws, the religion, the social structure, and the deep feeling for the land itself, which was Aboriginal culture in 1788. The invaders had not noticed any of this. They must acknowledge it for any type of covenant to succeed.

The 1967 referendum had left Ruby believing that

unquestioned equality for everyone was near-at-hand, but now this hope began to fade into a distant future.

The Pitjantjatjara and Yankuntjara people in the north-west of South Australia were campaigning for land rights, and this seemed to her a more worthwhile effort than the Makarrata. She threw herself into supporting it.

Pastoral leases and mining licences were increasingly sought by the settlers, and land rights were becoming more and more important to Aboriginal groups. Support was slowly coming from the wider community, especially from churches, unions and students. There was sympathy within the Labor Party with Don Dunstan advocating racial justice and equality. When they won government in 1965 he became Minister of Aboriginal Affairs. He began immediately to prepare the first land rights legislation in Australia – the Aboriginal Lands Trust Act (SA) proclaimed in December 1966. The act set up a trust that enabled Aborigines to obtain specific titles to reserves. This provided some land tenure for Aborigines in the south of the state.

The Pitjantjatjara and Yankuntjara people had occupied vast tracts of land in the far north-west and never doubted it was theirs until the 1960s and 1970s.

Don Dunstan became ill and retired in 1979, and the Labor Party lost an election held a few months later. The new government's election promises had included support for Pitjantjatjara land rights but it soon became clear that this would not protect their land from mineral exploration licences.

An Aboriginal Land Rights Support Group was set up in Adelaide to help the people put their claims to the new government. Ruby joined this group and was involved in the planning of a meeting of the Pitjantjatjara people with the new premier, David Tonkin. Buses and cars were hired to bring about 130 of them to Adelaide, and permission obtained for them to camp on the Victoria Park race course. Ruby was involved in arranging tents and cooking equipment, but her most significant help was in opening up her office to them, allowing them to use the telephone and photocopying machines, to receive messages and mail, and to make tea and have meetings there.

Sympathetic media coverage was helpful, and Aboriginal representatives were able to put their case to the government and also to the people. From the Aborigines' point of view the whole venture was a success.

Opposition continued from mining and pastoral interests, but serious consideration was given to the claims of the Aborigines and finally in March 1981 the Pitjantjatjara Land Rights Bill was passed, not pleasing everyone, but offering the Aborigines a compromise they were willing to accept.

In the following November about 1500 people gathered at Itjinpiri Creek, just north of Ernabella, to witness the handing over by David Tonkin of an inalienable freehold title to 102,360 square kilometres of land to the Pitjantjatjara and Yankunytjatjara people.

Ruby was delighted and felt that it was an example of what could be achieved by a positive but non-aggressive campaign.

The Department of Aboriginal Affairs (DAA) had not been pleased with Ruby's involvement in this episode. They told the ALRM executive that campaigning for land rights was not what the grant to the Aboriginal Legal Rights Movement was for, and that Ruby had misused the funds.

Ruby strenuously denied this. She saw her work for the Pitjantjatjara people as valid work for the Aboriginal Legal Rights Movement. Land rights were always legal rights as far as she was concerned.

A non-Aboriginal friend went to see the director of the DAA on Ruby's behalf. Surely this was a misunderstanding that could be put right by talking the position over with Ruby.

Perhaps, said the director, if this were the only problem. Regrettably Ruby had some 'unfortunate friends' who were giving her advice that was unacceptable to the department.

Her friend took this to refer to Ruby's membership of the Socialist Party. Nothing was said about this or about Ruby's visits to China and the Soviet Union, but Ruby's friend was aware of it all. She felt somehow that the word 'socialist' hung in the air and that the department related it to the Pitjantjatjara land rights campaign. The director did not mention it, and neither did she. She did not know how best to help Ruby, and she allowed herself to be shown politely to the door.

Premier David Tonkin handing over the title to the Pitjantjatjara lands to elders, Jimmy Tjutapai and Punch Thompson, on 18 November 1981. (*Advertiser*)

The executive of the legal service was divided on the issue, but the majority did not support Ruby. They felt that she had acted too independently, had failed to consult the executive, and that while they were funded by the department they must follow the department's directions.

She was told to resign or be dismissed and given fifteen minutes to leave the office.

Ruby left in a defiant mood, believing passionately that land rights should be a part of Aboriginal legal commitment, and that what she had done was correct. She set about suing the executive.

She consulted a solicitor and a Supreme Court writ was issued alleging breach of contract and unfair dismissal. After seven months the matter was settled out of court. The executive agreed to re-employ Ruby. She returned to work, but she saw her position as untenable and immediately resigned.

Suing the executive had brought her widespread disapproval within the Aboriginal community, but she felt that her stand had been right, that the executive was in the wrong, and that it was becoming a group of government lackeys who allowed themselves to be manipulated through control of their funding.

Obviously no Aboriginal group dependent on government grants was going to employ her. She looked about for another job. It was 1981 and the YWCA was looking for a project development officer. Five years after International Women's Year, Adelaide was moving only slowly from the social patterns that required married women, particularly those with children, to devote themselves wholly to their domestic responsibilities.

In this situation many women felt isolated, diminished by loss of status and income, lonely and bored. 'Only a housewife', the lowest rung of the female status ladder, was their designation. The YWCA was developing programs to help these women with activities that would raise their self-esteem, bring them new friendships, and prepare them for re-entry into the workforce.

Gene Wenham, publicity officer of the YWCA, had been president of the South Australian International Women's Year Committee. She knew Ruby as a lively, energetic committee member, and was delighted when she applied for the job.

Ruby was as non-racist as it is possible to be. People were people as far as she was concerned, and Gene was sure she would work well with everyone, including not only young Aboriginal women, with whom the YWCA was trying to make better contact, but also with the growing population of migrant women. She welcomed Ruby onto the staff with high hopes. Ruby too had high hopes.

Unfortunately neither Gene nor Ruby realised how stressful the ending of her job with the Aboriginal Legal Rights Movement had been. Ruby was still depressed, and as the year wore on she realised more and more that Aboriginal people were the ones she wanted to help. She saw them as more in need and more deserving than the women who came to the YWCA.

She was able to help with an Aboriginal Youth program, but it did not seem to reach the needs of Aboriginal women to the same degree as the work she had done with the Women's Council, or the legal service. Sadly, towards the end of 1982, she told Gene she could no longer continue.

Gene, who had become increasingly aware of Ruby's problems, talked with her sympathetically, and was one of the first people to put to her the idea of more formal qualifications.

A friend on the staff of the South Australian Institute of Technology told Ruby about the Task Force that was seeking to bring tertiary education to Aboriginal students in terms of their culture and history, and of their present needs. He too urged her on to further studies.

Ruby looked into it and found with pleasure that what the Task Force offered was very different from the Diploma in Business Administration that she had resisted in 1974. At that time the first beginnings of Aboriginal studies in Australia had been coming into place in Adelaide, but there was nothing then appropriate for Ruby's work in the legal service.

She had not heard of A.M. (Max) Hart, an Adelaide teacher who had served for some years with the Christian Missionary Society in Uganda and Kenya. He came back to Adelaide in the 1960s and tried to persuade the Western Teachers' College to adopt a unit of Aboriginal studies. He was told there was no place for anything of that sort in a tertiary institution. One senior official said to him, 'We would be the laughing stock of Australia.'

Max Hart persisted and in 1968 he gained approval to teach Aboriginal studies, the first time ever that such a subject was in the syllabus of an Australian teachers' college. The first students were mainly non-Aboriginal. They were people working with Aboriginal organisations, teachers, and others with a general interest in Aboriginal culture.

It proved to be a good time for such a course. Increasing attention was being given to the special needs of Aboriginal education, and Aborigines were being encouraged to train as teachers.

The Western Teachers' College was to become part of the Torrens College of Advanced Education, which later merged with the Institute of Technology to become the University of South Australia. Here, in January 1992, Australia's first university faculty of Aboriginal and Islander Studies was announced. Max Hart's persistence brought a brilliant result.

This was after Ruby had graduated, but by 1983 there was already a golden opportunity for her.

The Task Force had been set up in 1973. A new federal government had been elected with Gough Whitlam as prime minister. Commitment to the Aboriginal people had been a strong part of his election platform.

Within a few months he had introduced a self-determination policy for Aborigines, the first time self-determination had been acknowledged at so high a level. He also established a new Department of Aboriginal Affairs which introduced programs in education, health, legal aid, medical care, and housing, based on consultation with Aborigines. The Task Force was developed as part of these plans.

The Task Force was designed to train a group of Aborigines to work in the area of social welfare. Initially it was intended to operate for only two years but it was so successful it was decided to continue with it. Its growth and development were spectacular.

In 1969 the Aboriginal Study Grants Scheme (ABSTUDY) was introduced by the first Minister of Aboriginal Affairs, William Wentworth, to help Aboriginal students to undertake post-secondary studies. Very few Aborigines were enrolled in universities, and the grants were used mostly for apprenticeships and job-training programs.

However, by the early 1980s there were eighteen Aborigines throughout Australia known to be taking tertiary courses, and some had already graduated. Charles Perkins with a BA from Sydney University was, in 1966, the first Aborigine ever to graduate, followed two years later by Eric Willmot with a science degree from Newcastle University. In Adelaide John Moriarty and Ken Wanganeen graduated in 1970 and 1972 from Flinders University. There were no tertiary Aboriginal studies in those days, and their degrees were based on European university courses.

The Aboriginal graduates were a triumphant vindication of the determination and ability of Aborigines to demonstrate their equality, and to strive for justice. These four men had all been streamed into non-academic courses at school, each of them was the only Aborigine in his course, and the subjects available to them were not only unrelated to them but gave a gross distortion of their history and their worth. By 1973 a better scheme was long overdue.

The idea for the Task Force came from the South Australian Department of Community Welfare. One of their employees had returned from the United States where a similar program was in place for North American Indians.

The DAA was eager for it to develop in Australia and sought help from the South Australian Institute of Technology, which responded generously. A scheme was drawn up to improve access to tertiary education for Aboriginal students, to provide a supportive enclave for them, and to conduct areas of course work. By 1982 the preliminary plans had been made. The then director, Professor Eric Mills, presented the idea to the council, and it became a part of the institute.

The program had been originally designed to train a group of Aborigines to work in the area of social welfare, and to this end the institute co-opted Mary Ann Bin-Sallik, the first Aborigine to graduate as a nursing sister from Darwin Hospital. In 1975 she was the first Aborigine employed in higher education anywhere in Australia.

In her spare time she studied for an Associate Diploma in Social Work, and the quality of the papers she submitted for this, and of her practical work, won her a scholarship to Harvard University as a high achiever. Although she did not have a BA she was admitted to study first for a Masters Degree and then for a PhD. She graduated in 1990 as a Master of Education Administration and with a Doctorate in Education.

It was she who co-ordinated the Task Force to develop in four stages, in the last of which the Institute of Technology accepted full responsibility for it, incorporating it into its formal structure as the School of Aboriginal and Islander Administration. These developments were still in their early stages in 1982 but Ruby was excited by the promise of it all. She passed the mature age entry tests, qualified for a grant and enrolled to study for a Bachelor of Arts in Aboriginal Affairs Administration.

The next three years were a healing period for her. Once again she felt she was working well, and the work she was doing was related to the Aboriginal future she dreamed of.

Mary Ann was Student Counsellor for the whole period in which Ruby was an undergraduate. She guided her and the other students through what was a new environment for them. Ruby developed a high regard and a warm affection for her.

Ruby completed her course in the minimum time of three years. She graduated in 1985, having majored in Public Administration, Ethnology and Anthropology. It was a happy time in which she made lasting friendships with other students and the staff.

She made a valuable friendship on her first day. The students were urged to talk with someone they had not met before, and Ruby and Helen Liddle seemed to be drawn to each other across the room. Perhaps it was because they were both older than most of the students, but they felt that there was a mysterious element about it – that it was meant to be. They became very close friends and Ruby asked Helen to go with her to New Zealand on the last major assignment she undertook.

Helen is among the legion of women who have felt strengthened and enriched by Ruby.

'She cast a spell over me,' Helen says. She likes to recall a day when they came back from college at about five in the afternoon, both wearing casual clothes, and while Ruby had a way of lending style to whatever she wore, Helen felt she did nothing for the jeans and T-shirt and canvas shoes she was wearing.

Ruby suddenly remembered that the students had been invited to a Government House cocktail party.

'We can't go like this,' said Helen, 'there isn't time to go home and change. We won't be able to go.'

'Of course we can,' said Ruby. 'There will be a powder room where we can do our hair and put some make-up on. Come on.'

Helen remembers she went in very timidly, but she soon forgot what she was wearing and had a wonderful time. Afterwards Ruby said to her, 'Never say you can't go anywhere unless you've been told that you can't, and even then make sure you get a good reason.'

'Ruby offered so much of that sort of strength,' says Helen, 'and it stays with you.'

For Dr Olga Gostin, a senior lecturer, Ruby was a memorable student with special abilities. 'It became a two-way thing between us,' she says. 'While I had academic skills to pass on she had subtle knowledge and wisdom which she would share with great delicacy.'

There was still much to be learnt about Aboriginal studies. 'The School has since devised a code of ethical behaviour,' says Dr Gostin, 'and Ruby made a significant contribution. She was there at the beginning, and she had a grassroots understanding of what was needed.'

Ruby's graduation day was truly a great occasion for her. She was one of the two first degree course graduates, and she was chosen as a speaker at the ceremony. The occasional address was delivered by Eric Wilmott, the first Aboriginal professor in Australia. He had begun his working life as a drover on an outback cattle station, and by his own interests and abilities had gained a BSc. He was then a professor at James Cook University.

Ruby's one regret was that Mary Ann was not there in the PhD robes Ruby knew she would earn. She had just left for the United States. In 1990, when she returned as Dr Bin-Sallik, she became head of the Aboriginal Studies and Teacher Education Centre of the Underdale campus of the University of South Australia.

Ruby missed her on graduation day, but she knew she was at a distinguished gathering, and that Aboriginal equality was dazzlingly there for everyone to see.

She would not have been surprised to learn that equality would take time to filter through to the Australian community as a whole. She was used to that sort of delay, but she knew beyond doubt that it was there and that it would be seen. For herself she was now one of the small group of Aborigines with tertiary degrees. Government departments would open their doors to her once again.

By January 1985, before her graduation, she was Aboriginal Project Development Officer in the Equal Opportunity Branch of what was then the Department of Personnel and Industrial Relations (now the Department of Labor and Administrative Services).

'In her four years with this unit she made a great impact on the public service,' says Joan Russell, who was manager of the branch. 'She had a strong personal style which impressed all of us who worked with her. We were very proud of her.'

She remembers Ruby coming into the Equal Opportunity office on her graduation day, wearing her cap and gown and with long ribbons in black, red and yellow to emphasise her Aboriginality.

'She was full of confidence and pride that made her second to no one,' Joan says, 'and in small ways too she never let us forget she was an Aborigine. I remember reproving her on one occasion for not bothering with a saucer at tea time. She just laughed back at me and said, "Don't forget we only had pannikins in our wurlies."'

Gael Fraser, who became her immediate superior, remembers her first meeting with Ruby. Gael had been appointed to a newly-created job. She arrived in her office to find it sparsely furnished with a few chairs and a heavy desk, two metres long and one-and-a-half metres wide, placed squarely in the middle of the room on its threadbare carpet. She was looking at it with dismay when Ruby came in.

'It will probably take ages to get someone to move it,' said Gael.

'Let's do it together now,' said Ruby, and, kicking off her shoes, she persuaded Gael to help. It required considerable effort, but they managed to set it crosswise in the room, at a better angle to the door. Doing things 'together' and 'now' were two things Gael came to realise were typical of Ruby. Feeling much happier Gael organised coffee and they sat down to begin making plans for the work ahead.

Gael found Ruby invaluable in helping the non-Aboriginal staff to see more clearly the problems involved. She would arrange meetings that were totally confidential at which she would answer any questions – 'All you ever wanted to know but were too embarrassed to ask,' she would say. The staff respected her and really liked her. The work place was livelier because of her.

At this time Aborigines made up one per cent of the population in South Australia, and the government's aim was to achieve a level of one per cent Aboriginal staff in permanent employment throughout the public sector. This meant bringing in 150 Aboriginal staff, and seeing that they were prepared for the work. Ruby was involved in developing an Aboriginal Employment Unit to carry out this task.

From the beginning she realised that the disadvantages

which beset Aborigines meant that the unit would need to be different from other employment services. It would need to be concerned with education from the preschool level upwards, and she knew how Aboriginal problems intertwined so that housing, health, and aspects of social welfare would also be involved.

The unit would need to focus on young people but, given the nature of Aboriginal families, it would need to be careful that too much responsibility was not imposed on a young person who might be the sole earning member in the family. Training aspects would need to be widened to help some applicants to a better understanding of how to be employable, and they would need special support.

Ruby also wanted to ensure that there would be real opportunity for career development for Aborigines within the public service. In the past, she believed, they had been blocked from such advancement.

Leslie Wanganeen, who was appointed to assist Ruby, came to the unit with experience of working with many Aboriginal groups and committees. She had a Task Force Diploma in Community Service, and had been a member of the Recruitment Branch. Understanding Aboriginal viewpoints was among her special skills. She was eager to be involved in this new project of making the public service more accessible to Aborigines, and she understood, as Ruby did, that completely new attitudes and techniques would be needed.

Between them they made a great success of their task, producing a sixty-page plan of what was to be done to establish the framework, and outlining fifteen programs to carry out its objective.

Marking the end of this first stage, the Aboriginal Employment Unit was launched on 1 November 1988, in the Pilgrim Church Centre. It went off with all the flair that was

Ruby's hallmark. The centre was crowded, and the federal and state ministers, G.L. (Gerry) Hand and Greg Crafter, were both present.

Ruby and Lesley carried on the work of implementing the plans. For Lesley it was rewarding because she felt it was all worth doing and was being done well, but she was never entirely happy in the bureaucracy of the department. She felt both admiration and warm affection for Ruby, but she was also exasperated by her. She saw her as too ready to forgive the shortcomings of others, and too ready to accept the slow progress towards the changes that would give equality to the Aboriginal people.

At the end of 1989 Ruby left to become the head of the Aboriginal Unit assisting the Royal Commission into Aboriginal Deaths in Custody. Lesley became the head of the Aboriginal Employment Unit, and the task became more difficult for her.

She had a staff of four Aboriginal women with whom to initiate and develop the fifteen programs through which the work would be carried out. It was intensely hard work but they got it all 'up and running'. They knew they were there to do a job, and they did it to the best of their ability. Lesley was proud of their achievements.

At the same time her staff didn't take themselves too seriously. They were always ready to laugh and joke together. Lesley felt that this was misunderstood. Despite what they achieved they were regarded as time-wasters. She felt they were never seen as equals by their white colleagues despite their qualifications and abilities.

Lesley thought the non-Aboriginal staff had racist attitudes, although they did not recognise it in themselves. They had difficulty in accepting decisions made by an Aboriginal officer for white people. They saw reconciliation only in terms of Aborigines accepting European values and standards.

The idea of giving serious consideration to the different values of the Aborigines, or regarding them as possibly superior, never occurred to them.

She saw this as a reflection of the ignorance and indifference about Aboriginal problems that were endemic in the community.

Government departments were hierarchies built on ambition and competition. Aboriginal culture had evolved groups in which the members were interdependent in an atmosphere of physical and spiritual harmony. Their elders were graduates of their own education system, meeting on equal terms, and their decisions were made by the group discussing matters until consensus was reached. It was not like that in the South Australian public service.

Ruby could turn her back on what was negative in any situation, and always looked on the positive side. Lesley tried to do this too. She would ring Ruby up and they would have coffee together. Ruby would encourage her, strengthening her belief in herself, but back in the office it would seem again that Lesley and her Aboriginal staff were just 'window dressing'.

Sonia Waters came onto the staff as a clerical officer several months before the unit was launched. Her parents had known Ruby since before Sonia was born, but when Ruby interviewed her she was questioned in the same way as all the other applicants, and Sonia is convinced it made no difference to her getting the job.

She was impressed by the professional attitudes and dedication that Ruby and Lesley maintained in such a happy office. Laughter was never far from the surface and she agrees with Lesley that this was misunderstood.

Sonia was not worried by this. The unit was the achievement of their group and she was enormously proud of it. Ruby was in charge, and it was Ruby's approval she wanted. She saw Ruby as superior to most of the non-Aboriginal staff, not ethnically but in terms of the work they did. She thought Ruby and Lesley worked harder, achieved more and understood better what was needed. Ruby was not worried by other people's opinions and attitudes. She believed that racial equality was inevitable because fundamentally it was a fact. For Sonia, working with Ruby was a learning experience.

Lesley in the 1990s works happily as the manager of the Narungga Progress Association, the Aboriginal Community Welfare office in Maitland on the Yorke Peninsula. Andrea Mason, who replaced her in Adelaide, became the Aboriginal Staffing consultant for the Commissioner of Public Employment. She is a Bachelor of Arts in Aboriginal Affairs Administration as Ruby was. The unit has been renamed the Starting Programs Unit.

Andrea sees Lesley as having joined the staff to help plan and organise a unit that was to be unlike anything else in the public service. It was difficult for the Aboriginal women, and for the non-Aboriginal staff too.

'Lesley saw the Aboriginal point of view,' Andrea says, 'and she didn't hesitate to challenge the other staff, including senior officers, to consider new responsibilities and the duty that was owed to Aboriginal people. Ruby had had a lot of experience beforehand, but for Lesley it was a totally new situation and she carried it out with great courage.'

Like Ruby, Andrea had the advantage of a happy childhood. She belongs to the Wongi people of the Western Desert, growing up in a part of Australia where dispossession was less ruthless than in areas closer to European settlement, and where their heritage was better protected. She was always in a family situation with her parents and her brothers and sisters.

Her father was Pastor Ben Mason, MBE, a leader of his people who represented them at the first meetings of the National Aboriginal Consultative Committee in 1976, and many times since. Brought up at the Mount Margaret Mission he had a deep Christian faith which he melded well with his Aboriginality. He liked to make a positive approach to problems that arose, to hold to long-term commitments, to look for the best to happen, and for opportunities for people to change.

Andrea, who deeply admired her father, follows his principles. When difficulties arise she likes to say, 'Let's have a yarn about it and see if we can reconcile the differences.' She is a great believer in people talking things through, and listening to each other. It is people of her calibre who are paving the way to reconciliation.

It was amazing what Ruby could fit into her program. She seemed to be always there, always on the job, yet in March 1988 she found time to stand for parliament. A federal by-election was held in Port Adelaide on 26 March 1988, following the resignation of Mick Young, a senior minister in the Hawke government.

There were eight candidates. Ruby was one of five Independents. The leaflets she distributed described her as representing the Independent Aboriginal Cultural Party. As ever her first concern was the Aboriginal people, their rights to their land and their heritage, but she looked to the wider community also. Her policy supported the rights of all cultural groups, called for protection of the natural environment, and for the democratic rights of everyone. She attacked the increasing gap between the rich and the poor.

Port Adelaide is part of the Kaurna cultural region, the area of the Adelaide plains. The Aboriginal people belong to the Ibis Dreaming, and they allowed Ruby to use an ibis on her policy leaflet. Aborigines rallied to support her many meetings, and she took every opportunity to speak of land rights and human rights.

There were 72,571 electors on the roll, and Ruby won

1142 primary votes, about 1.8 per cent. Rob Sandford, the Labor Party candidate, won the seat. Judy Fuller represented the Liberal Party, and Meg Lees the Democrats. The five Independents all lost their deposit, which is not returned unless four per cent of the vote is polled. Three of the Independents scored fewer votes than Ruby.

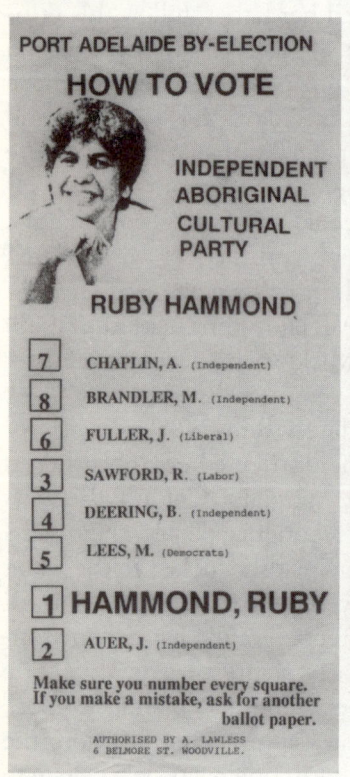

Left: Election leaflet, March 1988.
Above: Graduation, 1985. (*Advertiser*)

On the whole Ruby was pleased with the result and was quoted in the *Advertiser* on the following Monday as saying that a national Aboriginal political party was a possibility. She believed it could contest federal and state elections, and union and council ballots as well.

This did not happen, but Ruby was not worried. 'It will happen in the future,' she said.

Ruby was the first Aborigine in South Australia to stand for federal parliament. Since her death there have been major changes to electoral boundaries, and a new district has been named Hammond in her honour. It is an extensive rural area extending to the Victorian state border in the east, and including the townships of Murray Bridge, Strathalbyn, Meningie, Pinnaroo and Swan Reach.

Ruby received two awards for her work with the public service. In 1992 she was presented with the Australian Public Service Medal. By this time she was seriously ill and in hospital, but the medal was presented to her personally by the governor, Dame Roma Mitchell, who went to the hospital for the special ceremony that was organised.

A year later the Equal Opportunity Achievement Award was made in her name, but this time, on 20 May 1993, it was too late to present it to Ruby herself. Her son Bruce received it for her. Her daughter Sandra Southwell was not present, but it was for a happy reason. Not long before she had given birth to a daughter who was named 'Ruby Kathleen'.

Sandra Saunders, director of the Aboriginal Legal Rights Movement, and Elliott Johnston QC had nominated Ruby for the Equal Opportunity Award. Sandra Saunders spoke of 'her work to make South Australia a fairer place, firstly for her own people but not exclusively for them'.

Elliott Johnston said, 'Ruby's vision was of all people, black and white, working together to achieve a society free of discrimination, and free of the ills of poverty and deprivation.'

In 1990 Ruby became the head of the Aboriginal Issues Unit with the Royal Commission Inquiry into Aboriginal Deaths in Custody. The commission had been established in October 1987, and presented its final report to parliament in April 1991.

The opportunity to fill this position delighted Ruby. Ever since her time as executive secretary of the Aboriginal Legal Rights Movement in South Australia the law had been one of her major interests. It showed that Elliott Johnston still had faith in her. He had been a pioneer of Aboriginal legal rights in South Australia, and a member of the board of the ALRM. She looked forward to working with him again.

The commission inquired into ninety-nine cases of Aboriginal and Torres Strait Islander people who had died in custody between 1 January 1980 and 31 May 1989.

A particularly tragic case for Ruby was Kingsley Dixon, a young South Australian.[1] His mother, Alice, was a long-standing friend, and Ruby had known Kingsley since he was a little boy. He was nineteen when he died, and Ruby understood and shared in Alice's intense grief.

Kingsley had been a lively, intelligent little boy, the much-loved only son in a family with four daughters. He had a stable background but in spite of this he did not do well at high school, and by the age of thirteen he was in trouble with the police. When he was sixteen he served a period in a juvenile institution, where he appeared to be relatively content. He made friends there and had diversions to occupy his time.

But not long after his release he was in court again on a charge of 'illegally using a vehicle'. He was sentenced to five months' imprisonment, and spent it in the Adelaide Remand Centre and the Adelaide Gaol.

Perhaps the worst prison in the state, the Adelaide Gaol had been condemned in 1973 by the Criminal Law and Penal Method Reform Committee presided over by Dame Roma Mitchell, then a judge of the Supreme Court. It had been recommended that the gaol be internally modernised as a pre-release work centre, and its use as a correctional institute discontinued. This had not happened.

Fourteen years later, in July 1987, another report described the gaol as suitable for about 170 inmates. The average number of prisoners in that month was more than 300. The cells were not sewered, with buckets being provided for toilet requirements.

Kingsley was released in July 1986, but two months later, following a break-up with his girlfriend, he set fire to premises occupied by her and the young man she was living with. He pleaded guilty to arson and two lesser charges. He was sentenced to three-and-a-half years' imprisonment with a non-parole period of eighteen months. He was to serve it in the Adelaide Gaol.

Ruby was aware of Kingsley's problems and was one of the friends who tried to help and support Alice, who was in continual contact with him, in and out of prison.

Ruby knew what a lovely child he had been, and she felt certain his problems stemmed from racism suffered at school. From some deep-seated national ignorance many teachers treat their Aboriginal pupils as less intelligent than the others. They fail to see their potential because, from this inbuilt prejudice, they do not expect them to have the capacity for academic success. In the 1990s this is less likely to happen than it was in the 1970s when Kingsley was at school.

Many Aboriginal children came from homes where they were better cared for, and better disciplined, than some non-Aboriginal children, but this passed unnoticed. With a disturbing number of teachers, Aboriginal children were the second-class citizens of the classroom. In such schools racism went unchecked in the playground.

Ruby knew too that in prison, racism would have been more evident than it was in the outside community. She had heard of prison officers referring to Aboriginal inmates as 'black bastards', calling them 'dogs' and 'no hopers'. The Aborigines were given the most menial and dirty jobs although prison officers denied deliberate discrimination. Other prisoners also treated them with racist belittlement, often refusing to share the over-crowded cells with them.

Alice was worried about drugs, knowing that heroin was dangerously available in this and many other prisons. She knew Kingsley was smoking marijuana and took it to him when she could, as being a lesser evil. When she learnt that he had been 'manifestly under the influence of a drug or drugs' when he was taken to his cell shortly before his death, it was an added torment for her.

On 9 July 1987, Kingsley telephoned Alice in the morning. His speech was slow and slurred, and at about eleven she went to see him. At about 3.30 pm he was found in his cell hanging by a strip of sheeting.

In the Royal Commission report on his death the commissioner said, 'I do not find it probable that he deliberately killed himself, but his action and its tragic consequences were the situation the prison rules and regulations were designed to prevent. They were either not known or were ignored; he was not treated with the care his condition demanded. His death in my view would not have occurred had these rules and regulations been adhered to.'

He also referred to Kingsley's 'not anticipating that unconsciousness would intervene in seconds, as I believe it probably did'. He added here 'that the medical evidence assumes significance in as much as it proves how quickly inevitable death can occur when ligatures grip the sides of the neck – far more quickly than is commonly comprehended'.

The commissioner found that Kingsley had died by his own hand but not necessarily with the intention of taking his own life.

Alice Dixon died two years later. She never accepted that Kingsley's death was suicide. He had occasionally spoken to other prisoners of suicide but no one had taken him seriously. No member of the prison staff had considered him to be suicidal or of a depressed personality. At home he had been a lively, outgoing person. His death was a tragedy not only to his family but to the whole Aboriginal community of South Australia. Alice Dixon's dissatisfaction with the original finding on Kingsley's death was among the factors that led to the setting up of the Royal Commission.

The story of Kingsley's death and of the other ninety-eight prisoners who died in custody in the period under review made up the basic report of the Royal Commission. On the whole they were young, only two had completed secondary schooling, eighty-three were unemployed at the date of last detention, forty-three had been separated as children from their natural families, seventy-four had been charged with an offence before the age of nineteen.

The commissioners did not find that any of the deaths were caused by deliberate violence or brutality by police or prison officers, but they did find that the standard of care shown towards people in custody was generally poor, and that a lack of proper care contributed to some of the deaths. They found little evidence of appreciation by prison officers of the duty of care owed to those in their custody, and no apparent policy to overcome this situation.

To the basic report were added 399 recommendations for changes, mainly to criminal law and prison procedures. These were directed towards preventing the shortcomings in treatment and care of prisoners which had been revealed by the inquiry. Importantly they went beyond this, examining the historical, social, cultural and economic factors that had led to the Aboriginal and Torres Strait Islander people being the most disadvantaged in Australia. There was also a final overview written by Elliott Johnston, the last of the commissioners, summing up the causes of this tragic situation. Recommendations in the overview point to ways of eliminating disadvantages, promoting independence and self-confidence among the Aboriginal people, and making the community generally aware of the baselessness of the racist assumption of an ingrained superiority.

Ruby endorsed every one of the recommendations.[2] The overview continually echoed her own thinking, which was based on her experiences as a field officer with the Council of Aboriginal Women, and as executive secretary with the legal service. It was nearly twenty-five years after the referendum and she felt very little had changed.

By the mid-1970s Ruby had perceived that welfare issues, including health, housing, education and employment, were all inextricably woven into the problems that brought Aborigines into conflict with the law. In those days when she had tried to put this idea forward it had been dismissed as irrelevant. In this inquiry, it was accepted as fact.

She had always regarded imprisonment as a last resort, a punishment quite unsuited to those whose 'crimes' arose from poverty and the disadvantages which were the daily lot of so many Aborigines. It had seemed to her particularly stupid to keep sending such people into prisons which were overcrowded and substandard, while the government complained of the high costs of keeping them there.

Here was the commission recommending that 'positive initiatives to reduce the number of Aboriginal people in custody ... constitutes a more pressing priority as far as resources are concerned than in improving police cells'.

And adding: 'Where, however, it is determined that new cell accommodation must be provided in areas of high Aboriginal population, the views of the local Aboriginal community and organisations should be taken into account in the design of such accommodation.'

In the 1970s a recommendation that Aboriginal organisations be consulted on such a matter would simply have been ignored, but in the commission's findings such consultation was urged repeatedly.

Consultation was recommended in matters concerning health, schooling, alcohol dependency, housing, youth programs, non-custodial alternatives to prison, recruitment and training of Aboriginal staff for police officers, prisons and courts.

Two recommendations concerning verbal abuse and offensive language by police recalled one of Ruby's constant concerns in the 1970s. She remembered many Aborigines bewildered by arrest for offensive language, arrests in which, particularly if it were resisted, police used much the same language themselves.

She had always been troubled when she feared that prisoners did not understand what was happening, or what was being said to them. She felt that if the prisoners knew only a little English the court often failed to understand that a problem existed.

Now it was being recommended that 'where there is doubt as to whether the person has the ability to fully understand proceedings in the English language and is fully able to express himself or herself in the English language, the court be obliged to satisfy itself that the person has that ability. Where there is doubt or reservations as to these matters, proceedings should not continue until a competent interpreter is provided to the person without cost to that person.'

And 'that governments should take more positive steps to recruit and train Aboriginal people as court staff and interpreters in locations where significant numbers of Aboriginal people appear before the courts'.

The breadth of the recommendations and the final report amazed Ruby. There seemed to be no problem on which they did not touch.

The media, which so often angered, frustrated and even

grieved Aborigines, was not overlooked. A detailed recommendation urged 'that the media industry develop formal and informal contact with Aboriginal organisations, and that they be encouraged to develop codes and policies relating to the presentation of Aboriginal issues'.

There was a further recommendation that consideration be given to an annual award for excellence in Aboriginal affairs reporting.

Obviously the two major needs were an end to racism and an end to the constant interfering and overseeing of Aboriginal affairs by government and bureaucratic organisations. Ruby saw these two factors as linked.

Elliott Johnston said in his overview that he had realised to some extent the petty tyranny to which Aborigines were subject, but until he worked with the commission he 'had no conception of the degree of pin-pricking domination, abuse of personal power, utter paternalism, open contempt and total indifference with which so many Aboriginal people were visited on a day to day basis'. He says, 'It is an attitude that is deeply resented by Aboriginal people.'

This appalling state of affairs has filtered down from government officials at the highest level to the lowliest behind-the-counter clerk, and reflects the degree of racism which is endemic throughout non-Aboriginal society.

These evils, for evils they are, were recognised by the commission, and the report and recommendations condemn them.

Ruby, whose whole philosophy tended to optimism, liked to remember the more than ninety per cent 'Yes' vote in the 1967 referendum. It was, for her, glowing evidence of goodwill in the community, evidence that, despite racism and its attendant tyranny, a sense of justice was latent in the community. 'It is ignorance that holds it back, and ignorance is curable,' said Ruby.

She dreamed of Australia creating a society in which her grandchildren would live with special pride in their Aboriginal inheritance, knowing that its contribution was of special value.

Ruby realised that the way forward would be slow, for it was a case of winning over a whole community. But she knew too that ideas can spread within a community like plants on a hillside. Her dream might not come true in her lifetime, but she was certain it would be there for her children and grandchildren. She would have been truly saddened to have found how little notice was taken of the Royal Commission recommendations. Very few of them have been implemented.

In August 1995 an Australian Institute of Criminology study found that already ten indigenous people had died in custody that year, the same number that died in custody in 1994, and nearly three times the average number of people who had died in custody each year during the period investigated by the Royal Commission.

Dr David McDonald, who presented the report, said the figures would get worse unless governments made a serious effort to implement the Royal Commission's findings.

FOURTEEN

MAKING RECONCILIATION A REALITY

understanding
Aboriginal
Dreaming

RUBY'S LAST POSITION WITH THE PUBLIC SERVICE WAS AS Aboriginal adviser to the Department of the Arts and Cultural Heritage, a position that delighted her. She had long believed that the arts – painting, story-telling, dancing and acting – were powerful ways of communicating, sharing ideas and promoting points of view, and that it was through the arts that people discovered themselves and expressed their innermost feelings. She loved to be part of it, and when it came to the theatre she was a 'natural'. She had vitality, charm and a beautiful voice.

She had discovered theatre and its magic in the 1970s. These were good years for the theatre in Adelaide. The time was right, the place was right. They were blossoming years, and Adelaide, with its population of just over one million, a perfect city to develop new theatre. In that decade Adelaide established itself as the Festival City of Australia, building up a great celebration of theatre, art and music to be held every two years. To some extent it was based on the Edinburgh

Festival, but every city is different and this is reflected in its arts.

A *Festival Fringe* grew up with amateur and semi-professional groups developing and displaying their talents in little theatres and halls around the city. It was among these groups that Aboriginal women found an outlet, not only during the festival month but also at other times to suit themselves.

National Aborigines Day had been established in the 1960s and marches were held in every capital city on the second Friday in July. In Adelaide they were small, quiet and rather unimaginative demonstrations that attracted very little publicity. Ruby decided they must do something more spectacular.

Her secretary, Helen Monten, told her she had a sister at university who was interested in marketing, and would be willing to help with publicity. So Anne Monten came on the committee.

'You will have to *do* something,' Anne said. 'Newspapers won't give you publicity unless you do something that will make news.'

They took up this challenge eagerly. They decided to invite Wanjuk Marika, chairman of the Aboriginal Arts Board, an excellent speaker and a colourful figure. He played the didgeridoo in the Rundle Mall and spoke to the crowds that gathered.

It was Muriel Van Der Byl who suggested a bi-cultural supper. They decided on witchetty grubs[1] and pie floaters.[2] They managed to arrange for witchetty grubs to be sent down by rail from the Northern Territory, and Muriel went to the station to collect them. She was almost overwhelmed to find two huge plastic containers full of them. Not easily deterred, she took them home and cooked them in garlic butter – not an authentic Aboriginal recipe but, after all, it was to be bi-cultural.

This was the most successful Aborigines Day they had ever had, not only in terms of publicity, but in terms of having fun. The year was 1977. What would they do in 1978? Anne, with her university experience, suggested a revue. The men were dubious, but a group of women with singing, dancing and acting talents were enthusiastic and managed to persuade some of the men to join in.

Soon they were relating stories and ideas to develop into sketches. They needed help and it came generously from non-Aboriginal women. Anne Dunn and Chris Westwood joined them as director and stage manager. (Anne was later to chair the Festival of Arts Board, and Chris became executive producer for the State Theatre Company.) Students from the Centre for Aboriginal Studies in Music at Adelaide University agreed to take part in the revue, and the Aboriginal Arts Board provided funds.

The result was *When I Die You'll All Stop Laughing*, which ran for three nights in the Union Hall at the university. The title was taken from the opening number, a song written by Eva Johnson, telling a story of the Brolga Dreaming that warns of death if we do not care for the land.

The aim was to take a light-hearted look at the plight of Aborigines, but to be thought-provoking at the same time. The critics liked it and it was a success. John Kirby in the *Sunday Mail*, 16 July 1978, said, 'If the allegations made in some of the sketches – police forcing Aboriginal girls to have sex and falsifying evidence – were meant to be taken even remotely seriously, then there should be a federal inquiry into the treatment of Aborigines.'

There was no inquiry, but it had been a great success. The group felt a sense of achievement. The revue was the basis of lasting friendships, it was the beginning of the Aboriginal Women's Theatre, and it led to other shows.

Ruby had been part of it all, and for her there had been an

extra bonus. She had urged her brother Kingsley to take part. He had been going through an unhappy period, in and out of prison and in trouble with the police. It took a lot of persuading to get him to come on stage and to dance with his sister, but in the end he thoroughly enjoyed it. He found himself a valued part of a group, and he has never looked back. He became involved with the Uniting Church, working with them as part of their Aboriginal Reconciliation team.

Three years later it was decided to have another revue. Once again the group contributed their own stories, but this time they were shaped into a single theme. Eva Johnson, with her flair for words, called it *Faded Genes*. The revue was performed modestly in an empty warehouse on Magill Road.

The curtain rises on an Aboriginal youth playing a didgeridoo by a camp fire in a clearing in the bush. A young girl stands listening nearby, and gradually Aboriginal people emerge to talk and sing to her of the Dreaming and its continuing relevance to their lives. The other side of the stage lights up slowly and the audience becomes aware of a group of European young people talking and laughing in a milkbar. Gradually the girl is drawn to this group, and then called back to her Aboriginal friends, back and forth until finally she stands in uncertainty in the centre of the stage. The cast, who were almost equally Aboriginal and non-Aboriginal, came to take their curtain calls, standing alternately hand-in-hand on each side of her.

At the first performance they began to sing *We shall overcome*. Led by Ruby on the extreme right of the stage they came down among the audience, up and down each row, taking hands until everybody, singing together, had moved into a great circle.

Eva Johnson, author of this play, is a talented writer, telling of what she knows. She was a stolen child, taken from her mother at a very early age. Her best-known work,

Tjindarella, was a bitter commentary on this. Tjindarella is an Aboriginal girl, scrubbing floors at the mission and dreaming, as Cinderella did, of a better life. But there is no happy-ever-after ending for her. Her godmother is the Department of Aboriginal Affairs whose magic wand gives false promises. Government policy represents the glass slipper, which does not fit at all, and Tjindarella realises that only land rights, which she despairs of ever getting, will mean a happy ending. It was a witty play, and the symbolism was cleverly done.

Tjindarella was staged in the Space Theatre, an experimental theatre section of the Adelaide Festival complex. In 1985 the Aboriginal Women's Theatre held a festival in Adelaide, and players came from all over Australia. Eva Johnson won the South Australian Aboriginal of the Year Award for her work in producing *Tjindarella*. It played to full houses.

In 1989, when Ruby was still working with the Department of Personnel and Industrial Relations, she remembered these revues and was one of the women who initiated the brilliant cabaret show, *Is This Seat Taken?*. The talents of more than ninety women as performers, musicians, writers, directors and general stage hands went into its making. There were Aboriginal and non-Aboriginal women in equal numbers.

The term 'reconciliation' was not then in use, but this clever piece of theatre was the absolute embodiment of it.

The show was the sort of project Ruby rejoiced in, and her hand can be seen in much of the early planning. Those who were there at the beginning remember meetings in Ruby's living room, with everyone sitting round on the floor telling stories which became part of the script. They shared stories about their own lives and about growing up, finding common ground in being women, telling jokes about their experiences, talking about their differences, and discovering that they were not so different after all.

These sessions were serious, creative and productive, but without doubt they were also fun. There was a feeling of joy about them.

The revue was staged in the Space Theatre. *Is This Seat Taken?* was set up as a cabaret. Place-mats at the tables gave the ninety names of those taking part. In the centre of the mat was a statement prepared by Ruby, defining the show. It was, she said:

- the first Australian production to bring together Aboriginal and white women on an equal basis in a major theatre production.
- recognition of common ground and shared ideals; concern for the environment, for the future of our children, and for the development of a just and fair society.
- a representation of Aboriginal and white women working together as women in partnership. We won't forget the past – collectively we acknowledge what has been wrong and are working to change it.

It was a deeply moving event, not only for those taking part but also for those who came to see it. It expressed in dramatic style one of Ruby's cherished beliefs – that a group of women, no matter what their ethnic backgrounds, could always make common cause, for they are all of the same gender, and in the end all of the same race, the human race. 'Hand-in-hand together' was her way of problem solving, and she preferred co-operation to confrontation. She was a 'people person' rather than a feminist, but she had great faith in women, related to them easily and loved working with them.

Ruby wore yellow satin in the show, and shone throughout every performance. Among the songs she sang was one she particularly loved:

You know the sun and the moon and the stars up in the sky,
You see the mountains and the flowers and the trees,
You see the rivers and the sea,
Feel the wind that blows so free,
That is where, and from them all you come from.

Our ancestors in the past made the land and made the law
Making all living things just the same.

We may be different in many ways
But we should live in harmony
With each other, and all things, all our days.

This was Ruby's song. She identified with it, she sang it often, and it expressed her philosophy so well that many people thought she had written it, but it is one of Bob Randall's songs.

Bob Randall is one of the best-known song writers in the Aboriginal community, and one of the sweetest singers. He spent some time in Adelaide in the 1970s and was a student at the Aboriginal Community College when he met Ruby. He encouraged her to sing and this became the basis of a strong friendship. They shared a spiritual commitment to their Aboriginal inheritance which Bob expressed in his songs.

Afterwards Ruby spoke of *Is This Seat Taken?* as the first time there had been a real community event at the state theatre.

'It was both women's theatre and Aboriginal theatre,' she said, 'and it was tremendously exciting. It was like fireworks, like a laser beam going across the room, and we were all on that beam. We had come together to make a statement, to display our strength, our talents and our togetherness as women.'

Muriel Van Der Byl remembers it as a wonderful experience. At the beginning there had been times of tension, with people complaining about the way things were going.

'I don't want to hear any more of that,' said Anne Dunn, one of the producers. 'I want to look at the best there is, and the best that can be. We'll have a complaints session next week.'

But when next week came nobody had complaints any more. What they had to say was constructive.

'We all grew,' Muriel says. 'We wanted to change the world, and we certainly changed ourselves. Our white sisters wanted us to be up-front, and it wasn't a do-gooder thing. It was what it was about for all of us.'

The stories they acted out were real. They told of happiness and sadness, and before long they were satirising racism.

The audience quickly saw that racism was nonsense. They were laughing at the woman at a function in the Lady Mayoress's parlour to which Aboriginal women had been invited. 'You can't be Aborigines,' this woman said. 'You are too pretty, too well dressed, too well behaved.'

They also laughed at the Guides, who were teaching their Brownies how to set up camp, how to light a fire, and what to do if they got lost. 'True brownies like us don't get lost,' said the young Aboriginal girls.

Among the moving songs they sang was *Land My Mother*, by Eva Johnson, and, at the end, Val Power sang *My brown-skinned baby, they take him away*, a song that can move people to tears. It is another of Bob Randall's songs.

The women could see that they were all sisters, and that those who, from some absurd notion of skin colouring, had deeply wronged a part of the human family must seek, hand-in-hand, for a new understanding.

In October 1991 Ruby joined the Department for the Arts and Cultural Heritage. She saw the arts as a highway to the reconciliation she dreamed of – a reconciliation within which the Australian community would understand Aboriginal culture and philosophy, accepting its spiritual links with the land, and the unique qualities that make Australia different from every other country.

She knew it must come from sharing, and that in Australia this would be a difficult challenge. Since the war, people from every culture on earth had become Australians, and mutual understanding would be a long, slow process. Aboriginality would be the thread that would weave it together. As always Ruby wanted to do something about it.

She had heard of the bi-cultural approaches that were becoming an increasingly important part of Maori exhibitions in New Zealand. Ruby felt that she could learn something from this, and decided to go to New Zealand to see it first hand. She set off in March 1992, taking Helen Liddle as a companion.

In 1985 in Adelaide Ruby had met Dame Georgina Kirby, who was a member of the Maori Arts Board and a leader among Maori artists. Ruby and Helen were able to stay with Georgina in Auckland. She took Ruby to art galleries and museums, and they spent long hours talking into the night about their faith in art as a communicator in human understanding.

In 1990 Georgina Kirby had established the Te Taumata Art Gallery, which is a centre for exhibitions not only of Maori art but also of indigenous art from all around the Pacific, and from other international centres.

'Te Taumata' means 'to set the eyes on excellence', and Georgina Kirby has kept this as the basic theme of her gallery. They visited it together, and Ruby made copious notes on the gallery's bi-cultural arts policy, the various exhibitions, and their administrative and funding methods. They went to other galleries that exhibited Maori work, and to intricately carved meeting houses.

At the beautiful Kotuko Marae at the Rutherford High

School there was a celebratory dinner at which Ruby was asked to speak and sing. Helen remembers this occasion for a typical moment of encouragement from Ruby. The dinner was an important occasion with distinguished guests, and Ruby and Helen arrived late. They had to walk through the crowded hall and Helen was blushing with embarrassment. 'Don't worry,' said Ruby. 'They are all saying to each other, "Here come the Aborigines at last – always late. Their minds are on the Dreamtime, never on the right time."'

Museums in both Auckland and Wellington excited Ruby with their splendid displays of Maori carving.

'You were aware of it as soon as you went through the doors,' she said. 'You knew instantly that you were in a country with an indigenous people who are richly artistic. It should be like that in Australia.'

She quickly saw that Maori art was symbolic in just the same way as Aboriginal art. Every line in a painting, every dot in a Western Desert picture, has a meaning, and the paintings tell a story or express a philosophy to those who can 'read' it. She saw that Maori carvings were relating the thinking and history of their people in a similar way, and were not just decorative.

Ruby liked the attitudes of the Auckland Museum where the staff were aware of the special nature of cultural collections, and recognised that such exhibitions were held in trust for the people and were pathways for social relationships.

The educational role that the museum was adopting impressed her too. She saw the museum as helping young Maoris to rediscover their heritage and culture, and as teaching pakehas to better understand the quality of the people whose land they had overtaken.

She knew that attitudes of this kind were developing in Australia, but she felt that New Zealand was ahead. Perhaps the two countries had lessons to teach each other, and Ruby hoped she would be able to play a part in developing the links between them.

But other work was awaiting Ruby on her return. She began a short initiation period in the Art Gallery of South Australia with Ron Radford, the director, and Jane Hylton, the curator of Aboriginal Art. Her New Zealand report was pushed to the back of her desk.

She was not well, although she continually expected to be better the next day. Those who loved her were worrying about her. Irene, Muriel and Helen tried to persuade her that she could not go on saying she was too busy to go to the doctor.

In the end Ruby was too tired to finish her New Zealand report, but her optimism did not fail her. She knew the South Australian Museum had the largest Aboriginal collection in the world, although most if it was in the basement storerooms. She knew that it could, and believed that it would, become a great international resource.

Her faith was well founded. In August 1994 the Arts Minister, Diana Laidlaw, announced that there would be a feasibility study for just such a gallery. The federal government would also contribute funds.

Dr Christopher Anderson, the museum's director, and his staff were excited. They knew the value of their collection, and that only lack of funds had prevented them from creating an international display that would bring scholars and tourists from all over the world.

They believed Adelaide had the capacity to be the nation's information centre, and they planned to consult with Aborigines all over Australia when creating it. They hoped tourists would come to Adelaide to see the country first through Aboriginal eyes, and then go on to explore it with greater understanding, but more importantly they wanted a centre where the Aboriginal people could renew their understanding of their past.

Cabinet considered further funding. Dr Anderson believed there were Cabinet ministers who understood the importance of Aboriginal culture in the welfare of Australia's mixed-race society, and who realised that by attracting people from overseas, the gallery would have an economic role too.

Dr Anderson and his staff are consulting widely with Aboriginal communities, and are expecting to engage more Aboriginal staff for this sensitive work. Dr Anderson is confident that an Aboriginal centre of international importance will be developed in Adelaide.

On 12 April 1995, the federal government announced that it had struck a land deal that would see the construction of a national Aboriginal museum as part of the National Museum of Australia in Canberra, but that this would not diminish the Adelaide plans.

Ruby's work with the art gallery involved a commemorative display of Aboriginal Art which opened on 27 May 1992, the twenty-fifth anniversary of the referendum that had given citizenship to Aborigines. The display was Ruby's suggestion and she and Muriel Van Der Byl did most of the planning and setting up. It was a varied display from the art gallery's extensive collection of Aboriginal work, much of which was highly political. The display included non-traditional paintings, and work by artists of the Western Desert. Commemorative posters were specially prepared by Aboriginal artists Muriel Van Der Byl and Maureen Cooke. The opening was crowded. Maureen was there to talk about the posters, Ruby gave a moving speech, and Val Power sang *My brown-skinned baby, they take him away*.

The display included a copy of the 'Limited Exemption

from the Provisions of the Aboriginal Act, 1934–39' issued on 20 October 1941 to Ruby Florence Ahang. To highlight this Ruby and Muriel had produced a 'Limited Exemption from the Pay the Rent Act', which non-Aboriginal people signed to obtain free admission. Aborigines were ushered in without any delay.

There was also a History of Invasion which ended by saying:

> By the time of the referendum in 1967, the Aboriginal people had achieved some gains. They finally achieved the right to vote federally in 1962, and in South Australia in the same year the government abolished all the so-called 'protective' laws. When ninety per cent of the people in South Australia in 1967 voted 'Yes' to the referendum, Aboriginal people expected major improvements in their lifestyles and opportunities.
>
> Such changes are still being fought for. It is 25 years since the people voted 'Yes' for justice for the indigenous people of this land. It's time to pay the rent!

The date of this exhibition, 27 May 1992, was memorable for Ruby's family and friends. It was on the day before this date that the doctor told Ruby she had cancer, and perhaps only a few months to live.

Typically Ruby's main concern was not to upset the others too much, but she had to let them know. When the display was over she said to them, 'I have something to tell you. It is going to be a shock for you. I am dying. It is time for me to go now.'

Soon she was saying, 'Now dears, we've done our crying. We don't know how long I've got, but I want to make the best of it.'

She was to have chemotherapy, and, knowing that her hair would probably fall out, she set about acquiring the most colourful and beautiful scarves she could find, scarves in which she managed to look stunning all through the last months of her life.

Before long she was admitted to the Queen Elizabeth Hospital for a major operation. The staff became aware that they had an exceptional patient. It was not possible for the operation to save her life but it helped her. She was soon up and about in a limited way, exclaiming with enthusiasm at the strained chicken soup which was all she could eat, and joking with the nurses.

They became aware that she was a VIP. Cabinet ministers came down to visit her, and the get-well messages that came in every day included one from John Bannon, then the premier of South Australia.

Ruby was moved to a smaller hospital, the Le Fevre Community Hospital at Port Adelaide. She knew that she was dying and that she would never go home, but she would always welcome warmly and good-humouredly the friends who came to see her. She tried to make the best of each day, and to the very end she could make jokes.

Once on a cold April morning Muriel arrived complaining that it was 'nippy' outside. 'That's the Japanese airforce flying over Australia,' said Ruby, and added, laughing but serious too, 'I mustn't make racist jokes, must I?'

There was always someone for her to talk to. Irene, her beloved sister, was almost always with her. Her daughter, Sandi, and Irene's daughter, Vicki, were constant visitors. Frank and John, Bruce, Kingsley and Kevin also came each day. Ruby had a single room and it was often crowded. Friends visited as well as family. Muriel came after work each day, and Julia Twohig, a naturopath, came to massage her. Hannah Middleton, who had led the study group to the Soviet Union, came from Sydney several times in the last weeks.

Ruby talked with them, rational to her last moment, about

her dream of Aboriginal justice and equality and how they were moving towards it, slowly but surely. Ever since her graduation she had known that it was becoming apparent to all but the ignorant that, intellectually, Aborigines were equal to every other group in Australia. She had long believed that in wisdom Aborigines were far ahead of most Australians. She did not see this as a genetic thing, but as something stemming from the Aborigines' deep and spiritual links with the land. They cared for the land, allowed it to care for them, and found in it the answers to everyday living and to everlasting life. Ruby believed the land would enrich the lives of everyone in Australia if they could come to understand and share it.

She was deeply grateful for her own life, for the love and caring she had known with family and friends, for the opportunities she'd had, for her work which had enabled her to serve her own people, and for her many friendships.

She was also grateful for the European and Chinese strands in her inheritance, but above all she was grateful for her Aboriginality. It had brought her faith and certainty; it had brought her a vision and enabled her to work towards it; it had given her a sense of identity that carried her back to the earliest Dreamtime, the very beginnings of life.

A balcony outside her room looked towards the west across the sea, and Ruby loved to sit out there in the evenings and watch the sun go down. She loved the sunset light dancing on the sea. 'It's like a waving cornfield, or a field of sunflowers,' she said.

She loved sunflowers. One afternoon in Ruby's last April, Muriel was driving out to the hospital when, in the window of a North Adelaide florist, she saw a large and perfect sunflower. The shop had shut, but Muriel banged on the door. When the staff came she begged them to sell it to her for her friend who was dying. They wouldn't take any payment, they gave it to her.

It was one of the happenings that made those close to Ruby believe that there was a mystically special quality about the last days of her life.

Ruby also loved the sense of the day ending that the setting sun brought her. 'That's just how I would like to go,' she said, 'just fading away like that.' And that is how it was for her. One evening as the sun was setting Ruby's life quietly ended.

On the previous night Kevin felt that he received a message. He felt that spirits came to his room, singing in an Aboriginal language, warning him that the time had come for Ruby to travel back into the Dreaming. He told the others, and Irene told Ruby that when she was ready everything was right for her to go.

On that last day there were more visitors than usual. Ruby talked with them all day without revealing how close the end was. It seemed to Irene that she waited for them all to leave. Muriel, the last of the visitors, went out for something to eat. Only Irene and Kevin remained.

'Come on, Kev,' Irene said. 'We must sit with her now.'

She took Ruby in her arms, and Kevin held her hand. Irene quietly sang her song, '*You know the sun and the moon, and the stars up in the sky . . .*'

As the song ended Ruby took two quiet breaths and slipped away.

'She's at peace now,' Irene said, and she turned to look at the sky. 'Wow!' she exclaimed. It was the most brilliant sunset she had ever seen. It seemed to have all the colours of the rainbow.

Muriel came back. Together she and Irene closed Ruby's eyes, brushed her hair and made her look beautiful. Kevin rang the family and others close to Ruby. They came quietly back – her husband, Frank, her children John, Sandi and Bruce, her brother Kingsley and her dearest friends.

The sympathetic staff found candles for them. They lit these, and turned out the lights. They sat with Ruby until the morning.

'It was a most spiritual time for us all,' Irene says.

It was not hard to feel Ruby was still with them. An inveterate planner, she had arranged her own funeral. They knew just what she wanted them to do. Her advice was with them in a very tangible way. She had written farewell notes to those who were close to her, urging them in terms she had used so often to carry on, reminding them of their special talents, their special abilities, and of the dreams and hopes each of them had. 'Of course you can do it, you can do anything you really want to do,' she said, and she urged them to carry on the things she would have been doing with them.

Ruby had, for a long time, been planning to go to Europe to seek out her European heritage with Muriel and Muriel's sister, Val Power. They had decided on Scotland because Muriel and Val's great-great-grandfather had come from there.

'You must all go,' she had written. 'Irene will go in my place.'

Knowing that Scotland would be cold, Muriel got a grey blanket for each of them to make into a cape. To her delight she and Irene quite independently decorated their capes in an almost identical way, with an eagle on the back, and an Aboriginal flag. Scotland is eagle country. They set off in September 1994, and for each of them Scotland has become a magical place. They saw eagles many times, and felt that Ruby was with them in spirit.

'The Scottish people are wonderful,' says Muriel. 'We didn't encounter racism anywhere, and there is something mystical about the people. They have a link with their land that is very like ours.'

Ruby died knowing that she had worked well, and that she had played a real part in the great struggle for justice and equality. She knew that it was not a project for any one person, or even for a few people. It was time for her to go, and for others to carry on the task.

Ruby with an Aboriginal painting that tells of women's beliefs.

It was as though the Aboriginal nation had at last taken the first few steps on a long march. Ruby believed she had been one of the leaders, but only one of many, and that what mattered was the great number following behind.

The Aboriginal people must maintain their faith in their spirituality which carries them back to the Dreaming, and gives them the strength, the hope and the courage with which they have come proudly through more than 200 years of mistreatment and belittlement.

At the end of Ruby's life her thoughts and messages were for those she loved, but she might have written to us all:

Make Reconciliation a reality. Aboriginal Dreaming sings to us of living in harmony with the land and with each other. You will find the Aboriginal people generous about Reconciliation.

Try to understand the vision and the spirituality of the philosophy and the laws they lived by for more thousands of years than we are yet sure of. It is their Dreaming. Land must be returned to them to keep it alive.

Care for the land as they did, seeing it as the source of life from the beginning of time and into the eternal future.

Care for the people with whom we share the land, and especially care for the Aboriginal people who belong to Australia in a way that no other Australians have yet learnt to do. Give them all they need to fulfil their lives as they would have done if they had not been invaded and dispossessed. To Australia's shame there are still Aborigines living in Third World poverty. This must be ended without delay. Aborigines wherever they live need health, education and employment, housing with good water, sewerage and roofs that do not leak. They need the right to organise their own lives and shape the future of their children. Make sure they get it.

Don't let Reconciliation be a political wrangle. Hand-in-hand together you can make Australia a truly wonderful place.

This was Ruby's vision. Don't dismiss it as an impossible dream. Together we can make it come true.

'Of course you can do it,' Ruby would say.

APPENDIX

COMMITTEES and PROFESSIONAL BODIES

Ruby never refused a request for help. Her advice and planning skills went into many committees, including:
- Department of Personnel and Industrial Relations – Commissioner's Panels (1991)
- *Ibis Dreaming Cultural Enterprise* (Member) (1991)
- National *South Australian Arts Week Committee* (1991)
- *Performing Arts Sub-Committee* (Chairperson) (Festival Fringe 1991)
- National Australian Women's Consultative Council (appt. 1990–1993)
- Focus: *Adelaide Festival Fringe Inc.* (Member) (elected 1990)
- Aboriginal Justice Advisory Committee (appt. 1990)
- Aboriginal Women's Forum (1990)
- Spastic Centre of South Australia (Member) (1990)
- *Aboriginal Cultural Institute* (Treasurer) (Tandanya) (elected 1991)
- Coalition Against Crime (Member) (appt. 1990)
- Aboriginal Legal Rights Movement Inc. (Secretary) (elected 3 years)
- Justice Freedom and Hope Committee, Uniting Church (Member) (appt. 1987)
- *Museum of Australia* Aboriginal Advisory Committee (Member) (appt. 1984, re-appt. 1991)
- *Indigenous Art Committee* (Executive Member)
- Aboriginal and Islander School of Management Committee (Member) (appt. 1990)
- Aboriginal and Island School of Management, Advisory Committee (Member) (appt. 1990)
- Aboriginal Employment Development Policy Committee (appt. 1988)

- Aboriginal Cultural Institute (Tandanya) (Vice-Chairperson) (elected 1990)
- Aboriginal Employment and Training Task Force
- S.A. National Aborigines Day Observance Committee (Member) (NADOC – 1987)
- South Australian Institute of Technology and Academic Board (Member) (1988)
- South Australian Institute of Technology Council (Member) (appt. 1986)
- Tertiary Education Authority of SA (TEASA) (Member) (appt. 1986)
- Aboriginal Women's Festival Committee (Member) (1984–86)
- The National Museum of Australia Council (Member) (1984–86)
- The World Peace Council (Helsinki) (Vice-President) (elected 1978–85)
- The Council of South Australian College of Arts and Education (SACAE) (Member) 1978–81
- The Prime Minister's Committee for International Women's Year (Member) (1975–76)
- The Steering Committee, National Aboriginal Consultative Committee (Member) (1974)
- Aboriginal Lands Trust, South Australia (Member) (appt. 1974–77)
- Aboriginal Housing Board (Founding Member and First Chairperson) (1971–74)
- The Aboriginal Legal Rights Movement Inc. (Founding Member) (1972)
- The Council of Aboriginal Women (Member) (elected 1968–74)
- Department of Personnel and Industrial Relations – Commissioner's Panels (1989)
- The Aboriginal Land Rights Support Group (Foundation Member 1973)
- Ombudsman's Advisory Committee (Member) (appt 1984)
- S.A. Women's Health Committee (Member) (appt 1988)
- Aboriginal Parent's and Children's Society of South Australia (President) (elected 1984)

Notes

CHAPTER 1
1. Ngatji – Central to all Aboriginal societies was some concept of a creative epoch, which set in place for all time major aspects of the cosmic order, embracing physical, human and spiritual domains of existence. Commonly known today as the Dreaming or Dreamtime, this era was when the creative beings are said to have left behind the first humans, together with the blueprint for their society – its language, structures and system of rules and values. To perpetuate the blueprint, the living were enjoined to obey the rules and perform the rituals that would guarantee an automatic continuation of the flow of power and fertility from the realms of the creator to the human world. In the Yaraldi case, there was a pre-eminent ancestral being, Ngurunderi, who founded the society and its culture ... In Yuraldi cosmology, what drew the creative period closer to human existence were the ngatji, totemic ancestors which were originally human but became birds or animals during the creative epoch. Unlike Ngurunderi, the aloof dweller in the sky realm, the ngatji remained eternally within the natural environment. They also retained their human qualities. These beings are emblematic representatives of the various Yaraldi clans (as well as individual Yaraldi) and are commemorated in songs and ceremonies.

    Foreword, Robert Tonkinson, Professor of Anthropology, University of Western Australia, to *A World That Was*,

Ronald H. Berndt, Catherine H. Berndt and John E. Stanton, Melbourne University Press, 1993, p xxv.
2. *After the Dreaming – 1968 Boyer Lectures*, Professor W.E.H. Stanner, Australian Broadcasting Commission, p 44.
3. Elliott Johnston QC – made a QC in 1970; Judge of the Supreme Court, South Australia 1985–1988; Commissioner for the Royal Commission into Aboriginal Deaths in Custody, 1990/1991.
4. Commonwealth Racial Discrimination Act, 11 June 1975.
5. Royal Commission into the Administration of the Juvenile Court Acts and other Associated Matters, South Australia, 1975.
6. House of Representatives Standing Committee Inquiry into Alcohol-related Problems, Adelaide, June 1977.

CHAPTER 2

1. Queen Ethel – Mrs Harry Watson (nee Wimpey), known as Queen Ethel, was the last full-blood native in Kingston. She died in 1954 and was buried in the Kingston Cemetery. In 1971 she was honoured at a ceremony at the National Trust Maria Reserve in Kingston. A memorial to her was unveiled by Mr Robert Edwards, curator of anthropology at the South Australian Museum.

    Kingston Flashbacks, Centenary of District Council of Lacepede, 1873–1973, p 14.
2. Verne McLaren AM – Member of the International Board of Advisors World Wilderness Congresses; foundation member World Wildlife Fund; South Australian National Trust Council member; Kingston Branch National Trust chairman 1964–1979; author of *Let the Earth Live*, *The Cape Jaffa Lighthouse*, and with Dick Roughsey, *To the African Wilderness*.
3. Protection – The Aborigines Act of 1911 was to control their lives for the next fifty years. It was 'designed to make provision for the better Protection and Control of the Aboriginal and

Half-caste inhabitants ... The emphasis was control. It eroded civil rights. It had a strong emphasis on segregation. It was restrictive and repressive ... The Act ratified institutionalisation as a way of life, and confirmed the status of Nungas as "inmates" whose affairs and families were to be controlled in almost every respect.'

Survivors in Our Own Land, Christobel Mattingly and Ken Hampton, Wakefield Press, 1988, p 45.

4. Exemption certificates – Section 11a of the State Aborigines Act Amendment Act 1939 made changes to the definition of 'Aborigines', extending it from 'full bloods and mixed bloods living with full bloods' to 'all people of Aboriginal descent'. It also provided for exemptions from the provisions of the act. It was not popular with many Aboriginal people. They say of it – 'In the wider community, Nungas who were exempt, resented having to carry a piece of paper which declared them "honorary whites".' ... Exempted people were not permitted to live on reserves and found it difficult to keep contact with relatives and friends. Because they were allowed liquor, pressure was often put upon them by those who were non-exempt to share the prohibited beverages. On the other hand exempted persons were not eligible for some of the assistance non-exempt Nungas received. Therefore they often felt deprived. ibid. p 49.

5. Aborigines Protection Board – established by the Aborigines Amendment Act 1939. It abolished the office of Chief Protector of Aboriginals and the Advisory Council, replacing them with an Aborigines Protection Board consisting of the Commissioner of Public Works and six non-Aboriginal members. ibid. p 57.

6. *Advertiser*, 25 May 1995, p 19.

Also, for evidence of an ancient culture see *Macquarie Book of Events*, Macquarie Library, Sydney, 1983 p 41.

CHAPTER 3
1. Rosemary Kyburz, MLA (Lib) for Salisbury, Queensland 1974–80. See 'Profile', *Age*, 26 April 1980, p 13.
2. *Pearls from the Deep* – the story of Colebrook Home for Aboriginal Children, Quorn, South Australia. V.E. Turner, United Aborigines' Mission, Adelaide, 1937.

CHAPTER 4
1. *Royal Commission into Aboriginal Deaths in Custody*, National Report, Overview and Recommendations, Australian Publishing Service, Canberra, 1991, p 20.
2. Eddie Le Sueur's reports – Hammond Papers, Mortlock Library, South Australia.
3. The South Australian Prohibition of Discrimination Act 1966–1970 banned all types of race and colour discrimination in employment, accommodation, legal contracts and public facilities. This was the first act of its kind in Australia.
   Macquarie Book of Events, op cit. 1960, p 45.
4. *Advertiser*, 5 October 1972, p 5.
5. *Poverty Among Aboriginal Families in Australia*, Research Report, Fay Gale and Joan Binnion, University of Adelaide – Commission of Inquiry into Poverty, Australian Government Publishing Service, Canberra, 1975, p 52.

CHAPTER 5
1. *The Original Australians*, A.A. Abbie, Seal Books, 1976, p 12.
2. Mutha puttaye – In 1995 the state government declared an area of 16 sq km of former pastoral land belonging to S. Kidman and Co. to be a conservation park as yet unnamed. It is an area of mound springs and includes 'the old bubbler'. *Advertiser*, 8 September 1995, p 11.
3. *The Mapoon Story by the Mapoon People*, International Development Action, Melbourne, 1976.
4. ibid.

CHAPTER 6

1. *Sydney Morning Herald*, 26 January 1972, p 7. Ministerial Statement, Hansard HR, 23 February 1972, p 122.
2. The idea for the Tent Embassy came from Charles Perkins. 'Lying at home sick a few days earlier, Perkins had suggested to two radicals, Michael Anderson and Kevin Gilbert, that they erect a couple of tents outside Parliament House and call them the Aboriginal Embassy.'

    Charles Perkins – A Biography, Peter Read, Viking, Penguin Books Australia Ltd, Ringwood, Victoria, 1990, p 129.
3. Sir Douglas Nicholls – Knighted in June 1972 for distinguished services to the advancement of the Aboriginal people, he was the first Aborigine to receive a knighthood. A distinguished footballer and a deeply religious man he became a pastor of the Gore Street Church of Christ in Fitzroy in Melbourne and was a leader in many of the struggles of the Aboriginal People in Victoria, working with the Aboriginal Advancement League and the Federal Council for the Advancement of Aborigines and Torres Strait Islanders. In January 1977 Don Dunstan appointed him Governor of South Australia, but unfortunately he suffered a stroke in the following April, and retired from active involvement in Aboriginal affairs.
4. Committee of Inquiry into the Role of the National Aboriginal Consultative Committee – set up by Ian Viner, Minister for Aboriginal Affairs in 1976. Committee members were dissatisfied, feeling their advice was ignored. Viner blamed previous governments for lack of clear statement of aims, duties and procedures. Report presented in May 1977. Following recommendations, the National Aboriginal Conference (NAC) was set up to replace the NACC.

    Hansard HR, 9 November 1976, p 2440.
5. Neville Bonner – filled a casual senate vacancy for the LCL in Queensland, 1971. In the following year he became the first, and still in 1995 the only, Aboriginal to be elected to parliament.

6. Aboriginal Land Rights Commission – Mr Justice A.E. Woodward, commissioned February 1973. First Report, July 1973 Parliament of the Commonwealth of Australia 1973, Parliamentary Paper No 138. Second Report, April 1974 Parliament of the Commonwealth of Australia 1974, Parliamentary Paper No 69.

   A bill based on the Woodward Report was introduced in October 1975, but lapsed with the dissolution of parliament on 11 November 1975.

   An amended bill, the Aboriginal Land Rights (Northern Territory) Bill, 1976, was introduced by Mr Ian Viner, Minister for Aboriginal Affairs in the Fraser government. He had had 'many discussions with Aborigines and others including members of the Northern Territory Legislative Assembly and other interested groups'. The bill was passed without further amendment. Hansard HR, 4 June 1976, p 3081.
7. *Canberra Times*, 18 January 1974, p 1. Also Read op cit. p 160.
8. *Canberra Times*, 15 February 1974, p 1.
9. *Canberra Times*, 27 February 1974, p 1.
10. *Canberra Times*, 1 March 1974, p 1. Also Read op cit. p 168.
11. *Canberra Times*, 2 March 1974, p 10.
12. *Sydney Morning Herald*, 16 November 1975, p 4.

CHAPTER 7
1. 'Fear Favour or Affection', Elizabeth Eggleston, No 13 in *Aborigines in Australian Society*, Academy of Social Sciences in Australia, ANU Press, Canberra, 1976.
2. Hammond Papers, Mortlock Library, South Australia.
3. *Advertiser*, 30 July 1974, p 3.
4. Huffa v. Power, SA Supreme Court, Zelling J 28 May 1977. Judgement No 3270.
5. Queen v. Williams, SA Supreme Court, Wells J, May 8, 11, 12, 13, 14, 25 – 1976.

6. R. v. Anunga, Northern Territory Supreme Court. Forster J. 11, 1976. ALR, p 412. Guidelines cited.
7. Eggleston, op cit. p 137.

CHAPTER 8

1. *A Study of Assimilation*, Fay Gale, Library Board of South Australia, Adelaide, 1964, esp. chapter 5.
2. Brian Butler – chairman of the National Aboriginal and Islander Child Care Agencies Inc and chief executive officer of the South Australian Child Care Agency Forum. He is from the Aranda people in Central Australia and from a traditional point of view has the status of a senior trusted counsellor in Aboriginal law. With a long history of working for Aboriginal rights, he has been particularly concerned with the rights and welfare of children.
3. Hansard SA Assembly, 28 April 1977, p 3849.
4. *West Coast Sentinel* – 23 February 1977, p 3; 20 July 1977, pp 1 and 10; 10 August 1977, p 14; 24 August 1977, p 1; 14 September 1977, p 1.
5. *Advertiser*, 20 October 1977, p 9.
6. William Wordsworth 1770–1850. Untitled Sonnet.
   The world is too much with us, late and soon
   Getting and spending we lay waste our powers ...

CHAPTER 9

1. Hansard, 17 November 1976, p 2275.
2. *Advertiser*, 18 November 1976, p 1.
3. *Advertiser*, 19 November 1976, p 1.
4. Protectors – The Colonial Officer in 1835 stipulated that before the first ships would be permitted to sail for South Australia the South Australian Colonisation Commission should 'prepare for securing the rights of Aborigines, which plan should include the appointment of a Colonial Officer to

be called Protector of the Aborigines, and arrangements for purchasing the lands of the Natives'.

The commission's plans, based on the Wakefield scheme, depended on the sale of Crown lands, which the commissioners had assumed were there for the taking. Believing this, the commissioners undertook to 'secure to the natives their proprietary right to the soil wherever such rights may be found to exist'.

The Emigration Officer, John Brown, noted in his diary, 7 January 1836, that 'the Commissioners were exceedingly anxious that the office (Protector of Aborigines) should be in the hands of the one who ... thoroughly understood the principles of the Colony'.

In the event Protectors were appointed to take over the lives of the indigenous people in a way that suited the commissioner and the settlers.

The Law of the Land, Henry Reynolds, Penguin, 1992, pp 100, 114, 115, 117, 121.
5. These hearings were open to the public. Margaret Forte attended them.
6. *Advertiser*, 10 June 1977, p 1.

CHAPTER 10

1. 'Native title' was the phrase used in a powerful legal synthesis by Chief Justice John Marshall in the American Supreme Court between 1810 and 1835. In a series of famous cases he enunciated the basic principles of 'native title'. These principles have been evoked since in Canada, the United States and New Zealand, and have acquired a status of international law. The High Court of Australia chose to follow this legal tradition, and also to uphold the view that taking of Aboriginal land, piece by piece without compensation, was directly contrary to the spirit of English property law.

Henry Reynolds, op cit. pp 47, 195–202.

2. Chief Seattle (Sealth), 1788–1860, Duwamish – Suquamish tribal leader at the signing of the Fort Elliott Treaty.

    Louis Hooban, chief executive officer, Indian Heritage Council, Tennessee, in correspondence with the author.

3. Captain Cook's instructions, which were denoted secret, were signed by the Lords of the Admiralty on 30 July 1768. The primary purpose of the voyage was to observe the transit of Venus from the island of Tahiti, but there were additional instructions relating mainly to the 'southern continent'. They included a direction that the discoverer was 'with the Consent of the Natives to take possession of Convenient Situations in the Country in the Name of the King of Great Britain, or if you find the Country uninhabited take Possession for His Majesty by setting up Proper Marks and Inscriptions as first discoverer and possessor'.

    The Life of Captain James Cook, J.C. Beaglehole, Adam and Charles Black, London, 1974, p 147.

4. Sir Joseph Banks appeared before the Commons Committee on transportation in May 1785. In answer to questions he told them that there were very few inhabitants, and that although 'they seemed inclined to hostilities they did not appear at all to be feared'. Asked whether, in case it was resolved to send convicts there, any district of the country might be obtained by cession or purchase he replied that 'there was nothing we could offer them that they would take except provisions, and those we wanted ourselves'. He admitted to knowing very little about them.

    Questioning of Banks, cited in full in Reynolds, op cit. pp 53–4.

5. *The Destruction of Aboriginal Society*, C.D. Rowley, Penguin, 1974.

6. Kylie Tennant in *Mary Gilmore, a tribute*, Australasian Book Society, 1965, p 27.

7. C.D. Rowley, op cit. p 7.

8. The Encyclopaedia of Aboriginal Australia, Aboriginal Studies Press for the Australian Institute of Aboriginal and Torres Strait Islander Studies, 1994, p 359.
9. The Encyclopaedia of Aboriginal Australia. op cit. p 1164.
10. Frank Hardy spent many months with the Gurindji people. The story is told in his book *The Unlucky Australian*, Rigby Ltd, Adelaide, 1968.
11. Hansard HR, 13 August 1968.
12. *Politics of Pauperisation*, F. Stevens, Australian Quarterly, Vol 41 No 2, September 1969.
13. Millirrpum and others v. Nabalco Pty Ltd and Commonwealth of Australia.
    NT Supreme Court, Blackburn J, 13 December 1968, Vol 17 FLR 141.
14. Hansard HR, 9 April 1963, p 481.
15. Hansard HR, 12 September 1963, p 927.
16. Hansard HR, 20 August 1963, p 277.
17. Hansard HR, 18 September 1963, p 1177.
18. Hansard HR, 18 November 1965, p 2879.
19. *The Mapoon Story*, op cit. (ref. 2, chapter 5).
20. NT Supreme Court, April 1971, Blackburn J, Vol 17 FLR 140.
21. Ministerial Statement, Hansard HR, 23 February 1972, p 122.
22. *Canberra Times*, 9 February 1972, p 3.
23. Aboriginal Land Right Commission – First Report, 19 July 1973, Second Report, 3 May 1974.
24. *Black News Services*, Vol 3, No 1, March 1977.

CHAPTER 11

1. *Advertiser*, 6 November 1972, p 3.
2. Socialist Party – The Invasion of Hungary in 1956 caused a split in the Communist Party of Australia. Many of them broke away to form a new communist party, an independent group advocating Marxian socialism without allegiance to the Soviet Union. Other communists saw in Hungary a treachery

to their cause that seemed to them to justify the invasion. They resented the loss of the word 'communist' but, making the best of what was left, they formed the Socialist Party of Australia, retaining their old links with Moscow.

CHAPTER 12
1. *The Trials of Nancy Young*, F. Stevens, Australian Quarterly, Vol 42 No 3, September 1969.
2. *Aboriginal 'Dreamings' and Town Plans*, J.H. Downing, Institute of Aboriginal Development, Alice Springs, 1974.

CHAPTER 13
1. Royal Commission into Aboriginal Deaths in Custody. Report of the Inquiry into the death of Kingsley Richard Dixon, Commissioner J.H. Muirhead QC., Australian Government Printing Service, Canberra, 1989.
2. Royal Commission into Aboriginal Deaths in Custody. National Report – Overview and Recommendations, Commissioner Elliott Johnston QC, Australian Government Printing Service, Canberra, 1991.

    Recommendations referred to: 2:53, 3:64, 3:79, 3:91, 3:250, 3:312, 3:329, 4:59, 4:282, 4:322, 4:367, 4:459, 5:53, 5:65.

CHAPTER 14
1. Witchetty grubs – the edible larva of moths, which Aboriginal children dig out of the bark of trees, and regard as superior to chocolate.
2. Pie floater – a meat pie served in pea soup was developed as a supper delicacy by a pie cart operating for many years outside the Adelaide railway station. It is a South Australian speciality.

Acknowledgements

My first thanks must go to the many Aboriginal men and women who have helped me. I am deeply grateful for the warm and generous hospitality so many of them have shown. Not all of them have had faith in what I have been doing. They are suspicious, with good cause, of the motives of white people interesting themselves in their concerns, but all of them have treated me with great courtesy.

Many non-Aboriginal people have helped me – members of Ruby Hammond's staff, public servants, members of non-government organisations, welfare officers, librarians, members of parliament and members of my own family.

These are thanks I prepared for the unpublished *Brightening Landscape* which became a basis for *Flight of an Eagle*. I wish I had given more personal thanks, especially to Charles and Phyllis Duguid, Gladys Elphick, Miriam Dadleh, Faith Thomas and Arthur Ahang, none of whom have survived for me to thank them now.

I have further thanks for the help I have had in the past two years. Thanks to Ruby's sister, Irene Allen; her children, Sandi Southwell and John and Bruce Hammond; her brother Kingsley Ahang; and also Christopher Anderson, Mary Ann Bin-Sallik, Hugh Bray, Brian Butler, Andrew Collett, Danny Coulson, Jennifer Dann, Chicka Dixon, Anne Dunn, Vi Deuschele (nee Watson), Dick Finlay, Gail Fraser, Irene Gale, Olga Gostin, Michael Gray, Jane Hylton, Phillip Jones, Georgina Kirby, Frank Lampard, Helen Liddell, Jan Lowe, Andrea Mason, Maud McBriar, Verne McLaren, Sheridah Melvin, Hannah Middleton, Anne Monten, Alan O'Connor, Lewis O'Brien, Shirley Peisley, Lynn Poole, Geoffrey

Pope, Val Power, Bob Randall, Joan Russell, Marlene Stewart, Muriel Van Der Byl, Leslie Wanganeen, Sonia Waters, Peter Waye, Gene Wenham, Mary Woodward; staffs of the South Australian State Library, the South Australian Supreme Court Library, the State Electoral Office, the Equal Opportunity Commission, the Australian Bureau of Statistics and the Payneham Public Library.

I must thank Simon MacDonald, a knowledgeable and sympathetic editor; Margaret Blaber, whose enthusiasm for the book never flagged through typing two versions and what seemed like endless sub-editing; and Wilson Forte for his support as always.

The preparation of this book was greatly assisted by a Community History Fund grant in 1994.

Bibliography

Interviews and research on which this book is based, including long talks with Ruby Hammond, were carried out by Margaret Forte. Quoted statements are from these interviews, and unattributed comments are hers. General history is from the books and papers listed in the bibliography and the notes and references.

Abbie, A.A., 1969, *The Original Australians*, Rigby, Adelaide
Beaglehole, J.C. & Black, A. & J., 1974, *The Life of Captain James Cook*, London
Berndt, R. & C. & Stanton, J., 1993, *A World that Was*, MUP, Melbourne
Bin-Sallik, M., 1990, *Aboriginal Tertiary Education in Australia – How well is it serving the needs of the Aborigines?*, An Aborigines Study Key Centre Publication, University of South Australia, Underdale
Blainey, G., 1975, *The Triumph of the Nomads*, Macmillan, Australia
Bourke, C. & E. & Edwards, B. eds, 1993, *Aboriginal Australia*, UQP, St Lucia
Broom, L. & Lancaster Jones, F., 1973, *A Blanket a Year*, part of Aborigines in Australian Society by the Social Science Research Council of Australia, ANU Press, Canberra
Downing, J.H., 1974, *Abotriginal 'Dreamings' and Town Plans*, Institute of Aboriginal Development, Alice Springs
Duguid, C., 1963, *No Dying Race*, Rigby, Adelaide
Eggleston, E., 1976, *Fear, Favour or Affection*, part of Aborigines in Australian Society, ANU Press, Canberra
Elkin, A.P., 1974, *Aboriginal Men of High Degree*, Angus & Robertson, Australia
Fraser, B. ed., 1983, *Macquarie Book of Events*, Macquarie Library, Sydney
Gale, F. & Brookman, A., 1972, *Urban Aborigines*, ANU Press, Canberra
Hardy, F., 1968, *The Unlucky Australians*, Rigby, Adelaide
Harris, S., 1972, *This is Our Land*, ANU, Canberra
Harris, S., 1979, *It's Coming Yet*, Aboriginal Treaty Committee, Canberra
Lippmann, L., 1973, *Words or Blows, Racial Attitudes in Australia*, Penguin
Maddock, K., 1972, *The Australian Aborigines*, Penguin, London
Mattingley, C. & Hampton, K., 1988, *Survival in Our Own Land*, Wakefield Press, Adelaide

Nettheim, G. ed. with the International Commission of Jurists (Australian Section), 1974, *Aborigines, Human Rights and the Law*, Australian and New Zealand Book Co, Sydney

Parsons, M., Roberts, J. & Russell, B., 1975, *The Mapoon Books*, 1, 2 and 3, International Development Action, Fitzroy

Perkins, C., 1975, *A Bastard Like Me*, Ure Smith, Sydney

Read, P., 1990, *Charles Perkins: A Biography*, Penguin, Melbourne

Reynolds, H., 1992, *The Law of the Land*, Penguin, Melbourne

Rowley, C.D., 1970, *Aboriginal Policy and Practice*, part of Aborigines in Australian Society by the Social Science Research Council of Australia, ANU Press, Canberra

Stanner, W.E.H., 1969, *After the Dreaming – 1968 Boyer Lectures*, Australian Broadcasting Commission

Thorpe Clark, M., 1975, *Pastor Doug*, Rigby, Adelaide

Turner, V.E., 1937, *Pearls from the Deep,* (the story of the Colebrook Home for the Aboriginal Children, Quorn, South Australia), United Aboriginal Mission

Wright, J., 1972, *We Call for a Treaty*, Aboriginal Treaty Committee, Canberra

GOVERNMENT REPORTS

Armstrong, S., 1975, Legal Aid in Australia, *Inquiry into Poverty in Australia*, AGPS, Canberra

Gale, F. & Binnion, J., 1975, Poverty Among Aboriginal Families in Adelaide, *Inquiry into Poverty in Australia*, AGPS, Canberra

Hill, K., 1975, A Study of Aboriginal Poverty in Country Towns, *Inquiry into Poverty in Australia*, AGPS, Canberra

Johnston, Elliott, 1991, Overview and Recommendations by Commissioner Elliott Johnston QC, *Royal Commission into Aboriginal Deaths in Custody*, AGPS, Canberra

1974, *The Environmental Condition of the Aborigines and Torres Strait Islanders and the Preservation of their Sacred Sites*, AGPS, Canberra

1975, Aboriginal Land Rights Commission, in *Woodward Report*, 2nd Report, AGPS, Canberra

1976, May report, *Delivery of Services Financed by the Department of Aboriginal Affairs*, AGPS, Canberra

1976, *International Women's Year Report of the Australian National Advisory Committee*, AGPS, Canberra

1976, *The Role of the National Aborigines Consultative Committee*, AGPS, Canberra

1992, Overview of the Response by Governments to the Royal Commission, *Aboriginal Deaths in Custody*, AGPS, Canberra

1993, *Aboriginal and Torres Strait Islander Commission*, First report, AGPS, Canberra

1994, October, *Native Title Consultations*, First report of the Parliamentary Joint Committee during Ausgust 1994, Parliament of the Commonwealth of Australia

1994, December, *The Native Title Act 1993 – What it does and how it works*, Department of the Prime Minister and Cabinet

UNPUBLISHED PAPERS

Aboriginal Legal Rights Movement Annual Reports, 1974–77

Aboriginal Legal Service New South Wales, First Annual Report, 1971

Collett, A. & Graves, A., 'A study of the Nature and Origin of Aboriginal Petty Crime in Port Augusta in 1971'

Coombs, Dr H.C., Walter Murdoch Address, November 1976

Council of Aboriginal Women of South Australia, Annual Reports, 1968–72

Submissions and Transcripts of the Senate Standing Committee Hearings in Relation to Aborigines and Alcohol, Adelaide Sessions, June 1977

OTHER REFERENCES

Aborigines and the Law, 1976, December, *Legal Services Bulletin*, Vol 2, No 4

Australian Council of Churches, 1981, Justice for Aboriginal Australians, *Report of the World Council of Churches team visit to the Aborigines*, 15 June to 3 July 1981, Sydney

Brennan, F., 1992, April, The 'new partnership' of the 1990s, *Alternative Law Journal*, Vol 17, No 2

Brennan, F., 1994, Securing a Beautiful Place for Aborigines and Torres Strait Islanders in a Modern, Free and Tolerant Australia, *Constitutional Centenary Foundation Inc*, options paper

Carrick, J. & Robertson, G., 1970, June, The Trials of Nancy Young, *Australian Quarterly*, Vol 42, No 2

Council for Aboriginal Reconciliation, 1995, *Going Forward: Social Justice for the first Australians*, Canberra

Identity, 1974–77, *Australian Publications Foundation Journal*

Stevens, F., 1969, September, Politics of Pauperisation, *Australian Quarterly*, Vol 41, No 3

Yura Wangkanyi, 1977, *Port Augusta Aboriginal Newsletter*

Index

Abdullah, George, 141
Abbie, A.A. (Prof), 108, 358
Aboriginal Affairs,
    SA Department of, 145
    legal services policy, 7
Aboriginal Community College, 204, 295–6, 338
Aboriginal Cultural Centre, 14
Aboriginal Education Foundation, 71
Aboriginal Police–Steering Committee, 14, 15, 172
Aboriginal Progress Association, 71, 99
Aboriginal Legal Rights Movement, 4–6, 8–10, 12, 14, 16, 19, 21, 45, 46, 71, 133, 144, 160, 161, 173, 174, 176, 178, 186, 189, 191, 193, 205, 306, 309, 323, 324, 352
Aborigines Advancement League, 70, 71
Aborigines Protection Board, 52–3, 357–8
Adelaide Sobriety Group, 200
Agius, Charlie, 8
Ahang, Arthur, 23–6, 28, 30, 34, 36
Ahang, Ethel (nee Ellis), 24, 26, 28, 29, 30, 31, 32, 33, 38, 39–41, 44, 46, 48, 49, 50, 66, 68
Ahang, Fred, 28–30, 32, 36, 56, 58
Ahang, Jack, 28, 30, 48
Ahang, John, 64, 65, 68, 80
Ahang, Kevin, 30, 38, 345, 347

Ahang, Kingsley, 30, 32, 42, 335, 345, 347
Ahang, Marie, 30
Ahang, Maureen, 28–30, 36, 46, 47
Allan, Irene (nee Ahang), 30, 32, 38, 40, 47–51, 59, 64, 65–8, 82, 94, 95, 118, 342, 345, 347, 348
Allan, Terry, 67, 94
Allan, Vicki, 94, 345
Allan, Wayne, 94
Anderson, Michael, 226, 230, 358
Angas, Marjorie, 29
Arabunna people, SA, 112, 118
Austin, Willy, 183
Australia–China Friendship Society, 243
Australian Legal Aid Office, 6, 174

Ball, Robert, 207
Bandler, Faith, 159, 223
Banks, Joseph, 362
Barnard, Lance, 233
Beazley, Kim, 221–2
Bennett, Frank, 288
Bennett, John, 168
Binnion, Joan, 107, 358
Bin-Sallik, Mary Ann, 312, 315
Blackburn, Justice, 223–4, 364
Black News Service, 237, 365
Blackford, SA, 3, 22–6, 28–30, 32, 34, 37, 39, 43, 45, 48, 49, 52, 64, 114

Bonner, Neville, 21, 139, 140, 261
Bonney, Lola, 25
Bostock, Jerry, 244, 251, 253
Boyer Lectures, 4, 356
Brady, Marceil, 262
Bryan, Laurie, 70–1
Bryant, Gordon, 139–40, 145, 202, 221, 230
Buchanan, Cheryl, 244
Bullocky Town, SA, 29
Butler, Brian, 182

Calder, E.L., 199
Cameron, Mary, 28, 39
Casey, R.G. (Lord), 216
Caterer, Helen, 92
Catley, Robert, 160
Cavanagh, Jim, 144, 146–7, 149
Chalkner, John, 87
Changsha (China), 258, 260
Chapman, W.E., 198–9
Coe, Paul, 135, 141, 158, 230
Colebrook Home
 (for Aboriginal Children), 72–7, 188, 358
Coleman, Basil, 190–1
Collett, Andrew, 45, 46, 160–3, 170, 178–9, 186, 190, 194, 195
Commercial Motor Vehicles Foundation, 88, 97
Community Welfare,
 SA Department of, 9, 124, 182, 201, 312
Cook, James (Capt), 212, 363
Coombs, H.C. (Dr), 219, 224, 299–302
Corporal, Maude (Mawunka Yanindah), 119
Coulson, Danny, 180, 186–7, 189
Coulthard, Faith, 72, 74, 78, 87

Council of Aboriginal Women (CAW), 4, 6, 79, 83, 85, 87, 108, 130, 133, 135, 137, 139, 154, 282, 284, 285, 328, 352
Crawford, J.A., 88
Crown Hotel (Kingston, SA), 56, 58, 60
Cunnamulla Reserve Qld, 287, 288
Curkpatrick, Shirley, 47

Dadleh, Larl, 122
Dadleh, Miriam (nee Khan), 26, 109–11, 113, 118, 120–2
Daunton-Fear, Mary, 161
Davenport Reserve, SA, 179, 182, 182, 185, 296
Davies, Vonnie, 181
Davis, Mary, 262
Dexter, Barry, 139, 146, 149
Dixon, Chicka (Charles), 201, 226, 244, 246, 252
Dohnt, Betty, 182
Downing, J.H. (Rev.), 293–4
Duguid, Charles (Dr), 69–71, 77, 83, 188
Duguid, Phyllis, 70
Duncan, Graeme (Prof), 160
Dunstan, Don(ald), 9, 156, 305, 359

Eaton, Mary, 70
Edwards, Ray, 183–4, 186
Eggleston, Elizabeth (Dr), 155, 175, 361
Ellis, Charlie, 27
Ellis, Ethel see Ahang, Ethel
Ellis, Ernie, 27, 109, 112, 118
Ellis, Ruby (nee Smith), 26, 42, 108, 111
Elphick, Gladys, 69, 71, 78, 79, 81, 83–5, 88–90, 95, 101, 103, 105, 106, 108, 285, 286, 291, 292

Enderby, Keppel, 225, 230
Ernabella Mission, SA, 70, 187, 194, 195, 196, 306

Federal Council for the Advancement of Aboriginal and Torres Strait Islanders (FCAATSI), 70, 100, 139, 159, 215, 217, 223, 229, 282, 358
Fielding, Bruce, 178
Foley, Gary, 135, 227, 230
Forster, Justice, 171–2, 361
Fox, Justice, 230
Fraser, Gael, 316
Fraser, Malcolm, 152, 236, 299, 300, 360
Fudge, Olga, 9

Gale, Fay (Dr), 67, 69, 88, 106, 179, 297, 358, 361
Gaskill, Joan (Sr), 183
Gilmore, Mary, 214, 364
Gostin, Olga (Dr), 314
Graves, Adrian, 161, 178, 186
Gurindji people, NT, 216–8, 364

Hacket, J.V., 162–4
Haman, Ellen, 62
Haman, Emmy, 61, 62
Haman, Hans, 61, 62
Haman, Ingelore, 62
Haman, Sylvie Ann, 65–6
Hammond, Bill, 65–8, 80
Hammond, Bruce, 11, 30, 35, 36, 51, 81, 95, 111, 114, 117, 118, 174, 323, 345, 347
Hammond, Frank, 11, 65, 66, 68, 69, 81, 94, 109, 263, 345, 347
Hammond, John, 11, 59, 64, 65, 67, 68, 80, 81, 345, 347

Hammond, Sandra, 11, 66, 68, 81, 82, 95, 111, 114, 118, 174, 323
Hardy, Frank, 216, 364
Harris, Stewart, 229, 230, 301
Hartman, Bill, 28
Hartman, Dossie, 28
Hermannsburg mission, NT, 26, 27, 120
Hiatt, L.R. (Dr), 152
Horner, Musgrave, 87
Howson, Peter, 104, 135, 230–2
Hull, Joseph, 178
Hunt, Ralph, 230–1
Hyde, Ruby (Sr), 73–76

International Women's Year, 38, 62, 272, 276, 278, 281, 282, 284, 286, 308, 309, 352
Is This Seat Taken?, 336–8

Jimmy, Jean, 128–31
Johnson, Bertie, 62
Johnson, Eva, 334–6, 339
Johnson, L., 203, 206
Johnston, Elliott, 5, 85, 155–6, 160–5, 327, 330, 356, 365
Jones, Caroline, 278
Juvenile Court, SA, 8, 9, 19
Juvenile Court Acts
    Royal Commission, 14, 169, 172, 356

Kalumburu mission, WA, 240
Kalogerinis, A. (Dr), 287, 289
Karpany, Ron, 62
Kartinyeri, Pat, 185
Kate Cocks Home, Adelaide, 59
Khan, Alison (nee Stokes), 121–2
Khan, Nemith, 120–1
King, L.J., 92, 97

Kingston, SA *see also* Blackford, 3, 22–6, 28, 35–7, 39, 41, 45–7, 50, 52, 56, 58, 60, 61, 64, 198, 214, 250, 252, 269, 356
Kinnear, Audrey (Sr), 186, 189
Kirby, Georgina (Dame), 340
Kuo Mo-Jo, 258–9
Kyburz, Rosemary, 64, 358

Lang, Bruce, 180
Larrakia people, NT, 300
Lawrence, John (Prof), 159
Lawrie, Margaret, 72, 78
Lennon, Lallie, 183
Le Sueur, Eddie (Edwin), 88–9, 93–4, 97–9, 358
Lewis, J.W., 190
Liddle, Helen, 313, 340
Lindner, Barry, 166
Loveday, Ray, 159
Lumbers, Eugene, 71
Luther, Maurice, 152

McAdam, Elliott, 13, 14, 169–70, 172, 205–7
McLeod, Robert, 150
MacDonald, Colin, 101, 103
McGuiness, Bruce, 168
McGuinness, Joe, 142
McLaren, Verne, 24–5, 28–9, 33, 356
McMahon, William (Sir), 133–4, 224–5, 299, 300
MacNamara, Natascha, 9, 79, 82, 84, 97, 137, 234, 281
Mahomet, Gool, 122
Manski, Kevin, 262, 269
Mao Tse Tung, 247, 251, 258, 260
Mapoon Reserve, Qld, 127–32, 222, 358

Maria Creek, SA, 24, 28, 46, 268
Marika, Wandjuk, 127, 333
Marree, SA, 27, 44, 108–10, 112–13, 115, 117–20, 122–6
Middleton, Hannah (Dr), 262, 269, 272, 345
Millar, C.J., 84
Millhouse, Robin, 92
Mitchell, Ivy, 77
Mitchell, J., 262–3
Mitchell, Marcia, 263
Mitchell, Roma (Dame), 2, 323–4
Mohr, Justice, 169
Monten, Anne, 333
Monten, Helen, 333
Morley, John, 90–92, 104
Moy, F.H., 150
Muirhead, Justice, 171, 364
Mutha puttaye (Coward Springs, SA), 44, 114–17, 359

National Aboriginal Conference, 153, 299, 360
National Aboriginal Consultative Committee, 138–9, 150–3, 320, 353, 359
National Aborigines Day, 100, 184–5, 228–9, 333, 352
National Black Theatre, 246
Newbury, Alan, 217
Nettheim, Garth (Prof), 159
Newfong, John, 135, 230
Ngarrindjeri people, Coorong, SA, 2
Nicholls, Douglas (Sir), 21, 168, 229, 358

O'Clerkin, Con, 262
O'Donoghue, Lois, 72–4, 76, 135, 152, 153, 189

Parkside Hotel, SA, 60–1
Patterson, R. (Dr), 145–6
Peisley, Shirley, 8–9, 16, 53, 59, 61
Penny, Harry (Dr), 87
Perkins, Charles, 21, 139, 142, 145–50, 311, 358
Phillip, Arthur (Capt), 213
Playford, Thomas (Sir), 76
Point McLeay, SA, 9, 61, 98, 102
Point Pearce Aboriginal mission, SA, 9, 11–12, 61, 69, 92, 98, 286
Pope, Geoff (Rev), 67–8
Powell, Barry, 176, 178
Power, Val, 144, 164–6, 169, 339, 343, 348, 361
Pratt, Noel, 140

Queen Ethel see Watson, Ethel

Randall, Bob, 269, 338–9
Rankine, Leila, 97, 285
Reid, Elizabeth, 277–9, 282
Rowley, C.W. (Prof), 302
Rutter, Delia (Sr), 73–6

Samuels, Gordon, 159
Saunders, Sandra, 323
Sanz, Seraphim, 240–1
Schluter, M., 190–2
Seattle, Chief, 210–11, 363
Shao Ci-Mar, 256
Stanley, James, 144–5, 152–3, 178
Stanner, W. (Prof), 4, 302, 356
Stevens, F., 219

Task Force, 8, 14, 144, 309–12, 317, 352
Taylor, Harry, 8
Tennant, Kylie, 214

Tent Embassy – Canberra, 100, 104, 134–6, 138, 148, 225, 228, 230–3, 244–5, 359
Tent Embassy – Adelaide, 100–3
Tonkin, David, 199, 305–7
Thompson, Lynette, 244
Tongarie, Maude, 72

Van Der Byl, Muriel, 86, 333, 338, 343, 347–8
Viner, Ian, 152–3, 166, 235–6, 359–60

Walker, Dennis, 135, 138
Walker, Mark, 180
Walsh, Pat (Sr), 182
Wanganeen, Leslie, 317
Wanganeen, Ken, 311
Ward, Alan (Dr), 169

Ward, Justice, 171, 235, 237
Watkins, Cherie, 90, 97
Watson, Bill, 37
Watson, Betty, 59, 61
Watson, Bruce,
Watson, Colin, 36
Watson, Ethel (Queen Ethel), 24–5, 36, 356
Watson, Harry, 24–5, 37
Watson, Lilla, 244
Watson, Linda, 37, 60–1
Watson, Vi, 37, 57, 60–1
Wauraltee Hotel, SA, 11–12
Waye, P.N., 166–7
Wells, Justice, 166, 168–70, 361
Wenham, Gene, 309
Wentworth, W.C., 85, 160, 216, 311
Westley, Ian, 185

Whitlam, E. Gough, 124, 138, 148–50, 161, 195, 201, 225, 233, 235, 243, 279, 310
Whitlam, Margaret, 278
Williams, Dorothy, 166
Williams, Gary, 158–9
Williams, Mary, 285
Williams, Sydney, 166–70
Willmot, Eric, 311
Willmot, Joanne, 8
Wilson, Milton, 2, 45
Winder, Kenneth, 244
Wintinna Mick, 177
Withers, R., 168
Woma Committee, 180–1, 200, 203
Woodward, Justice, 233, 235, 237–8, 295, 299, 360
Wootten, J.H. (Prof), 156, 159
Wright, Judith, 302

Yirrkala people, NT, 221–3
Young, Nancy, 286–9

Zelling, Justice, 164, 360